Contemporary Community Health Series

Pitt Series in Policy and Institutional Studies

THE AGING:
A GUIDE TO PUBLIC POLICY

The Aging

A GUIDE TO PUBLIC POLICY

Bennett M. Rich
and
Martha Baum

UNIVERSITY OF PITTSBURGH PRESS

Published by the University of Pittsburgh Press, Pittsburgh, Pa., 15260
Copyright © 1984, University of Pittsburgh Press
All rights reserved
Feffer & Simons Inc., London
Manufactured in the United States of America
Second printing 1986

Library of Congress Cataloging in Publication Data

Rich, Bennett Milton, 1909–1984
  The aging, a guide to public policy.

  Includes bibliographical references and index.
  1. Aged—Government policy—United States. 2. Aged—
Legal status, laws, etc.—United States. 3. Old age
assistance—United States. I. Baum, Martha. II. Title.
HQ1064.U5R512 1984   362.6'0973   84-40228
ISBN 0-8229-3500-7
ISBN 0-8229-5364-1 (pbk.)

Contents

x / *Contents*

Introduction

Landmark legislation affecting the aging was enacted in the 1930s. In the intervening decades, the number and scope of programs have dramatically increased. Each program has been developed in response to some recognized need that is in large measure separate from other needs. Taken together, the many programs do not constitute a cohesive national policy affecting the elderly. On the contrary, each reflects the particular political and social conditions surrounding its origin and implementation. The multiplicity and complexity of resources and services available through programs for the aging make it extremely difficult to achieve even a reasonable grasp of this area. Scholars in the field of aging, educators, direct-service workers, agency administrators, and perhaps especially older people themselves who wish some comprehensive understanding of the evolution and current state of programs for the aging do not find assistance readily available. It is hoped that this study will help them achieve such an understanding.

The piecemeal development of legislation, the multiple layers of government involved, and the numerous sociopolitical forces that play a part in the development of programs for the aging are typical of policymaking in the United States. The context in which policy is made will be the focus of the first chapter. A general overview of policymaking in a historical context will be followed by an analysis of the principal forces most directly involved in the making of policy for the aged at the federal level. This discussion will set the scene to accomplish the two major goals of the book.

The first goal is to describe in summary form, and in the context of a brief historical overview, the major federal programs for older Americans. Discussion will focus on objectives, administration, and operations. As will be seen, the effect of some programs is direct—from the federal government to the individual. Through other programs, the federal government establishes guidelines and supplies financial resources to state and local levels. By means of still others, the national government protects the elderly through regulatory mechanisms. The descriptive overviews discuss the origin and content of programs in the context of the allocation of responsibility and the extent to which target populations are served.

The second goal is to analyze program areas to determine their relationships with one another, the degree of fit and consistency, and the extent of the coverage they offer to aged population groups. Statistical data on costs and people served are presented wherever possible, but data that would make feasible any comprehensive evaluation of programs for the elderly have not been collected. Similarly, it is not possible to quantitatively assess interrelationships among programs even to determine how many persons served by one program are also likely to be served by others. The analysis in this book is therefore limited to examining programs to identify their gaps and to determine the extent to which they overlap.

The book consists of nine chapters. Chapter I discusses the politics of aging in the United States, emphasizing the role of the federal government. Chapters II through VIII are organized around logical subdivisions within the programs for the aged. Each of these chapters includes a descriptive overview and an analytic summary of a particular subset of programs. Chapter II discusses what is called the Aging Network, a term that refers to the organization and substantive content of the Older Americans Act and its amendments. Chapter III pulls together retirement and economic programs that address the general financial well-being of older Americans. Chapter IV discusses the numerous retirement and economic programs directed at special groups within the older population, In chapter V, health programs for the elderly are the focus of attention. Chapter VI delves into two essential auxiliary programs, transportation and housing. Chapter VII is concerned with the ways in which the federal government attempts to protect the older worker from discrimination and to provide opportunities for meaningful work for older Americans. Chapter VIII concentrates on aged American veterans, a unique population that has received federal benefits from their inception and that occupies a special status in relation to the beneficiaries of other programs. The last chapter, chapter IX, is devoted to both a condensed descriptive portrait and an analytic synthesis of all the programs for older Americans. Some implications for the present and forecasting for the near future are also included in the final chapter.

As has other social legislation in the United States, enactment of programs for the elderly has proceeded incrementally and in relatively small steps. Although the legislation of the thirties represented a radical departure since it embraced intervention at the federal level, it covered only a relatively small proportion of the older population. Over the next two decades, most of the programs for the aging related to economic concerns. In a half-dozen steps, social security benefits were extended to more and more worker groups across the labor spectrum. The late fifties saw the enactment of a modest health assistance program. In the sixties, the expansive days of the Great Society, Medicare and Medicaid health programs were introduced, primarily to meet the needs of elderly persons. In 1965, the same year that these two programs were enacted, the Older Americans Act was passed. Initially modest in scope and in funds allocated, the act was amended several times to allow ever-increasing levels of financial investment and of activity. Even in the 1970s, when concerns about federal intervention and budgetary expansion were mounting, legislation was enacted to protect the elderly against inflation by trying social security payments to a cost-of-living index. Thus, though the investment in the fate of older people in the United States was initially modest, a very significant proportion of the federal budget is now expanded on this population group.

It is not difficult to relate these developments to the changes in the age structure of the population of the United States (for more detailed demographic information, see the Appendix). Between 1900 and 1930, the number of persons aged sixty-five and older more than doubled, growing from about 3 million to almost 7 million. The percentage of this age group in the total population increased from 4.1 percent to 5.5 percent. Between 1930 and 1950, the number of older persons almost doubled again, reaching close to 12.5 million. By 1950, this group constituted 8.2 of the population. A decade later, in 1960, the Bureau of the Census counted almost 17 million Americans aged sixty-five and over, or 9.3 percent of the population. The figures expanded again in the seventies, and by 1980 there were over 25½ million Americans aged sixty-five and over, constituting 11.3 percent of the population. The expression "every ninth American" is used to emphasize the major shift in the nation's population makeup. Projections for the foreseeable future show that this population group will continue to expand both numerically and proportionately.

A general profile, however, obscures other changes in the older population. Increasing recognition of the diversity of needs of the over-sixty-five age group has recently begun to focus attention on specific populations cohorts. For example, the growth of the population in the upper reaches of the age structure, those persons over seventy-five and even eighty-five, is nothing less than startling. The high vulnerability of these groups poses an array of problems requiring wide-ranging governmental attention. As this study endeavors to demonstrate, the government is already involved through a host of aging programs. In the next decades, virtually every current policy will be subjected to intensive scrutiny as competing forces strive to effect change. Some of the changes already enacted in recent years will be discussed in subsequent chapters.

THE AGING:
A GUIDE TO PUBLIC POLICY

I / The Politics of Aging

1. Introduction to the Policymaking Scene

There is a direct link between how the elderly fare and the politics of aging in industrial societies. In modern society people look to government to solve social problems and to regulate social life much more than they did in the past. An impressive increase in the scope of governmental tasks is one of the uncontroversial facts in the history of modernization. The United States is obviously no exception to this general rule. Yet the policymaking process in the United States is unusually complex and confusing. Lindbloom refers to the process as "muddling through."[1] The area of programs for the aging is an excellent example. The United States enacted legislation granting retirement pensions, that is, allowing persons to leave the labor force at sixty-five with guaranteed economic support, only comparatively recently. Germany passed the first such legislation in 1889. Most of the Western industrialized world followed suit during the next twenty-five years.[2] The United States resisted, holding out until the middle of the devastating depression of the 1930s. The array of programs available to the elderly is now extensive, as we shall see. However, these programs have developed very slowly and in small steps that have often seemed unrelated, and the number of political forces and regulatory mechanisms involved stagger the imagination. No other industrial nation seems so reluctant to ensure the social welfare of its population, in this case the elderly, as our own.

The main purpose of this chapter is to present a description and analysis of some of the most prominent features of the politics of aging in the United States. This discussion will provide a context in which to view the contents of programs for the aging, which will be the focus of subsequent chapters. But before we move to an examination of the contemporary political scene, some factors from the historical past that could help the reader understand to some extent how we arrived at our present political circumstances will be briefly discussed.

The first factor crucial to this understanding is the American value system, which is rooted in the colonial past.[3] The early settlers in this country sought

3

to escape the religious, political, and social constraints of more developed European societies. The strong religious overtone in the value base can be traced to the Protestant ethic, particularly to Calvinism.[4] In this stern, puritanical faith, the notion that each individual stood alone before his God and could be saved only through hard work and demonstrated achievement was accepted as gospel.[5] In the young American society, the traditions of individualism, hard work, and independence from auxiliary support flourished. It seems that this ethos ideally suited the pioneers, who were, and to some extent remain, our heroes.[6] In a territory where there was unlimited room for expansion and an unbelievably rich resource base, these rugged individualists found an excellent opportunity to demonstrate that the ethos did in fact work. Accordingly, dependency was allowed only to the very few who because of serious illness or very advanced age were forced to abandon work. This value base made it difficult to accept any need for social welfare and helps to explain both the late entry of the United States into the welfare field and the American approach to assisting the elderly or, for that matter, any group claiming to be disadvantaged. Because of the continued suspicion that those who do not work are somehow unworthy, we make it as difficult as possible to obtain any kind of assistance from the government and spend inordinate amounts of time and money searching for welfare cheaters and freeloaders, despite evidence that few such persons exists.[7] Coser points out that this approach may discourage many eligible persons from seeking assistance because of the degradation inherent in the process.[8] It is not that Americans are unwilling to help people in need; they tend to be very responsive to appeals from individuals, families, and communities demonstrated to be suffering from physical diseases or natural disasters through no fault of their own. As President Reagan, who quite evidently embodies the more traditional values, points out, the federal government has a commitment to provide a minimal floor of support for the "truly needy," and most governmental programs, at least those with eligibility requirements, are designed so that the less-than-truly needy do not receive benefits.

A second factor, still closely related to the ethos discussed above, is the complexity of governmental structure. In the United States, governing bodies exist at federal, state, and local levels. Hundreds of thousands of governing bodies at all these levels have some measure of political authority.[9] This unusual system of checks and balances reflects the early settlers' mistrust of governmental authority. The individualized value base also fed into the philosophical position of laissez-faire. Allowing private forces in free competition to work out problems in the marketplace was thought to be the best route to an affluent society. A natural corollary to this thinking was the belief that the government that governs least governs best. Another historical development also reinforced the belief in decentralized government. Early settlements in this country tended to be sparsely distributed, and most affairs of government were settled at the community level, usually through a remarkable American invention called the town meeting. This preference for citizen participation at the grass-roots level is evident in much of the legislation on behalf of the aging, particularly the Older Americans Act. As during the passage of much of the Great Society legislation, policy makers may be said to be trying to turn the vast electorate into one national-scale town meeting.

Another historical influence that must be taken into account is the Revolution, which produced among the original thirteen colonies a coalition that was based primarily on their mutual desire to gain independence from the British Crown. Achenbaum notes that the original constitution, intended to unify the colonies, had to be modified twelve years after its inception because it provided almost no role for the "federation."[10] Even with the new modifications, states' rights were still relatively strong. Compared with European countries, America remained predominantly rural and decentralized until relatively late.[11] The changes that occurred in the process of modernization—primarily industrialization, the development of technology, and urbanization—eventually produced a national political economy, but not until about the 1920's.[12] Although the central role of the federal government was eventually recognized, multiple layers of government, with their own separate jurisdictions and powers, persist to this day. Individual states and local communities staunchly defend their vested powers against suspected intrusions. In fact, a major role of the Supreme Court is to interpret the Constitution in cases involving federal versus states' rights. This division of power has been a major influence on the development of the policy maze in this country today.

A third factor, which is probably subtly connected to the first two, is the relative weakness of national political parties in the United States. Unlike political parties in other modern democratic states, our national parties exert an influence on the electorate only just before a national election. Obviously, the two-party system offers a limited choice to a huge and highly diverse electorate. Voter turnout therefore tends to be comparatively low, and there is an increasing inclination on the part of the voters to declare themselves as independents rather than committed to either party. The readily definable "blocs" of voters who could be depended upon to back one party or the other during the era of the New Deal and for some years thereafter no longer exist. Stable, party-based coalitions have practically vanished from the national scene. It seems that a large proportion of the citizenry has turned toward the interest group rather than the ballot box as a means of exerting pressure on government. The political influence of organized pressure groups and their associated lobbies has been increasingly evident in the United States. These groups often disagree about the solutions to given issues and compete with one another for scarce resources.[13] This complicated pressure field can occur even when the interest groups claim to represent the same constituency, as we shall see in the third section of this chapter.

The fourth factor is only too clearly related to the third: the enormous size and diversity of the population of the United States. Each of the parties in a two-party system tries to present a platform that has overarching appeal, and as a result party platforms tend to be ideologically general and lacking in specifics. In fact, since political parties seek to please everyone, national party spokespersons often sound as if they are saying the same things. Witness, for example, the attempts of the Reagan administration to pacify constituencies such as blacks and especially women—groups it once considered "uninteresting." Over the past twenty years, virtually every group in the total population has claimed to be a "minority" deserving special consideration from the legislators. Some groups are better organized than others, and some represent larger and/or potentially more influential constituencies than others, but all must to some extent be considered. Given the decline in bloc voting on the basis of race, ethnicity, religion, and socioeconomic status, legislators must make difficult choices about how to appeal to the widest possible audience. They willingly turn to interest groups for assistance because these groups offer baseline data that facilitate decision making in addition to propaganda for their particular causes.

Thus far, then, we have discussed the impact of some historical forces on current policymaking at the federal level. The emphasis on individual achievement, work, laissez-faire economic stance, and competition set the stage for a very reluctant approach to social welfare policy. As the nation grew older and more industrialized, the persistence of these values contributed to the very slow and piecemeal approach to welfare legislation. The same values also brought about the division of legislative powers, which in this huge, complex society has become extremely unwieldy.[14] At the same time, as the nation grew, it became more and more difficult to organize the citizenry except through the mechanism of interest groups, which resulted in a multiplicity of messages from an almost infinite variety of sources.

Out of the conditions just described began the long journey into federal policies for the aged. We are now involved in a confrontation about those policies. The struggle is complicated by shifts in both the age structure of the population (the increasing proportion of elderly relative to younger age groups) and the aging structure (the startling growth in the number of very old people). The economic problems this nation now faces have naturally helped bring about the current conflict.

We turn now to a description and analysis of the politics of aging on the national scene, first from the perspective of the legislative process and then the major interest groups which interrelate with the activities of the legislators.

2. The Legislative Process

Programs for the aging normally evolve from a complex series of political and administrative actions. Rarely is a piece of legislation the handiwork of one member of a legislative body. Nor, for that matter, is the legislative body itself the sole author. The original idea may have come from any one of a number of sources. Usually, a legislative act is the final preliminary step in putting a new program into operation. However, beyond the formulation of a new policy and its authorization are the indispensible administrative operations essential to translating the initial idea into reality. Politics—if broadly defined as the art of influencing the development of governmental policy—is an essential element of each facet of the entire program.

The central objective of this section is to present, in capsule form, a picture of the individuals and groups involved in the formulation of programs for the aging. The immediate presentation will be limited to the role of Congress. The principal interest groups representing the aging will be discussed later. Obviously, the president, and through him, his immediate staff, together with executive agencies and operating departments, may propose new legislation or changes in existing law. The dramatic proposals of the Reagan administration in the early eighties attest to the enormous impact of the executive branch. However, any major shift in direction depends upon the approval of the Congress. The members of that body are influenced not only by the president and those in charge of the machinery of government at both national and state levels but also by a host of organizations claiming to represent the people.

To those interested in promoting the concerns of the aging, the organization of Congress seems to present insuperable obstacles. One might assume that the solution to a problem concerning the aging depended upon the two committees with the word *aging* in their titles, namely, the Senate Special Committee on Aging and the House Select Committee on Aging, and that once these committees were persuaded of the appropriateness of a given proposal, the membership of each house of Congress, in its desire to promote the interests of the aging, would quickly approve the recommendations of the committees. Unhappily for the sponsors of a proposal, this scenario has no relation to normal congressional procedures.

The problems of the aging cover such a broad spectrum that to concentrate all proposed legislation in the hands of one committee in each house would place an extraordinary burden upon the membership. Moreover, and of critical importance, such an approach would be contrary to the operational procedures that have been painstakingly worked out over many decades.

Both houses of Congress, as well as most governmental departments, are organized by function. For example, legislation relating to the defense of the nation is the primary responsibility of the Armed Services committees in the House and the Senate. Similarly, because of the predominantly fiscal nature of social security, responsibility for legislation in this area is allocated to the Committee on Finance in the Senate and the Committee on Ways and Means in the House. Major exceptions to this structure, that is, committees organized on the basis of clientele rather than function, are the Veterans' Affairs committees of the Senate and the House.

THE SENATE SPECIAL COMMITTEE ON AGING

Congressional recognition of the concerns of the elderly dates from 1959, when the Labor and Public Welfare Committee of the Senate established the Subcommittee on Problems of the Aged and Aging. Over the next months, the subcommittee, under the chairmanship of Senator Patrick McNamara of Michigan, conducted extensive hearings and issued sixteen reports.[15] One conclusion of the subcommittee was that the problems of the elderly were of "such grave concern to the Nation as to require the full time and attention of a special committee of the Senate."[16] A resolution to that effect, enacted February 13, 1961, established the Special Committee on Aging, which would consist of nine senators to be appointed by the president of the Senate, six from the majority party and three from the minority. Senator McNamara was appointed chairman.

The authorizing resolution prescribed that the duties of the committee be as follows: "to make a full and complete study and investigation of any and all matters pertaining to problems of older people, including but not limited to problems of maintaining health, of assuring adequate income, of finding employment, of engaging in productive and rewarding activity, or securing proper housing, and, when necessary, care or assistance."[17]

The new committee was given the status—or lack of status—of a special committee. The authorizing resolution declared that "no proposed legislation shall be referred to such committee, and such committee shall not have power to report by bill or otherwise have legislative jurisdiction."[18] The committee was instructed to report its conclusions and recommendations by January 31, 1962, and to "cease to exist" on that date.

These strictures might have been crippling, but, in fact, they were not. Instead they offered a number of advantages. The membership could be drawn from the Senate as a whole, thus attracting those most interested in either the subject matter or the potential political value of the appointment. Interest in the committee proved to be so great that the membership was shortly enlarged to twenty-one. A second advantage of the special committee status was the relative freedom it gave the membership to operate in a wide area without arousing the jealousy of the members of standing committees. For example, had the new committee tried to assume control over Medicare legislation, it would have infringed upon the territory of the Finance Committee. Had it proposed legislation in the field of housing, it might have incurred the wrath of members of the Banking and Currency Committee. Instead, although its recommendations ultimately had to be approved by the appropriate standing committee, the special committee was free to study and recommend without seeming "to poach on another committee's jurisdictional domain."[19]

Nor did the resolution providing for termination at the end of one year prove to be a stumbling block. Time after time, the life of the committee was extended—always for one year. In 1977, a Senate committee to study the committee system proposed the reduction of the number of committees from thirty-one to fifteen. The Senate Special Committee on Aging was one of those scheduled for extinction. The issue was finally decided on the Senate floor. By a vote of ninety-six to four, the Special Committee was retained. Moreover, it was given permanent status, although the membership was reduced from twenty-three to nine.[20] The membership was increased to ten in 1979, then to twelve in the same year, and to fifteen in 1981.

The principal function of the Special Committee is to act as a legislative catalyst focusing upon issues of vital concern to older Americans. In part, this function can be performed within the halls of Congress as the members of the committee keep a watchful eye upon legislative developments. But one facet of their work lies beyond the internal pulling and hauling associated with the originating and nurturing of legislative measures. This facet relates to the work of the committee in learning about problems firsthand, in testing public reaction to proposals for new legislation, and in obtaining information about the actual administrative operation of ongoing programs.

The committee has learned about problems of the aging largely through the public hearings it holds, chiefly in Washington. By the end of 1981, approximately 350 hearings had been held in roughly 100 cities and towns. In addition, the committee has published dozens of documents, some prepared by government agencies, or consultants, and some by the staff, on a variety of subjects pertaining to the aging.[21]

One of the committee's contributions to the literature on aging has been an unusual report that has assumed the stature of a major public policy document.[22] Entitled *Developments in Aging*, the report in recent years has consisted of two parts. For example, the first part of the 1981 report, prepared chiefly by the staff, consists of a 549-page exposition of issues concerning the aging. Part 2, amounting to 331 pages, was prepared by concerned administrative agencies. Reports vary widely in character. Nevertheless, the total two-part document provides a remarkable storehouse of information.

THE HOUSE SELECT COMMITTEE ON AGING

The House did not act to create a committee on aging until 1974. At the 1971 White House Conference on Aging, the Section on Government and

Nongovernment Organization recommended that "a special committee on the aging should be established in the United States House of Representatives, functioning in a comparable role to that of the United States Senate Special Committee on Aging."[23] There were five other similar recommendations. Within the next three years, according to Congressman C. W. Young of Florida, "nearly two hundred members of the House of Representatives endorsed the recommendation." By that time, he said, there were twenty-one committees of the House . . . that [had] some jurisdiction with legislation relating to older people," and the time had come to create a select committee "to try to keep coordination, to make recommendations."[24] On October 2, 1974, the proposal was approved by a vote of 323 to 84, to take effect January 3, 1975.

The Select Committee on Aging was given to the unusual status of a permanent committee. Its principal role, a supportive one, is to seek out facts and to make recommendations to standing committees. It has no legislative jurisdiction. For example, it can not report out bills. The committee started out in March 1975 with twenty-eight members. This number increased to thirty-four during the 95th Congress, to forty-five during the 96th, and to fifty-four during the 97th. From its inception, the committee has followed the House rule for standing committees requiring those with over twenty members to form a minimum of four subcommittees. The chairman and the ranking minority member of the full committee are ex officio members of each of the following subcommittees: Retirement Income and Employment; Health and Long-Term Care; Housing and Consumer Interests; and Federal, State, and Community Services (redesignated Human Services in 1978).

Major oversight investigations—those that "examine the application, administration, execution, and effectiveness of legislation intended to benefit the elderly"—may, at the direction of the chairman, be conducted by the full committee.[25] A principal investigative tool is the public hearing, which may be held in Washington or in the field. Hearings may be conducted by the full committee or by a subcommittee. Occasionally, hearings are held jointly with other House committees. A less formal device, the briefing, may be used to obtain information quickly; persons knowledgeable in special fields may be invited to appear before the committee, sometimes in executive sessions.

The full committee has a professional and secretarial staff, including a minority staff director and minority secretaries. With the assistance of the staff, the committee conducts studies and prepares reports on subjects of particular interest to committee members.

Although the Select Committee on Aging has no legislative jurisdiction, members of the committee, through membership on other House committees, may be able to introduce legislation of interest to the Select Committee. They may also testify at the hearings of other committees. In addition, the full committee or any of its subcommittees, with the assistance of the professional staff, analyzes and develops data concerning pending legislation.

The committee endeavors to be a one-stop information source not only for members of the House but also for private individuals. The committee has published an extensive series of hearings and reports. During the 94th Congress, for example, it published eighty-six items with such titles as "Elderly Crime Victimization" and "Problems of the Elderly in Arkansas."

OTHER CONGRESSIONAL COMMITTEES

Both the Senate Special Committee on Aging and the House Select Committee on Aging are authorized to investigate and study any area of interest to the aging, but neither one has the power to introduce legislation. This lack of authority might seem to downgrade the importance of the committees. However, were it not for such a limitation, constant friction with other substantive committees might result. In practice, the prohibition simply requires that a committee member who wishes to propose legislation either request help from a member of another committee or, since each member normally serves on more than one substantive committee, make the proposal through another committee. The combined membership of the two committees on aging reaches into a substantial portion of the total congressional committee structure. The accompanying table lists the committees in each house that have jurisdiction over major program areas relating to the elderly.[26]

Senate

Committee	*Program Area*
Special Committee on Aging	Oversight responsibilities
Agriculture, Nutrition and Forestry	Food Stamp Program
Armed Services	Retirement for military personnel
Banking, Housing and Urban Affairs	Housing: nursing homes; Mass Transportation Act services
Finance	Social Security; Medicaid; Medicare; private pensions; Title XX social services; supplemental security income; taxation
Governmental Affairs	Civil service retirement
Judiciary	Crime Prevention
Labor and Human Resources	Older Americans Act programs; senior opportunities and services; educational programs; manpower programs; black lung; health care programs; action volunteer programs; age discrimination in employment; railroad retirement; private pensions

Veterans' Affairs   Programs for elderly veterans
Appropriations   Participation to some degree in all
                                         programs
Budget   Participation to some degree in all
                                         programs

House of Representatives

Committee	Program Area
Select Committee on Aging	Oversight responsibilities
Agriculture	Food Stamp Program
Armed Services	Retirement of military personnel
Banking, Finance and Urban Affairs	Housing
Education and Labor	Older Americans Act programs; senior community services employment; black lung, ACTION volunteer programs; private pensions; age discrimination in employment
Energy and Commerce	Medicaid; National Institute on Aging; nursing homes; railroad retirement
Judiciary	Crime prevention
Post Office and Civil Service	Civil service retirement
Public Works and Transportation	Urban Mass Transportation Act services
Veterans' Affairs	Programs for elderly veterans
Ways and Means	Taxation; private pension plans; Social Security; Medicare; supplemental security income; Title XX social services
Appropriations	Participation to some degree in all services
Budget	Participation to some degree in all services

In a foreword to the publication *Federal Responsibility to the Elderly,* the chairman of the House Select Committee on Aging, Representative Claude Pepper, speaks of the "fragmented, inefficient, unmanageable, and incomprehensible way in which the Federal Government provides necessary benefits and services to the elderly.[27] As the table demonstrates, however, the structure of Congress adds further confusion to an already "incomprehensible" administrative organization of services for the elderly. On occasion, congressional committees vie with each other for control of a particular program. The result may be a division of responsibility between two committees. An example, and by no means an isolated one, is the Senate's Black Lung Program, jurisdiction over which is divided between the Labor and Human Resources Committee and the Finance Committee. The possibility of strife within each house and between the two legislative bodies is ever present.

3. Interest Groups Representing The Aging

Interest groups representing the aging, play an increasingly important role in both formulating policies for the aging and reviewing and evaluating the administration of these policies. As mentioned previously, interest groups have become important segments of the total political structure. During the 1981 White House Conference on Aging, for example, a number of interest groups were represented by a relatively new body, the Leadership Council of Aging Organizations. Some interest groups participating in the conference were mass membership groups. Some were associations of professionals in the field of aging. Some were interested in a particular aspect of a service for the elderly. The following section briefly describes the origins and current status of interest groups representing the aging.

THE AMERICAN ASSOCIATION OF RETIRED PERSONS (AARP)

The largest of these organizations is the American Association of Retired Persons. Organized in 1958, AARP grew rapidly, overtaking, at least in membership, the group responsible for its formation, the National Retired Teachers Association (NRTA). Indeed, in 1982, the teachers' association became a division of AARP. In 1984, the total membership numbered roughly 15 million.

NRTA was founded in 1947 by Dr. Ethel Percy Andrus, a retired high school principal. Dr. Andrus and the association achieved national recognition in 1955 when group health insurance was offered by the Continental Casualty Company, through Leonard Davis, a young group-insurance specialist, to the twenty thousand members of the association. The interest shown by both teachers and nonteachers led Dr. Andrus to conclude that there was a need for a national organization of older persons. With the assistance of Davis, a new corporation was founded—the American Association of Retired Persons.

The two associations operated from one headquarters in Washington. Each had a board of directors. While NRTA and AARP had the same executive director, each association had its own membership roster. In 1978, the associations declared that "eight out of every ten retired teachers in America" held membership in NRTA and that "one out of every four Americans over the age of fifty-five" was a member of AARP.[28] Each association was made up of separate area, state, and local units. NRTA had over twenty-four hundred local units prior to the merger; AARP had about three thousand.

The associations provided a remarkable array of services for their members. For example, all members of NRTA, for an annual fee of five dollars (in 1982), received the *NRTA News Bulletin,* an eight-page paper published eleven times yearly, and the *NRTA Journal,* a magazine published bimonthly.

The masthead of the magazine described NRTA as a "nonprofit, nonpartisan, social welfare, philanthropic, educational and scientific membership organization." AARP published a similar newsletter with a similar format and articles that were often identical, as well as the magazine *Modern Maturity*. Following the merger of 1982, *Modern Maturity* was retained. A special news section for those who are also members of NRTA was added to the magazine.

Although the annual dues were modest, the associations generated a large income from special services. A number of health and accident insurance plans were developed through the initiative of Leonard Davis, a substantial owner in a group of insurance companies called Colonial Penn. A portion of the premiums—4.9 percent in 1979—was remitted to a joint account called the NRTA and AARP Administrative Fund. Colonial Penn also paid into a fund for advertising in the associations' publications.

The long-standing relationship with Colonial Penn brought with it a number of issues that plagued the associations for many years. For example, there were charges that the associations were being used as a front by Colonial Penn to distribute advertising at postal rates reserved for nonprofit organizations. In 1979, the executive director of the associations, Cyril F. Brickfield, announced that "misunderstandings about the relationships have begun to obscure our larger role and distract volunteer and staff leaders from our essential task of serving all older Americans." As a consequence, NRTA/ AARP found it necessary to reappraise the relationship that, admittedly, had enabled the associations "to pioneer a host of immensely valuable and needed services."[29] Subsequently, the relationship was severed, and in July 1981, the Prudential Insurance Company of America became the carrier for the group health insurance programs.

A second source of income was pharmacy service. Members of the associations were able to obtain medications at prices considerably below those charged by individual pharmacists. By 1979, a separate corporation and its subsidiaries had sales of over $62 million. The associations received royalties from these sales and from advertising in NRTA/AARP publications. Other enterprises from which the association boosted their operating funds included a travel service, an automobile insurance service, and a temporary employment service. The associations were among the early contractors with the Senior Community Service Employment Program. Federal grants amounting to over $38 million in 1980 covered the cost of projects administered by the associations.[30]

Many programs are operated by volunteers. For example, in 1979, eighty-three hundred tax aide counselors at thirty-two hundred sites assisted three-quarters of a million older people. The National Consumer Assistance Center in Washington, staffed by volunteers, answers members' questions by mail. Programs related to health, education, crime prevention, and other areas provide a wide range of services to association members. In addition, professional staff members prepare booklets and other training materials.

The income generated by the associations' relationships with various business enterprises led to the establishment of the Ethel Percy Andrus Gerontology Center at the University of Southern California. Intended initially as a site for research and training, the center, dedicated in 1973, later came to house the Leonard Davis School of Gerontology and the Andrus Foundation, which supports research at the center and at a number of universities. Individual research awards usually cover one year of study.

The associations were once considered to be sympathetic toward business. For example, in 1965, they did not oppose but neither did they promote the passage of Medicare. Later, in the early seventies, the associations tried to project a nonpartisan attitude toward issues involving the aging.[31] In recent years, through a legislative council representing both associations, state and federal issues relating to the elderly have been debated and solutions to some concerns of the elderly have been promoted. Because of their joint state committees, the associations claim to be "the only national organizations representing older people with concerted, effective legislative representation in every state."[32] Proposed legislation affecting the elderly at both the state and federal levels has become a matter of increasing concern to AARP.

THE NATIONAL COUNCIL OF SENIOR CITIZENS (NCSC)

The National Council of Senior Citizens was established in 1961 to promote one issue—Medicare. "Built around the remnants of the Senior Citizens for Kennedy, which had been organized for the 1960 campaign, the council was supported by funds from the AFL-CIO, the Democratic National Committee, and member dues of one dollar per year."[33] The Democratic National Committee's support was based upon its analysis of the 1960 election and its finding that "elderly voters had contributed significantly, and in some key districts decisively, to Kennedy's victory."[34]

The political activism associated with the origin of NCSC has been retained over the two decades of its existence. But while one observer has declared that "the leadership of NCSC is . . . securely in labor union hands,"[35] the council's interests have broadened to include virtually every need of the elderly that can be met by governmental action.

The strength of NCSC—"the life force of the organization"—according to its long-time executive director, William R. Hutton, has been its over three thousand senior citizen clubs,[36] many of which are made up largely of retired union workers. In the past, all members of an affiliated club were considered members of NCSC.

A revision of the constitution in 1979 requires any new club to have a minimum of twenty Gold Card members, that is, individual dues-paying members. At that time, NCSC claimed that 3½ million persons belonged to its affiliated clubs. Since then, renewed emphasis has been placed upon clubs having memberships made up of only Gold Card holders. In 1982, a major membership campaign was launched with the slogan "a million more by eighty-four."[37]

NCSC is governed by a general board consisting of national officers, state council presidents, at least twenty-six members elected at large, and a minimum of thirty-four members elected by regions. The board receives its authority from a biennial constitutional convention, the "highest governing body of the National Council of Senior Citizens, Inc."[38]

Club, area, and state councils are grouped into ten regions corresponding to the ten Federal Standard Regions. This organizational structure was adopted in 1979 in recognition of NCSC's relationship with three agencies, the former Department of Health, Education, and Welfare; the Department of Housing and Urban Development; and the Department of Labor. The report on the development of this structure states that "the pattern of the Federal Standard Regions was adopted since many important program decisions of the federal agencies are delegated to their regional offices and contact between such regional offices and the National Council of Senior Citizens affiliates in the region should be encouraged and facilitated."[39] Each region's representation on the general board depends on the number of Gold Card members in that region. Since 25 percent of the total number of Gold Card members are in Region V, this region was divided into subregion a, Ohio, Indiana, and Michigan; and subregion b, Wisconsin, Minnesota, and Illinois.

In order to buttress the revenues of the association and provide a service to the membership, NCSC sponsors a drug and vitamin program through National Pharmacies, Inc. The NCSC Travel Service has similar objectives. A Medicare supplement insurance program is operated by Maxon Administrators.

Through the NCSC Housing Management Corporation and in conjunction with the Department of Housing and Urban Development's Section 202 program, NCSC cosponsors, with local groups, the construction of rental apartment buildings for the elderly. In November 1982, the *Senior Citizen News* declared that NCSC's $300 million housing program made it the "largest nonprofit developer of Section 202/8 housing in the United States."[40] For many years NCSC has been a sponsor of the Department of Labor's Senior Community Service Employment Program. Through this program, part-time employment is offered to low-income persons over the age of fifty-five.

NCSC communicates with the membership by means of a monthly newspaper, *Senior Citizen News*. Among other features of the paper is an annual evaluation of the voting records of all members of Congress on ten issues of special concern to the elderly. A second publication, entitled *The Senior*

Leader, was introduced in 1979. It provides club leaders with background information on legislation supported by the organization and with ideas for local projects.

THE NATIONAL COUNCIL ON THE AGING (NCOA)

Described as "essentially a society of subject matter specialists," the National Council on the Aging, has ties with senior centers throughout the country, giving the organization a "quasi-mass-membership" status.[41] The origins of NCOA date from 1950, when a national committee on the aging was created by the National Social Welfare Assembly following the Federal Security Agency's declaration of its intention to hold the National Conference on Aging. The present title of the organization was adopted in 1960.

NCOA has a small dues-paying membership. Its sponsorship of the National Institute of Senior Centers, founded in 1967, resulted in connections with over five thousand centers in all parts of the country. Beginning in 1984, the board of directors will consist of from eighteen to thirty-six persons. Past presidents constitute a president's council. The staff of about eighty is head-quartered in Washington. In addition, there are four regional offices.

The financial banking for NCOA has come principally from grants. From 1956 to 1969 the Ford Foundation was a principal supporter. In recent years, major grants from the federal government have enabled NCOA to conduct studies and operate programs on a contract basis. For example, as one of the contract organizations with the Department of Labor's Senior Community Service Project, NCOA arranges with roughly two hundred public agencies in over fifty communities for the employment of four thousand low-income persons over the age of fifty-five. In 1978, NCOA had contracts and grants from seven federal agencies and nine states and contributions from over forty corporations, four major labor unions, and numerous foundations, associations, and educational institutions, including over twenty units of United Way.[42]

NCOA publishes a bimonthly magazine, *Perspective on Aging,* and a quarterly magazine, *Aging and Work: A Journal on Age, Work and Retirement* (formerly *Industrial Gerontology*). The organization also issues a quarterly bibliography of literature on aging and a monthly publication called *Senior Center Report.* The library in the Washington headquarters, according to NCOA, is the "most comprehensive . . . in the nation for materials in the field of aging."[43]

Some of the many institutions and programs sponsored by NCOA are the National Institute on Age, Work and Retirement (NIAWR), the National Institute of Senior Centers (NISC), the Senior Center Humanities Program (SCHP), the Center on Arts and Aging, the Housing Corporation, the Public Policy Center, the Media Resource Center (MRC), and the Intergenerational

Services Program. NCOA also sponsors the National Voluntary Organizations for Independent Living for the Aging (NVOILA), which provides technical assistance to over 160 national voluntary organizations, and Voluntarism in Action for the Aging (VIAA), a program that helps coordinate the efforts of national voluntary organizations.

Over the years, NCOA has maintained a relatively low-key advisory role. Indeed, the articles of incorporation include the statement that "no part of the activity of this corporation shall be attempted influence of legislation by propaganda or otherwise."[44] The governing board violated this stricture by endorsing the Older Americans Act. The following year the board resolved that "as an educational institution, NCOA may wish to express an opinion on certain issues and to establish appropriate mechanisms for this purpose."[45] The Public Policy Committee was created, and occasional statements were issued in the early seventies "on a number of the rather narrowly circumscribed aging issues."[46] However, by the late seventies, the board was issuing an extensive public policy agenda setting forth its position on major issues.

THE GRAY PANTHERS

The Gray Panthers originated because of the determination of one woman. Retirement at sixty-five led to fame, if not fortune, for Margaret (Maggie) Kuhn, who over two decades had worked in the Office of Church and Society at the national headquarters of the United Presbyterian Church, then in Philadelphia. Upon retiring in 1970, she called together five friends who were also retiring from religious or social organizations. Over subsequent monthly meetings, the group grew in size. Two topics were paramount in the group's discussions: the special problems of retired people and opposition to the Vietnam War. Students at Haverford College were invited to join the group, and over subsequent meetings the Coalition of Older and Younger Adults was formed. The name Gray Panthers was first used half-jokingly by a New York television producer. But on May 20, 1972, in Denver, Colorado, reporting on a press conference at the General Assembly of the United Presbyterian Church, the major newspapers featured the name Gray Panthers. A few days later, when Maggie Kuhn appeared on the "Today Show," the name was all but official.[47]

At first, the group considered itself a movement rather than a formal organization. A 1974 statement defined a Gray Panther as "a person who, either alone or with others, actively promotes the interaction of young and old people and the maximum involvement of all ages in areas of social and political life." The statement declared that the Gray Panthers were distinguished by several characteristics: "a movement instead of an organization," "a struggle against ageism," "a coalition of age and youth," "militant . . . (in nonviolent ways)," "concerned with actions for change rather than service."[48]

Initially, there were no dues or formal identification cards. But people from all across the country wrote asking to be made members. A central steering committee acted as a link with groups in other areas, and workshops were held in leadership development. In time, a network of community groups was operating in several states. A national newsletter, at first made possible only by contributions, began publication.

What distinguishes the Gray Panthers from other organizations is its coalition of young and old people who work together not only to combat ageism but also to oppose social injustice at all levels. In the mid-1970s, for example, the group's largest single project was the promotion of a national health service. In 1974 not one of the seventeen national health bills before the Congress was acceptable to the Gray Panthers. All were condemned as ignoring the consumer in favor of the insurance industry and the medical profession. Gray Panther groups in various cities have developed their own special interests: low- and middle-income housing in Washington, D.C., a women's center in San Francisco, and continuing education for both young and old in Philadelphia.[49]

Organizational and financial problems have been difficult to overcome. An enlarged nation steering committee guides the movement. Articles of agreement define the purposes and goals of the Gray Panthers Project Fund, as it is officially called, and establish operating procedures.

Biennial national conventions adopt resolutions covering a wide range of social issues. At the fourth biennial convention, held in Washington in December 1981, resolutions on the following topics were adopted: Social Security, peace, mental and physical health, housing, legal services, long-term health care, nuclear energy, the Family Protection Act, hiring under the Older Americans Act, defense, the right to die with dignity, employment, and priority for those in greatest economic or social need under the Older Americans Act.[50]

According to a management study in 1979, the principal contribution of the Gray Panthers has been in raising the nation's consciousness about ageism. A questionnaire sent to readers of *Gray Panthers Network* drew responses from twenty-eight states, with over 50 percent of the replies coming from three states: New York (24 percent), California (20 percent), and New Jersey (9 percent). Fifty-nine percent of the respondents were under sixty-five.[51]

Gray Panthers and their friends distinguish between this organization and "establishment aging organizations." The latter, with Washington offices, sizable professional staffs, and financial support from travel, insurance, and other businesses, including those subsidized by government contracts, operate in a manner totally different from that of the Gray Panthers. A leading scholar has declared that the Gray Panthers are "the only organization working to solve the problems of human beings rather than those of the profession and the industry."[52]

THE NATIONAL ASSOCIATION OF RETIRED FEDERAL EMPLOYEES (NARFE)

Founded in 1921, this association of retired federal annuitants has a current membership of approximately one-quarter million. Roughly twelve hundred chapters are units of state federations. These are grouped into ten regions, each headed by a field vice president. National officers are elected at biennial national conventions. The national officers and the field vice presidents make up the board of directors. Day-to-day operations are the responsibility of the president.[53]

For six decades, NARFE has held consistently to one objective: service to retired federal employees. It has, through the Civil Service committees of Congress, sponsored legislation relating to the retirement of federal civilian employees and has monitored legislative proposals that might act to the detriment of annuitants.

A monthly magazine, *Retirement Life,* is the principal means of communication with the membership. Membership in NARFE opens the door to participation in a wide range of insurance programs. However, the organization is quick to point out that it has "no financial interest in any of the companies underwriting these policies."[54] Opportunities for group travel are also provided.

NARFE is active in providing preretirement guidance to federal employees. At no charge to the government, the organizaton holds panel discussions led by NARFE members. The meetings also enable the panelists to acquaint prospective annuitants with the objectives of the organization.

The organization lays claim to various legislative accomplishments, all of which are meant to improve the status of the retired federal employee. In *The Gray Lobby,* Henry J. Pratt declared that "NARFE is essentially an 'interest' group, concerned with the narrowly-defined needs of its dues-paying retired-civil-service constituency. Its leaders do not concern themselves as part of a social reform vanguard, and their policy views reflect this fact."[55]

THE LEADERSHIP COUNCIL ON AGING (LCOA)

In the months before the 1981 White House Conference on Aging, representatives of a number of organizations formed the Leadership Council on Aging. A committee of roughly a dozen LCOA members endeavored to develop common positions to which all might subscribe. The result was an eight-point policy agenda entitled "8 for the 80s," which set forth recommendations for the twenty-two hundred delegates. In November 1981, twenty-three organizations adopted the eight-point statement, thus providing a series of guideposts for the consideration of the fourteen White House Conference committees.

During the conference, the council pursued the role of "advocate for the rights and opportunities for older people." This advocacy role involved, the council declared later, acting on "the premise that, notwithstanding efforts to manipulate outcomes for partisan purposes, our organizations had a responsibility to secure the best possible set of recommendations from the Conference with the view to putting them into practice over the 1980s."[56]

The chair of the council is rotated annually among the three members with the largest number of subscribers. Eight members constitute an executive committee. Following is a list of the organizations making up the council as of May 1982 (asterisks indicate members of the executive committee).[57]

American Association of Homes for the Aging
Asociación Nacional Pro Personas Mayores*
Association for Gerontology in Higher Education
Concerned Seniors for Better Government
The Gerontological Society of America*
The Gray Panthers
National Association of Area Agencies on Aging
National Association of Foster Grandparents Program Directors
National Association of Mature People
National Association of Meal Programs
National Association of Nutrition and Aging Services Programs
National Association of Retired Federal Employees
National Association of Retired Senior Volunteer Program (RSVP) Directors
National Association of Senior Companion Project Directors
National Association of State Units on Aging*
National Caucus and Center on Black Aged
National Council of Senior Citizens*
National Council on the Aging, Inc.*
National Indian Council on Aging
National Interfaith Coalition on Aging
National Pacific/Asian Resource Center on Aging
National Retired Teachers Association/American Association of Retired Persons*
National Senior Citizens Law Center
Older Women's League
Retired Members Department/United Auto Workers*
Social Security Department/AFL-CIO
Urban Elderly Coalition*
Western Gerontological Society

4. Summary Analysis

This chapter has indicated some of the complexity of social welfare policy-making, focusing on federal programs for the aged. Even within this limited area, it is clear that the United States will probably never develop a comprehensive policy for the aged or, for that matter, any other population group. One reason for this is the complex structure of Congress, our major policy-making body. Because of the historical development of a number of committees that are empowered to develop and introduce them, bills for the aging often fall under multiple jurisdictions; for example, one aspect of a program might belong to Finance, another aspect to Agriculture, and so on.

Responsibility for the same aspect of a program may be shared by two or more committees. Beyond that, the two houses of Congress go their separate ways to some extent and frequently must reach a compromise that is reasonably satisfactory to both the Senate and the House of Representatives. Additionally, the influence of the executive arm of government, the president and his staff, is very powerful. Even when the two bodies of Congress do come to an agreement, there is always the threat of a presidential veto. Such a threat may lead to further compromises, reservations, and restrictions. Former President Ford, for example, exercised his will almost exclusively by vetoing legislation he considered unacceptable.

The House and Senate committees on aging are largely information-gathering bodies, although they have access to committees that are empowered to introduce bills, especially through the coordinating arrangements developed in the House Select Committee on Aging. Nevertheless, the committees spend much of their time and energy producing studies and reports that are responses to a variety of specific concerns rather than a comprehensive, cohesive search into the needs of the elderly, thus generating volumes of fragmented material. A part of this diversity may be because senators and congressmen, while national figures, must also respond to their constituencies at the state and local levels. The public hearings held around the country are not merely fact-finding strategies; they are also intended to demonstrate that national political figures are responsive to the will of the people. Depending on where the political figure happens to come from, the will of certain people is stressed over that of others. This is inherent in the structure of American political life, as has been discussed previously.

In contemporary politics in the United States, the concerns of people are often represented by interest groups. As might be expected, each of the major associations representing the concerns of the aging has developed its own operational stance. The Gray Panthers and the National Council of Senior Citizens do not hesitate to take to the streets to call attention to an issue. Comparatively speaking, the Gray Panthers are in the early stages of development. They are lacking both the resources and the professional expertise necessary to carry out extensively researched studies on issues involving the aging. They have neither expressed an interest in this approach nor endeavored to improve their financial standing by contracting for services with the government. As a result, they have a degree of independence that the National Council of Senior Citizens, the American Association of Retired Persons, and the National Council on the Aging do not.

The National Council of Senior Citizens has maintained close ties with the labor movement. On occasion, its energies have been directed first toward the needs of labor and second toward the needs of the elderly. In October 1979, for example, NCSC served as the "official voice" of the Citizen Labor Energy Coalition and the Progressive Alliance during demonstrations in Washington, D.C., on BIG OIL Protest Day. NCSC has differed with other associations representing the aging on features of the Social Securities Act such as the earnings test and on legislation relating to mandatory retirement. In general, however, the organization has been an outspoken advocate of the aging.

The American Association of Retired Persons has moved from a position of almost extreme caution to one of outspokenness on many issues of immediate interest to the elderly. The group's activities have been confined to the presentation of views at legislative hearings and to the urging of members, through the association's newspaper, to communicate with legislative bodies. With a membership of approximately 15 million, AARP could occupy center stage in speaking on issues involving the aging.

The number of associations of the aged has increased substantially in the past decade. The political potency of these organizations will almost certainly increase. But other interest groups are also gaining strength. Moreover, many of these have greater financial ability to promote their positions.

Making even slight progress toward the passing of legislation on behalf of the aged, then, means listening to an almost infinite variety of voices, both inside and outside the halls of Congress. In addition, it is hardly necessary to mention that legislation on behalf of the aging is only one part of the agenda and that competing interest groups also have access to legislators' ears. Except during the Roosevelt and early Johnson administrations, it has been difficult to mobilize coalitions of "disadvantaged" groups, although it would seem that these groups have many goals in common. However, even persuading all those interest groups who claim to be operating to benefit the elderly to work together has not been possible.

Complicated as this discussion has been, it has dealt only with policymaking at the federal level. The next chapter, which deals with what is called the Aging Network, will describe the administrative complexity resulting from organizing social service programs to operate on the federal, state, and

regional levels. The next chapter also deals with substantive programs implemented under the Older Americans Act. Although this act is relatively recent,
it is discussed next because it has implications for structure as well as substance in public policy for the aging.

II / The Aging Network

1. Introduction: A Prelude

In 1965, the Older Americans Act was born. The act and the machinery involved in carrying out its objectives are often referred to as the Aging Network because of the extensive linkages on several levels that have been built up for its development and implementation. Technically speaking, the concept refers primarily to administrative structure.[1] However, since it is via this structure that services are delivered, the Aging Network has a more encompassing function. Since the structure is so central to the understanding of the Older Americans Act and its amendments, over the next pages we will focus first on the provisions for its administration and later on the services it provides. Finally, in the analytic summary we will look at the two parts in relation to one another.

Although of modest beginnings, the Older Americans Act has expanded over the years. The various White House conferences have been highly instrumental in promoting its growth. Before the formal introduction of the act itself, however, a number of forces were being mobilized to induce the federal government to take legislative action on behalf of the elderly. The more influential of these forces are briefly discussed below.

In 1950, the Federal Security Agency sponsored a National Conference on Aging, which was said to be "the first expression of the executive branch's coordinated concern for older persons."[2] Directed by Dr. Clark Tibbetts, the 816 persons in attendance were representatives of federal and state agencies and private organizations.[3] One year later, the interdepartmental Committee on Aging and Geriatrics was formed by the head of the Federal Security Administration to promote the exchange of information within the federal agencies. In 1956, the Special Staff on Aging was established in the office of the Secretary of the Department of Health, Education, and Welfare. In that same year, the interdepartmental committee was renamed the Federal Council on Aging; it is a forerunner of the present body of the same name.[4]

Growing attention to aging as a topic of general concern was not confined to the federal agencies. In 1945, Connecticut, by legislative act, established the Commission on the Care and Treatment of the Chronically Ill, Aged and Infirm as an operating administrative agency. The legislature of New York state focused upon the entire range of problems of the aging through the creation of a joint committee in 1947. State governors, through the Council of State Governments, sponsored a major study, published in 1955, setting forth a fifteen-point "program for action." By that time, twenty-four states had organized official bodies such as councils or commissions on aging.[5]

Congressional interest in the late 1950s was demonstrated by hearings held in several cities. The Senate Committee on Labor and Public Welfare, for example, organized the Subcommittee on Problems of the Aging. In the House, a subcommittee of the Committee on Education and Labor heard proposals for the Bureau of Older Persons and for the White House Conference on Aging. Proposed in 1958, the conference was finally held in January 1961, notwithstanding the administration's lack of support. Federal grants to the states made possible preliminary preparatory conferences, a procedure designed to promote citizen interest. Approximately twenty-eight hundred delegates, under the chairmanship of Dr. Arthur S. Flemming, the Secretary of the Department of Health, Education, and Welfare were in attendance.[6]

The conference was held in the weeks following the election of John F. Kennedy but prior to the departure of Dwight D. Eisenhower. The conference's call for federal grants to the states in order to expand services to the aged and to establish a federal coordinating agency undoubtedly influenced the new president. However, two years were to elapse before he sent a special message to Congress. In February 1963, in a message entitled "Elderly Citizens of Our Nation," the president declared that the nation had an "opportunity" to utilize the "skill and sagacity" of older persons and to give them "the respect and recognition they have earned." He continued that "it is not enough for a great nation merely to have added new years to life—our objective must also be to add new life to those years."[7]

Nothing was said in the message about the increasing support of some members of Congress and certain of the groups representing the aging for a separate administrative entity. On the contrary, there was considerable dissatisfaction on the part of these members and groups with HEW Secretary Anthony Celebrezze, who transferred the Special Staff on Aging from his office to that of the commissioner of welfare. The special staff was renamed the Office of Aging, but this did not satisfy those who objected to the relationship with what appeared to be an office primarily concerned with welfare.[8] Congressional committees, including the newly created Senate Special Committee on Aging, were the principal instigators of a drive for legislation giving increased recognition to the elderly. In July 1965 the Older Americans Act was passed unanimously in the Senate and by a vote of 394 to 1 in the House.[9]

2. The Older Americans Act:
Development and Administrative Structure

The new act set forth ten objectives. Each was an ideal that is as valid today as it was in 1965, notwithstanding the substantial progress that has been made in the interim. The objectives follow.

1. An adequate income in retirement in accordance with the American standard of living.
2. The best possible physical and mental health which science can make available and without regard to economic status.
3. Suitable housing, independently selected, designed and located with reference to special needs and available at costs which older citizens can afford.
4. Full restorative services for those who require institutional care.
5. Opportunity for employment with no discriminatory personnel practices because of age.
6. Retirement in health, honor, dignity—after years of contribution to the economy.
7. Pursuit of meaningful activity within the widest range of civic, cultural, and recreational opportunities.
8. Efficient community services which provide social assistance in a coordinated manner and which are readily available when needed.
9. Immediate benefit from proven research knowledge which can sustain and improve health and happiness.
10. Freedom, independence, and the free exercise of individual initiative in planning, and managing their own lives.

Precisely how these objectives were to be accomplished was not spelled out. The list, in fact, has little relation to reality. The first objective, for example, calls for "adequate income in retirement." However, the Congress gave the commissioner of aging no authority to alter the responsibilities of the thirty-year-old Social Security Administration. The second objective deals with "the best possible physical and mental health which science can make available." Again, the act gave the commissioner on aging no authority over the various federal health programs such as Medicare and Medicaid. The third objective calls for suitable housing for the elderly, a subject central to the function of the Department of Housing and Urban Development (HUD). Thus each of the ten objectives is only a statement of an ideal. Although the Older Americans Act authorized a new governmental agency, it gave the agency neither the authority nor the financial support to make an impact upon the national scene.

The Older Americans Act terminated the Office of Aging. In its place it established the Administration on Aging to be headed by a commissioner on

aging appointed by the president and confirmed by the Senate. Congress intended the agency to serve as a focal point at the federal level for matters
concerning the aging. Initially, the AoA was placed in the Office of the
Secretary of Health, Education, and Welfare and had equal status with the
Public Health Service and the Social Security Administration. As the result of
being downgraded, however, within two years, the agency was reporting to the
head of the newly formed Social and Rehabilitation Service. The commissioner
reported to the administrator of the service rather than to the secretary.[10]

As enacted in 1965, the Older Americans Act provided limited funds for
social services. Through state units on aging, grants were to be made to public
agencies and private nonprofit organizations. Monies were to be distributed
by the Administration on Aging on a formula basis, each state with an
approved state plan receiving 1 percent of the annual appropriation plus a
second amount based on the proportion of the population over the age of
sixty-five. Federal monies were to cover up to 75 percent of the cost of a
project the first year, up to 60 percent the second year, and up to 50 percent
the third year. The states could also receive up to fifteen thousand dollars to
cover one-half the administrative costs, a figure raised to twenty-five thousand
dollars in 1967. At the end of the third year, the project was expected to
continue without further federal support. However, following some states'
protests concerning their inability to assume full responsibility, the act was
amended in 1969 to provide up to 50 percent federal funding for the fourth and
subsequent years.

The act authorized grants for projects that would test out various methods
of providing services. Grants were to be made, also, for training projects and
for research on identifying new approaches to improving the lot of the elderly.
The fifteen-member Adivisory Committee on Older Americans was authorized to be appointed by the secretary.

The new agency grew slowly. There was much to be done, yet there was a
dearth of funds and a lack both of expertise and awareness on the part of the
public of the problems of the aged. With a view to remedying these deficiencies, proposals for a second White House conference were approved by the
Congress, and authorizing legislation was signed by President Johnson in
September 1968.[11] A year later the Senate Special Committee on Aging
signaled the need for further action: "The role of AoA . . . remains ambiguous. Its funding levels are lower than required for healthy growth of State and
community programs. It does not have the 'visibility' envisioned for it by the
Congress. Serious thought should be given, before and during the White
House Conference on Aging in 1971, to far reaching proposals for constructive change that will enable the AoA to fulfill the vital missions assigned
to it."[12]

Dissatisfaction with the progress in improving the lot of the aging was
again pointed out by a twenty-one member advisory group called together by

the chairman of the Senate Special Committee on Aging in 1971. The group's report, given a few weeks before the White House Conference, declared: "AoA falls far short of being the Federal 'focal point in aging' sought by Congress. Instead, its concerns are splintered and scattered; there are limited, if any, policies and few clear-cut goals. Recent reorganizations have not strengthened Federal programs and commitment in aging in any way. Rather, they have fragmented an already flawed and feeble agency still further. This situation has created chaos as well as a lack of direction in Federal and State programs."[13]

THE 1971 WHITE HOUSE CONFERENCE

The conference was in session from November 28 through December 2, 1971, but an extensive amount of preparatory work had been done before the actual convening of the 3,574 delegates. Beginning in the fall of 1970, over six thousand Older American White House Forums were held. Over one-half million persons participated. Responses to 194,000 questionnaires were analyzed to find out what the elderly perceived as their greatest needs. Reports from the forums were considered by state White House Conferences on Aging held from April through July 1971. Over thirty-eight thousand attended.

The conference was not without its problems. Resentment developed because national senior groups were involved to only a minor degree in these early stages. Resentment began to build up, also, over the system of selecting conference delegates, and because of the failure to include representatives of the elderly poor.[14] In an effort to reduce friction, Dr. Arthur S. Flemming, former head of HEW, was appointed chairman of the conference. Flemming was successful in conciliating the warring groups, and over the next months took steps to assure that the interests of various groups were represented and that individual delegates were given an opportunity to be heard.

Because of its size and scope, the conference required substantial planning. Fourteen subject areas were identified for study, nine being classified as Needs Areas and five as Needs Meeting Areas.[15]

Subject Areas

Needs Areas	*Needs Meeting Areas*
1. Income	1. Planning
2. Health and Mental Health	2. Training
3. Housing and Environment	3. Research and Development
4. Nutrition	4. Services, Programs, and Facilities
5. Education	5. Government and Nongovernment
6. Employment and Retirement	Organizations
7. Retirement Roles and Activities	
8. Transportation	
9. Spiritual Well-being	

The conference was divided into fourteen sections conforming to the fourteen subject areas. In order to meet the demands of various groups that were not satisfied with the subject area classification, seventeen Special Concerns Sessions covered a variety of topics, such as long-term care, aging and blindness, the Spanish-speaking elderly, the elderly Indian, and aged blacks. Each section and special session brought forth recommendations. The groups worked independently, with the consequence that there was some duplication of effort. For example, there were six separate proposals for the establishment of a committee on aging in the House of Representatives. All told, 663 recommendations, many of a multifaceted nature, were published in the two-volume final report of the conference.[16]

The success of the conference could be measured only in the light of succeeding actions over a period of months. Observers differed greatly in their assessments of the results. In March 1972, President Nixon sent a special message to the Congress entitled "Recommendations for Action on Behalf of Older Americans." The chairman of the Senate Special Committee on Aging, Frank Church, scathingly referred to the message as a "summation of the Executive Branch bent for 'game plansmanship,' long on promises and dismally deficient in substance . . . pathetically unresponsive to the strong and clear recommendations of the White House Conference."[17] A year later, however, the committee report declared that "reviewing the progress since the White House Conference on Aging, the Committee finds that bipartisan interest and support in the Congress—together with some initiatives by the Administration—have resulted in far-reaching accomplishments."[18]

In the months following the conference, substantial legislative changes were made in the Older Americans Act. Amendments in 1973 gave a new impetus to governmental services for the elderly.

THE 1973 AMENDMENTS TO THE OLDER AMERICANS ACT

The "Older Americans Comprehensive Services Amendments in 1973" substantially changed the original act. The ten objectives were left intact, except for number 8, which was amended. After the phrase "efficient community services" the phrase "including access to low cost transportation" was inserted. The Administration on Aging was removed from the Social and Rehabilitation Service and made a unit of HEW's Human Development Administration. The commissioner, who would now report directly to the secretary, was directed to establish a National Information and Resource Clearing House for the Aging. The federal Council on the Aging was created to evaluate the government's policies toward the aging.

Through expanded grant programs, the states were to be encouraged to develop "comprehensive and coordinated service systems to serve older persons." In order to receive grants, the states would be required to designate one agency as the unit responsible for developing an operating plan. Local units, designated Area Agencies on Aging, were to operate within planning and service areas in arranging for a broad range of social services. Each area agency on aging would be required to submit an area plan to the state showing the extent of the social services to be delivered. The area agency was to be primarily an arranger of services rather than a direct provider. The grant formula was altered so that each state would receive a minimum of one-half of 1 percent of the annual appropriation. The remainder of the appropriation for grant purposes was to be distributed according to the ratio of the state's population over sixty to the nation's population over sixty. The maximum federal payment was to be 90 percent of the cost of the services provided.[19]

The amendments provided for model projects; expanded training and research programs, including multidisciplinary centers for gerontology; and grants for acquiring, altering, or renovating multipurpose senior centers. The amendments incorporated as Title VII of the Older Americans Act a 1971 statute establishing a nutrition program for the elderly. Other changes authorized grants to states for providing library services to older persons and for establishing a community employment service program.

In the years following the amendments of 1973, there was considerable expansion of the programs authorized by the Older Americans Act. Nevertheless, much dissatisfaction remained. The executive director of the National Council of Senior Citizens declared: "As important as the legislation has been in the day-to-day lives of so many older people and as much as it has grown in its capacity to serve people, it has barely scratched the surface of the numerous and diverse needs of the elderly."[20]

Between its passage in 1965 and its extensive amendment in 1978, the Older Americans Act was revised on seven other occasions. A staff study by the House Select Committee on Aging declared that "in some years Congress thought that a tune up was all that was needed. In other years, as in 1973, a major overhaul was undertaken."[21]

As the expiration date of the act approached (September 30, 1978), there was increasing speculation concerning the nature and extent of the changes that would be made. Each house passed an amending measure. The conference committee had to settle roughly ninety points of difference.

COMPREHENSIVE OLDER AMERICANS ACT OF 1978

The Comprehensive Older Americans Act of 1978 effected substantial changes.[22] These, evolutionary rather than revolutionary in nature, were meant to remedy recognized deficiencies rather than to establish new systems. The objectives of the 1965 act were retained except for one change. Once again, an addition was made to number 8. Between the words *provide* and *social* was inserted the phrase "a choice in supported living arrangements and."

Several programs were consolidated under one title (III) in order to strengthen the concept, set forth in the 1973 amendments, of a "comprehensive and coordinated service system." Thus, social services, nutrition services, and multipurpose senior centers were to be administered as integral parts of a single effort rather than by separate funding and supervisory channels as in some states. This change was expected to promote the concept of a single community focal point for services for the aging. The basis for the allocation of funds was to remain the same, namely, the state's proportion of persons aged sixty and above. The amendments extended the act through 1981, required that each state have an ombudsman program to investigate nursing home complaints, and, in a new title, give Indian tribes the opportunity to receive funding directly from the commissioner on aging.

THE 1981 WHITE HOUSE CONFERENCE

A final feature of the 1978 amendments was the provision for another White House Conference on Aging, to be held in 1981. Resolutions introduced in both the Senate and the House in May 1977 came to fruition in Title II of the 1978 amendments.[23] In eight successive findings, the Congress declared "a great need" for policy changes that would improve the position of older individuals in the areas of economic well-being, health care, housing, the social service delivery system, long-term care, employment, retirement, and medical research.[24]

Initial plans for the conference were developed during the Carter administration. The enabling legislation made the Health and Human Services secretary responsible for planning and conducting the conference in cooperation with the commissioner on aging, the director of the National Institute on Aging, and the heads of other appropriate departments and agencies. In December 1976, more than one year later, an executive director was appointed. At that time a chairperson and four deputy chairpersons were sworn in. The chairperson was eighty-two-year-old Sadie T. M. Alexander of Philadelphia, an attorney, who according to President Carter was the first black woman in this country ever awarded an earned Ph.D.[25]

In order to generate discussion of the problems to be considered by the conference, local community forums were organized by area agencies on aging and other organizations. Groups and organizations interested in specific issues, such as the rural elderly or the Hispanic elderly, were designated to hold White House miniconferences. Background materials were prepared by sixteen White House Conference Technical Committees made up of professional and lay experts. Each of the fifty governors appointed a state coordinator who would be responsible for organizaing a State White House Conference. Beginning with those in Florida and Montana in September 1980, fifty-eight state and territorial conferences were held in succeeding months.

Early plans called for the selection of 1,800 delegates who would have voting privileges and receive travel cost reimbursement. An equal number of observers, who would have neither voting nor reimbursement privileges, were to be selected. One thousand of the delegates were to be divided among the states and territories according to the proportion of those over fifty-five in each jurisdiction. At least half of each state's delegation was to be female. Minority groups were to be represented in accordance with their proportion in the state's population. Operating within these guidelines, the actual method of selection was to be determined by the individual states. An additional 539 delegates were to be selected by the members of Congress and roughly 150 other individuals were either to be granted delegate status because of their membership on technical committees or be named as governor-appointed state coordinators. Finally, the executive director and national organizations representing the aging were to appoint delegates to round out the race, sex, age, and rural/urban profile.[26] In June 1981, the decision was made to add 400 delegates. These were appointed from lists made available by the White House and federal agencies.

That the political clout of the aging had increased in recent decades was amply illustrated by the maneuvering to control the conference. Following the change of administrations in early 1981, the chairman, the executive director, and forty-four members of a fifty-six-member national advisory committee were replaced. An executive director appointed in March 1981 was replaced in October. He had apparently not taken seriously the possibility of "political embarassment to the administration" resulting from delegates' reaction to the president's advocacy of some reductions in social security.[27] Just before the opening of the conference, the Republican National Committee conducted a telephone poll of approximately one-third of the convention delegates. The chairman of the committee declared that the purpose of the poll was "to see what the concerns of the seniors were." Opponents argued that the purpose was to intimidate the delegates.[28]

Many delegates were also unhappy over procedural rules that were looked upon as deliberate attempts to stifle debate. For example, instead of being permitted to debate and vote on each committee report, delegates were allowed one vote, for or against, the combined reports.

The approximately 2,260 delegates met from November 30 through December 3. Aside from opening and closing general sessions, the work of the conference was conducted by the following fourteen committees:

1. Implications for the Economy of an Aging Population
2. Economic Wellbeing
3. Older Americans as a Continuing Resource
4. Promotion and Maintenance of Wellness

  5. Health Care and Services
  6. Options for Long Term Care
  7. Family and Community Support Systems
  8. Housing Alternatives
  9. Conditions for Continuing Community Participation
 10. Education
 11. Concerns of Older Women: Growing Number, Special Needs
 12. Private Sector: Roles, Structures, Opportunities
 13. Public Sector Role and Social Security
 14. Research

The issue of immediate concern to a large number of delegates related to social security. The charge was made that the Committee on Economic Well-being, which had jurisdiction over the issue, had been stacked with delegates favorable to the administration. Unable to make any progress within the committee, opponents had some of their proposals introduced in other committees. An estimated eight-hundred delegates, unhappy with the manner in which the conference was being conducted, met to air their protests on the evening of the second day of discussion. They were joined by Representative Claude Pepper of Florida, the chairman of the House Select Committee on Aging. The following morning, members of the group assembled outside the Economic Wellbeing committee room, where they sang "We Shall Overcome." Representative Pepper met with conference leaders and "a resolution we can live with," according to Pepper, was worked out and adopted.[29] The resolution urged Congress "to make every possible and fiscally reasonable effort . . . to maintain no less than the real protection which Social Security currently provides to all participants."[30]

The conference adjourned after adopting, in one vote of approval, the 668 recommendations of the fourteen committees. Following the adjournment, the president issued a statement declaring that the "challenge before us is to develop policies which are constructive, comprehensive, and compassionate."[31] Development of a final report hinged upon delegate and observer response to a lengthy survey that the Leadership Council of Aging Organizations declared to be "almost impossible to decipher."[32]

The immediate reaction from organizations representing the aging ranged from a reference to the song "Is That All There Is" to the claim that the conference had produced "a national policy and program broad enough and bold enough to meet all challenges of the transitional decade which lies before us."[33] Certainly the delegates demonstrated a commitment to the social security system. Moreover, women's issues came to the fore as "the new common denominator of aging."[34]

The final report of the conference, a three-volume package, was issued in June 1982. The five well-written, substantive essays in volume one came under immediate attack for failing to "come to grips with the recommendations." For example, the general counsel of the National Council on Aging declared, "One searches in vain through this document's 115 pages, either in its text or in the 137 footnotes, for any reference to a recommendation approved by conference delegates."[35] Women's issues were totally ignored in the final report. So too were proposals that would have necessitated increased expenditures. One critic declared that "this is the report on the conference the Administration was hoping be held."[36]

THE AMENDMENTS OF 1981

The 1981 amendments reflect the policies of the new administration. Programs for the aging were extended by the Omnibus Reconciliation Act of 1981, which set limits on the amount that could be appropriated for fiscal years 1982 and 1983. A further extension and a number of substantive revisions made in December 1981 covered the period through fiscal 1984.[37] In general, the states were given a greater measure of control. For example, the requirement that 50 percent of social sevices funds be spent on specific programs such as access, in-home, and legal services were eliminated. Instead, these services were to receive an "adequate proportion." The states were also authorized to transfer 20 percent of federal funds between programs for supportive (replacing the term "social") services and nutrition services. Separate authorizations for home-delivered and congregate meals programs were extended. The act instructed the Department of Labor to establish training programs to help older workers find employment. In addition, funding was authorized for the continuation of the Older Americans part-time job projects.

THE ADMINISTRATION ON AGING

At this point, the administrative structure comes into focus. As indicated in the preceding pages, the leadership to activate the requirements of the Older Americans Act was placed with the Administration on Aging, headed by the commissioner on aging. Over the years, the organizational position of the commissioner had been less prominent than many desired. Renewed efforts in 1978 to elevate the position were unsuccessful. The House bill made the commissioner directly responsible to the secretary of Health, Education, and Welfare. But the Senate made no provision as to the commissioner's position. The conference agreement settled the issue as follows: "The House recedes from its position with assurance from the Secretary of Health, Education, and Welfare that the position of the Commissioner will be maintained at a high level in the Department with full access to the Secretary. The conferees will closely monitor the visibility accorded the Commissioner and his ability to serve as a focal point for all programs for the aging from his present organization position."[38]

The current law requires that the commissioner on aging be directly responsible to the Office of the Secretary. In practice, the Administration on Aging is one unit within the Office of Human Development Services. The commissioner's avenue to the secretary is through the assistant secretary of Human Development Services. A 1981 study by the General Accounting Office declared that the present organizational structure is in violation of the law since the administrative functions relating to contracts are centralized in a staff unit that is responsible to the assistant secretary of Human Development Services rather than to the commissionr on aging. Moreover, regional offices of fiscal operations responsible for monitoring grantees do no report to the Administration of Aging. Although bills to correct the organizational structure have been introduced , the 1981 amendments made no change in the commissioner's authority.[39]

The function of the Administration on Aging is to establish the organizational framework, to develop the guidelines, and to supply the direction that make a going concern out of the specific requirement of the Older Americans Act.[40] In addition, the 1978 amendments directed the AoA "to serve as the visible advocate for the elderly: not only within the Department of Health, Education and Welfare, but in 'other departments, agencies, and instrumentalities of the Federal government.' AoA's role as advocate, however, is limited to 'maintaining active review and commenting responsibilities over all Federal policies affecting the elderly.'"[41]

Beginning in 1973, the AoA began a sustained effort directed toward the development of detailed written working agreements with various federal agencies. These interagency agreements serve several purposes. They help to develop a consciousness of the problems of the aging, they commit the agencies to the use of a portion of their own funds for new programs for the elderly, and they emphasize the role of the Administration on Aging as the focal point of planning and action for the elderly. The same procedure was encouraged at the state level with the result that literally hundreds of special agreements were negotiated.

Current programs of the agency may be grouped into two major categories: those affecting the elderly directly and those supporting the concerns of the elderly. In the first category are the various state and community programs that make available to the elderly a vast range of services. The AoA develops regulations and, with the assistance of ten regional offices, supervises the remaining elements of the Aging Network; that is, the State and Area Agencies on Aging insofar as they provide specific services such as the operation of community-based multipurpose senior centers and nutrition programs. The second major category includes financing model projects that improve social services by aiding in the development of career training programs for those wishing to serve the elderly, funding research, and assisting in the establishment of multidisciplinary centers for gerontology.[42]

THE FEDERAL COUNCIL ON THE AGING

An explanation of the organizational structure at the departmental level must include mention of a related body that has review functions but is distinctly apart from the operational mainstream. One feature of the 1973 amendments to the Older Americans Act was the creation of a body that could stand somewhat aloof from the Administration on Aging and appraise federal policies relating to the elderly. The Federal Council on the Aging was created to advise the president on matters relating to the special needs of older Americans. But the council was to be more than just advisory. It was directed to be a "spokeman" by making recommendations on policies for the aging to the president, the secretary, the commissioner and the Congress. The fifteen-member body was to be appointed by the president and confirmed by the Senate and was to consist of at least five older persons. The council was to include representatives of national organizations of the elderly, the general public, business, and labor. The secretary of HEW and the commissioner on aging were ex officio members.

From an organizational point of view, the council was placed in a somewhat tenuous position with respect to the Administration on Aging. The secretariat for the council was within the Administration on Aging. Until 1976, when a separate line item was created, the budget was simply a part of the AoA budget. For a time, the council, which was directed to meet at least four times each year, concentrated on establishing its own identity. It did not have the staff to investigate many issues nor was it equipped to become an advocate of the aging. This concern was expressed to the Congress in the 1975 annual report: "The Federal Council does not want to be a passive advisory body, but neither does it want to be a chatterbox for superficial criticisms and proposals nor just an endorser of what others say about Older Americans."[43]

To some degree, the council was aided in its continuing struggle to establish an identity of its own by the 1978 amendments to the Older Americans Act. No longer was staff assistance to be dependent upon the administration. Instead, the amendments declared that "the Council shall have staff personnel, appointed by the Chairman, to assist it in carrying out its activities." Moreover, the secretary of the department and the commissioner on aging were no longer to be ex officio members of the council.

The changes in the act did not produce immediate results. In its 1978 annual report, the council complained the HEW procedures were, "for all practical purposes, in accordance with the pre-1978 act. If the Council is to meet its obligations effectively, means must be found to implement the clear intent of Congress with respect to the need to remove the Council from its subservient and dependent administrative position."[44]

During its early years, the council did not hesitate to make pronouncements on many issues. More recently, however, it has concentrated mainly on the status of the frail elderly, the rural elderly, and the very large issue of evaluating federal policies with respect to the aging. The 1978 amendments reaffirmed the desire of Congress that the council conduct a "thorough evaluation" of the programs conducted under the Older Americans Act.

However, this endorsement of the council's activities was not backed up by the funds for necessary research. On the contrary, a cutback in funding from $481,000 in 1981 to $200,000 in 1982, together with a substantial reduction in staff, raised serious doubts about the ability of the council to exist as a constructive presence in the field of aging.

STATE OFFICES OF AGING

With the passage of the Older Americans Act, State Offices of Aging assumed increasing importance. As indicated previously, by the early fifties a number of states had administrative units concerned with the problems of the aging. National recognition of the needs of the elderly spurred additional state action.

The passage of the 1973 amendments mandated that the states provide social services for those over the age of sixty. In order to receive federal support, each state was required to designate an agency that would be the sole unit for developing an annual state plan to be submitted for approval first to the governor and then to the commissioner on aging. The unit so designated was to administer the approved plan and coordinate all state activities related to the Older Americans Act. These functions included the determination of planning and service areas and the designation of Area Agencies on Aging. The 1978 amendments relaxed the previous requirements for an annual plan in favor of one covering a period of three years. The 1981 amendments gave still further flexibility by permitting the states to choose whether to submit a plan covering two, three, or four years.

The objective in requiring each state agency to have a plan was to enable the needs of the elderly and the precise steps to be taken in meeting those needs to be identified as precisely as possible. The 1978 amendments declared that in developing the plan, preference was to be given to "older individuals with the greatest economic or social needs."

Although federal regulations required that one state agency be responsible for the programs related to the Older Americans Act, no strictures were placed on the form of the administrative structure. Advocates for the aging insisted that the administrative unit be placed at the highest level of the state power structure. In 1969, Connecticut established the first separate department on aging. Some states have Offices on Aging that are directly responsible to the governor, others have independent offices or commissions on aging, still others have units responsible for services to the aging located in departments concerned with social services. A few of the states have intra-state regional offices that exercise immediate supervision over the Area Agencies on Aging.

The administrative unit designated as the State Office on Aging exists because of the federal requirement for a single agency that directs operations financed through the Older Americans Act.[45] Other state programs for the elderly may exist totally outside the network. Indeed, in many states there are numerous laws having special relevance to the elderly that are administered by a variety of agencies.

THE AREA AGENCY ON AGING

In order to supply a service—for example, the delivery of meals—to people on a national scale, an operational mechanism is essential. Under the original Older Americans Act, programs were fragmented and a the few funds available did not permit service on a national scale. The 1969 amendments authorizing the Areawide Model Project Program permitted some experimentation in the delivery service. With the passage of the 1973 amendments, a new concept, that of the Area Agency on Aging, solved the problem of the absence of an operational mechanism.

The first step was to persuade those states that wished to receive federal funds for the aging to improve their planning capabilities with respect to the elderly. Initially, in 1965, governors had been required to designate one unit of the state administration to supervise the various activities related to the Older Americans Act. Now they were directed to establish planning and service areas (PSA's). PSA's were to serve fifty thousand persons over the age of sixty or 15 percent of the population aged sixty and above. Within those planning areas having highest priority, operational entities called Area Agencies on Aging were to be created. The Area Agency on Aging could be related to a nonprofit organization serving one or more units of local government. Indeed, with the approval of the commissioner, the state could designate itself as the sole planning and service area and the sole Area Agency on Aging.

The 1973 amendments declared that the function of the Area Agency on Aging was to develop "a comprehensive and coordinated system for the delivery of social services within the planning and service area."[46] Achievement of this objective involved determining the need for social services and contracting with social providers to meet one or more of those needs. Instead of being involved directly in the provision of services, the area agency was to be a broker, or coordinator, of services.[47] Moreover, the agency was to "pool untapped resources of public and private agencies in order to strengthen or inaugurate new services for older persons."[48]

Each Area Agency on Aging was required to submit to the state office for aging an annual area plan that set forth in some detail the programs that would achieve a comprehensive and coordinated system. Public hearings were to be held prior to the submission of the plan in order that older persons, public officals, and others might comment. Priority was to be given to services for the low-income and minority elderly. The area agency could perform social services directly, if specifically approved, or it could make arrangements for the delivery of services through contracts with public or nonprofit agencies. Monitoring and evaluating the performances of the recipients of grants and contracts were the responsibilities of the area agency. Ninety percent of the cost of approved programs and 75 percent of the administrative costs were to be met by federal funds.

Establishing the concept of the area agency was a major undertaking. Theoretically, the idea of a comprehensive and coordinated service system made sense. Practically, however, the introduction of the new organizational unit was upsetting to existing organizations because of perceived encroachment on their "turf." Moreover, for many of the new area agencies, the question of how to coordinate services that were totally lacking constituted an enigma. Furthermore, the area agencies had no real authority over other agencies serving the aged. Although congressional committees were somewhat skeptical of the value of the new units, they withheld final judgment until the units could be developed. Appropriations were increased so that services could be made available, at least on a limited basis.[49] By March 1, 1974, 145 area agencies had become operative. Withing two years there were over 400. In 1981, the entire country was divided into 683 planning and service areas, with several states choosing to operate as single areas.[50] Within these planning and service areas there were 670 area agencies.

In authorizing the creation of Area Agencies on Aging, the 1973 amendments to the Older Americans Act gave the states considerable latitude in prescribing the precise structure of the agency. In many states, the area agency is a unit of the county government. A small percentage of the agencies are responsible to municipal governments. In 1978, more than one-third were nonprofit organizations that geographically, in some cases, embraced several governmental entities.

The nonprofit organization merits special attention. In many respects it is not unlike a unit of government. It is required to follow the instructions of the state agency on aging in administering the various programs stemming from the Older Americans Act. For example, the nonprofit organization contracts with service-providers for the delivery of, say, congregate meals. At first glance, procedures and methods of operation are no different from that of the area agency that is a unit of a county or city government. In fact, however, there is a vast difference between them. The not-for-profit organization is outside the mainstream of government and is also consequently, to a considerable degree beyond the concern of the local government's elected officials. This separation may have a deleterious effect upon the character of the service being performed and upon the clientele being served. Moreover, the employees are not governmental employees and thus lack the special protections established one by one over many years. This factor may accentuate greatly the problem of personnel turnover. Nationally, the future of the nonprofit corporation serving as an area agency of aging is unclear.

In one sense, the Area Agency on Aging is the end of the line as far as the network is concerned. By another measure, however, it is the beginning. The actual services for the elderly are performed in many states by a whole array of local organizations that contract with the Area Agency on Aging to deliver specified social services.

FINANCING THE NETWORK

The first appropriation to support the Older Americans Act covered fiscal year 1966. The amount appropriated was $7.5 million. Within five years, the appropriation had grown to $33,650,000. By 1971 the Administration on Aging could point with pride to a growth of 350 percent. The cynic, however, could observe that if one assumed a population of 21 million over the age of sixty-five, the appropriation amounted to $1.60 for each elderly person.

The momentum created by the White House conferences of 1971 and 1981 and the 1973, 1978, and 1981 amendments to the Older Americans Act were of vital importance to the Administration on Aging. Appropriations were increased, at first slowly, and then by large increments when the nutrition program was launched and received quick acceptance nationally. It was clear, however, from the 1981 amendments that the momentum was slowing down and that the federal role was weakening.

Funds are allotted to the states according to the ratio of a given state's population over sixty to the total population over sixty. Up to 8.5 percent of a state's allotment may be used to pay not more than 75 percent of the cost of administration. The remainder of the allotment is available for paying not over 85 percent of the planned expenditures for social services and nutrition services. Of the total expenditures set forth in the state plan, 25 percent of the nonfederal share must be paid in cash from state or local public funds. The balance may be in-kind expenditures.

In addition to services provided to the elderly through the Older Americans Act, in past years Title XX of the Social Security Act was a source of funds for most states. The Title XX appropriation was the federal government's largest funding source for social services, principally child care services. Some funds, however, were used for the aging. In 1978 the general accounting office conducted a survey of SSI recipients that revealed great variations among the states. In seven states studied, from 3 to 33 percent of the SSI recipients were aided by Title XX monies.[51] With the passage of the Social Services Block Grant Act in 1981, services previously funded under Title XX were incorporated into a block grant. As a consequence, states were given greater flexibility in determining eligibility, types of services, and the amount of financial support allocated for each service.[52] The federal appropriation, however, was reduced.

As noted above, the federal government does not bear the total burden of financing services for the elderly. The terms of the Older Americans Act require state participation on a limited scale. Moreover, the Area Agencies on Aging, through their pooling efforts, may obtain assistance from other federal, state or local agencies. County or municipal governments may make funds available from regular tax monies or from various federal grants to the local units. In some states, federal general revenue-sharing funds have been used to support the Area Agencies on Aging. However, the percentage of these monies expanded for programs for the aging has been extremely small—perhaps not as much as 1 percent.[53]

At the local level, senior centers and nutrition sites participate to some degree in the funding process through a variety of money-raising activities. Those benefiting from congregate or home-delivered meals are invited, but not required, to make contributions. Following years of uncertainty over the uses to be made of these contributions, the 1978 amendments conference declared that meal contributions shall be "used to increase the number of meals served."[54] The average contribution in fiscal 1983 amounted to about sixty cents per meal, generating $118 million "for area agencies to redirect toward the neediest older Americans."[55]

The proposed budget for fiscal 1981 allotted $997.9 million to be spent under the Older Americans Act. This figure included funds for the "reform and transfer" of the Department of Agriculture's Elderly Feeding program to the Administration on Aging. The figure also included funds previously administered by the Department of Labor for the employment of older persons. No request was made to fund the Senior Community Services Employment Program as a separate entity. The budget breakdown is on page 43.[56]

While the Aging Network has done well, comparatively speaking, the recent budget cuts place its future in some jeopardy. The New Federalism places both more autonomy and more fiscal responsibility in the hands of the states. However, as Tobin[57] predicted, it is wreaking havoc on the finances of many state and local communities.[58] Ironically for an administration bent on reducing taxes, cuts at the federal level have forced state and local governments to raise taxes or, alternatively, reduce services to disadvantages groups including the elderly.

Administration on Aging, 1984 Estimate (in thousands)	
State Agency Activities	$ 19.928
Title III Service and Meals	967.068
Grants to Indian Tribes	5.735
Research, Training, and Discretionary Programs	5.000
Federal Council on Aging	.175
Total	$997.906

3. Older Americans Act: The Services Content

Before moving to a discussion of the social services available through the auspices of the Older Americans Act, it may be useful to very briefly recapitulate the original goals of the act. The act had ten objectives, each of which seemed to promise the elderly optimal benefits and services in a given life sphere (see p. 27 of this chapter). These "promises" could not be kept, nor were they meant to be kept, at least within the confines of the limited authority of the Older Americans Act and the Administration on Aging. Rather they represent a compendium of ideals developed by those involved in the legislative process that led to the act. Nevertheless, to many who review the act, the expansive introductory statements produce a "credibility gap" when the fine print is actually reached. It is like an elephant giving birth to a mouse. Most of this country's social welfare legislation reads in very much the same way. Presenting "something for everyone" in the most glowing terms seems to be the best way to convince the legislators to do anything at all. This accomplished, the legislators then move to the harder task of achieving some kind of consensus on what will actually be authorized and implemented.

Other objectives expressed in later amendments were virtually impossible to achieve. Notable is the goal to provide a comprehensive and coordinated system of social service set forth in the 1973 amendments. Even though not expressed in the most ideal terms, the list of desired services is almost end-less. Comprehensiveness, thus, seems to defy any reasonable definition. Coordination, too, is very difficult, given the nature of the specific population groups. A good example is the recent concern with the rural elderly. Their geographic isolation makes it difficult to coordinate delivery of services to them with delivery of services to more urban population groups. At the same time, providing a sizable array of services to the rural elderly would be far too costly, even with a larger budget than the Older Americans Act has ever received. Again, a formally articulated goal seems beyond achievement. The ideals have been presented here so that they may be compared with what has actually been accomplished.

While some social services for the elderly have been in a developmental stage, others have been made available across the nation. Of these, however, some reach only a woefully small number of people. One reason for this uneven development and distribution is that the states and area agencies have considerable discretion in deciding upon the particular services to be emphasized in a given fiscal period. However, a 1975 amendment to the Older Americans Act produced some measures of uniformity by specifying that priority be given to four categories of services: transportation, legal counseling, residential repair, and in-home services, Certain percentages of the funds allotted were required to be expended on the priority categories. The categories were altered slightly in the 1978 Comprehensive Older Americans Act. The act declared that at least 50 percent of the amount allotted for social services "will be expended for the delivery of (a) services associated with access to services (transportation, outreach, and information and referral); (b) in-home services (homemaker and home health aids, visiting and telephone reassurance, and chore maintenance); and (c) legal services; and that some funds will be expended for each category of service."[59] As the New Federalism began to take hold, these strictures were relaxed. The 1981 amendments eliminated the requirement that 50 percent of the funds be allocated for a specific series of social services in favor of a clause requiring the expenditure of "an adequate proportion for those services."

Following are listed some of the services that area agencies provide.

Information and Referral   As the title implies, the objective of this activity is to inform the elderly of the availability of particular services. The aging person may be assisted in obtaining the service. The collection and maintenance of a bank of pertinent information is, obviously, an important feature of this service.

Outreach   Getting to isolated elderly persons and, if possible helping them.

Transportation   Meeting the individual's mobility requirements.

In-Home Services   Three categories of service, all intended to encourage independent living, are included under this heading: Homemaker Services (assistance with the work necessary to maintain a home, such as light housework and preparation of meals), Home Chore Services (assistance in performing tasks about the house, such as minor repairs), Home Delivered Meals (delivery of at least one hot meal a day to the homebound individual).

Legal Services Assistance with legal problems of a civil nature.

Protective Services Assistance to the mentally or physically impaired in the management of financial affairs.

Counseling Individual or group counseling to improve the ability to cope with others.

Socialization and Recreation Individual or group activities to lighten the burdens of living.

Education Short- and long-term courses to provide helpful learning.

SENIOR CENTERS

At the community level, programs sponsored by Area Agencies on Aging usually operate out of senior centers. The expression "senior center" is an old one and refers to the headquarters of a group of elderly persons. Not all senior centers are related to the federal program, although they may perform many of the functions noted above, especially those having to do with socialization and recreation. In recent years, the expression "multipurpose senior center" has been used to describe the federally supported community facility that provides a variety of services to older persons.

The centers supported by Title III of the Older Americans Act have increased in number or disappeared altogether, depending upon the level of funding. The center may have its own building or it may have its headquarters in a church, lodge, fire station, or other public or private facility. Under Title V, the 1973 amendments provided for assistance in acquiring, renovating, or otherwise altering a facility to serve as a multipurpose senior center, that is, one offering a broad spectrum of services. This program was first funded in 1976. At that time, the senior centers receiving federal support were serving approximately 2.5 million persons. The 1978 amendments support the concept of the multipurpose center as follows: "The conferees emphasize the importance of multipurpose senior centers in developing a comprehensive social service network and expect that area agencies will continue to place appropriate emphasis on their development and expansion."[60] In 1987, the Older Americans Act was supporting approximately twelve hundred multipurpose senior centers.

NUTRITION

Inadequate nutrition has been recognized for decades as a special problem of the elderly.[61] Major concern was expressed by the Congress in 1968 when the AoA received an appropriation of $2 million to finance a number of pilot projects. These projects were to obtain data about the specific causes of the inadequacies and to improve nutritional services to those elderly included in the projects by testing various delivery systems. Common to all demonstration projects were group meals, education on nutrition, and an evaluation of the results, taking into account the costs of various types of services. Over a decade ago an AoA nutritionist gave the following assessment:

The experience of AoA's nutrition program to date confirms the judgment that the problems of undernutrition and malnutrition cannot be solved independently of related problems of limited income and limited knowledge of nutrition, feelings of loneliness, rejection, and apathy; declining health, vigor and loss of mobility; physical handicaps that make food shopping and preparation difficult; and metabolic changes that accompany aging. No single approach can be fully responsive to the nutritional needs of the aging and no single system for the delivery of food and nutrition services is the total answer.

The provision of meals in a group setting is a highly desirable approach to these interrelated problems because it fosters social interaction, facilitates the delivery of other services, and meets emotional needs, of the aged while improving their nutrition. It offers an effective device for teaching by example the importance of a nutritionally adequate diet and what is essential to such a diet. It provides a framework for dealing with such everyday problems as transportation and housing arrangements which contribute to the nutrition problem.[62]

Nutrition problems received much attention at the 1971 White House Conference on Aging. Prior to the conference, the administration had indicated its intention to permit the pilot project to come to a close at the end of the trial period. However, the ultimate effect of the conference and of a bipartisan congressional push for legislation resulted in an administrative turnabout. In March 1972, the Older Americans Act was amended by the Nutrition Program for the Elderly Act.[63] Implementation of this legislation involved an ever-expanding program of grants for the operation of low-cost meals projects. The amount of funds made available was to be based on the number of elderly in a state. The first appropriation under the act was for $1 million in 1974. This figure had expanded in 1981 to $295 million for congregate nutrition and $55 million for home-delivered meals.

Food for the nutrition program is provided in part by the Department of Agriculture. In 1975, the secretary was required by an admendment to the Older Americans Act to purchase, on the open market, meat and other foods for distribution to the nutrition projects.[64] The department provides commodities or cash, as the individual states may request, to supplement the costs of providing meals. In 1981, 179.3 million congregate and home-delivered meals were served to the elderly at a cost of $350 million from Title III funds and $84.7 million in USDA assistance. Cash payments of USDA monies amounted to 73.9 million; commodities to $10.8 million.[65]

The nutrition program is now the largest single program of the AoA. By fiscal year 1981 it had organized roughly twelve hundred nutrition projects and established thirteen hundred congregate sites. The 1978 amendments provided separate funding for the congregate nutrition program and for the home-delivered meals program. This was done as a means of stressing the importance of providing nutritional meals to those unable to get to congregate meal sites.[66]

MINORITY PARTICIPATION

One of the nagging problems pertaining to governmental programs concerns the degree of participation by all elements of the elderly population. For example, do the programs discriminate against minorities? In 1982, the United States Commission on Civil Rights issued a report on this question as it pertained to the Older Americans Act. The study was based upon case analyses in six cities. In addition, it included interviews with Administration on Aging personnel and mail questionnaires to state- and local-level program administrators. The study endeavored to assess: (1) to what degree minorities were employed in carrying out Older Americans Act programs, (2) whether minority organizations were included in the awarding of contract funds, and (3) the degree of minority participation in the services provided.[67]

The six cities selected for analysis were Cleveland, Ohio; Bridgeport, Connecticut; Tucson, Arizona; Tulsa, Oklahoma; San Francisco, California; and Honolulu, Hawaii. Several cities contained substantial percentages of minorities. In Bridgeport, for example, 21 percent of the total population was black and 18.7 percent was Hispanic. In Tucson, 24.9 percent was Hispanic. In Honolulu, 73 percent of the population was classified as Asian and Pacific Island American.

The study showed that membership of the Area Agency on Aging advisory committees was frequently held by minority persons, occasionally in numbers beyond the population ratio. There was minority representation, also, on the staff of area agencies and of contracting agencies. Most of these positions, however, did not entail making decisions. Minority firms providing services received a relatively small fraction of contracting funds. This was true even in cities where the firms had established reputations.[68]

In each of the cities evaluated, the number of minority elderly receiving the services provided was a small percentage of the total number of eligibles. In Cleveland, for example, the "minority elderly were being underserved in relation to their representation in the eligible population . . . and even more so in relation to their relative social and economic needs."[69]

The study catalogued a number of reasons for the lack of participation. These included: (1) a belief on the part of the minority persons that they were unwelcome; (2) a feeling that the programs were not responsive to minority needs; (3) lack of knowledge of the programs; (4) lack of transportation.

The commission's recommendations of ways to increase minority participation were wide ranging. Among them were the following: (1) substantially increased outreach efforts; (2) publicity in languages other than English; (3) greater use of minority persons in planning and service implementation; (4) improvements in data collection; (5) bilingual staff in areas such as legal assistance and referral services; (6) greater use of minority service contractors.[70]

NEGLECTING THE "MOST NEEDY"

Another charge that has been leveled against government programs and especially those included in the Older Americans Act is that those who are poor and isolated are underserved. Senior centers and group meals attract primarily the healthy and active among the aged. Those who are homebound because of physical illnesses or other handicaps, who do not have the means to reach the service sites, and who have simply never heard of the programs receive no benefits from them. Senator John Heinz of Pennsylvania has protested that the major Older Americans Act services neglect the most needy among the elderly. He along with other senators at the 1981 Hearings on Older Americans Programs deplored the cutbacks in Outreach that would further discriminate against the poor and isolated.[71]

4. Summary Analysis

Through the original Older Americans Act, its amendments, and the procedures to implement it, the Aging Network has evolved gradually since its origins in 1965. As the funding for services grew, additional layers of administrative structure were added. The current structure could be depicted in the well-known flowchart format. Offices at the federal level have been allocated responsibilities for regulating and monitoring the activities carried out under the Older Americans Act. Although the Administration on Aging and the commissioner on aging are only nominally in charge of federal activities undertaken on behalf of the elderly, their administrative control, although circumscribed, has significant consequences for the network. The functions of the federal level are carried out through ten regional offices, each responsible for a geographically clustered group of states. These offices decrease the distance between the federal level and the state level. The next layer is composed of all the state offices responsible for activities on behalf of older Americans. Finally, a layer at the local level is composed of the Area Agencies on Aging that represent regional divisions within states.

In spite of numerous pressures, however, the goal of establishing a central agency at the federal level that would be responsible for all programs affecting the elderly has proved impossible to realize. There are simply too many congressional committees and government departments controlling relevant areas of activity to permit this coordination. The Administration on Aging has to manage as best as it can by making special agreements with other bureaus that control programs for the aging outside its jurisdiction. The need for an authoritative body that has a recognized place in the administrative structure of national decisionmaking bodies dates back to before the 1965 Older Americans Act. Yet the preceding account shows that, even with the establishment of the Administration on Aging, let alone prior to that formal decision, the status of programs for the aging has been subject to a number of forces working against their coordination. In spite of the commissioner on aging, the Administration on Aging continues to have a somewhat ambiguous status. The AoA has had its ups and downs, appearing sometimes to be gaining in authority only to be downgraded again a year or two later.

Interestingly enough, the ambiguous status of the federal office is reflected at other levels of the Aging Network. In spite of directives that states designate one agency to be in charge of programs for the aging, the jurisdiction of state offices is also generally limited. Whether this office is a special Office on Aging or a division within another department, Public Welfare, for example, it is subject to the influence of other political/legal vested interests. It has previously been noted that the local Area Agencies on Aging are often tied into entrenched political bodies or, to a lesser extent, linked with nonprofit organizations that are unregulated, untested, and private.

The system of regulating the dispensation of services under the Older Americans Act, then, is fraught with ambiguities, the lower levels of administration mirroring the situation at the top. The Area Agencies on Aging, the end of the administrative line, were instituted to provide a mechanism for the actual delivery of services to older Americans. They function as a gateway to that end. Like the higher-level governmentally authorized units, the Area Agencies on Aging are not in the service-delivery business. Such activities could presumably create a conflict of interest and interfere with other functions. Although some exceptions have been made in this respect, Area Agencies on Aging are brokers or coordinators for the service-delivery system. It is therefore through agencies and organizations that are not a part of the several tiers of the administrative structure that the true goal of the entire enterprise can be realized: services to older Americans.

Area Agencies on Aging have been directed to bring together all agencies and organizations that provide services to the elderly in a particular locality. Through this coordinating effort, duplication of services should be eliminated and identifiable gaps in the mandated services closed. This directive, however, ignores the realities of the situation. The Area Agencies on Aging simply do not have the clout to accomplish this task. About all the area agencies have to offer in exchange for cooperation from organizations outside the network is the "carrot" of potential federal and state funds. There is otherwise absolutely no way to ensure cooperative behavior. Local service agencies that do not find the "carrot" sufficiently tempting, given the paperwork necessary to receive funding, may simply decide not to participate.[72] Under these circumstances, quite naturally, there is no way to prevent service duplication. In other instances, gaps in the designated services may be identified, but it may not be possible to fill them. This would occur when a particular service was not being offered in a specific locality, and none of the existing service agencies were able or willing to provide it. Again, such a gap could be caused by insufficient reward for the amount of funding involved.

The question arises: Does the Aging Network serve the purposes intended? According to Estes, it does not.[73] In her view, the network represents a prime example of goal displacement. In other words, the network has become an end in itself, promoting the interests of the administrators and the service workers. The intended beneficiaries, older Americans, are relatively neglected. Only a trickle of services actually gets cranked out from the giant machine. Other investigators reach a more positive conclusion.[74] They agree that setting up the network was a cumbersome process that absorbed much of the time and energy of those involved. However, once the network was in place, it became much more effective in reaching and serving older people. The locally based Area Agencies on Aging have, in their view, performed an important function: making the elderly aware of the service system in their communities. Because this seemingly cumbersome administrative layer is locally based and visible, the Area Agencies on Aging are forced to be responsive to the needs of the people they are directed to serve.

Between these two extremes, the one so negative and the other so positive, there are many shades of opinion about the efficacy of the Aging Network. Since the evidence to support either judgment is very scattered, no final word on the subject can be offered here. In earlier pages, it was possible to provide statistics showing that hundreds of thousands of older persons are receiving services of some kind or another under the Older Americans Act. This certainly appears to be a significant accomplishment, although by some standards it could still be called a trickle. After all, there are now many millions of Americans who are formally labeled "old." Even the growing segment of the elderly who are very, very old—those eighty-five years of age and older—and are presumed to be the most in need of services now number several million. Beyond such considerations, the statistics are cited to prove accountability for past expenditures and to justify expenditures. They are then purely quantitative. The statistics deal only with numbers served and not with the quality of the services rendered and the impact of those services on the lives of participating older Americans. One evaluative study reported by Jones provides evidence that older persons served through senior citizens centers show improvements in well-being as a result and that they are satisfied with the services they receive.[75] Such studies are few and far between. It must also be remembered that participants in the multipurpose centers are the more physically active older persons. There has so far been little objection to this segment of the older population receiving services that enhance the quality of their lives, although in tightening financial conditions, this attitude may be changing. But questions have been raised in the last section of this chapter about whether the practice of "counting heads" to justify funding expenditures and to secure new funds leads to the neglect of the elderly who are the most difficult and costly to serve: the financially impoverished, the socially and geographically isolated, and the minorities, who are overrepresented in both groups. Given limitations on monetary resources, it is abundantly clear that only a fraction of the persons intended to be served under the Older Americans Act and its amendments will actually be served. The discussion revolves around whether, given those limitations, the funding is being appropriately allocated. If numbers served is the criterion for accountability, it seems obvious that the healthy elderly are going to be served extensively. By contrast, the impoverished, ill, and isolated elderly will necessarily be underserved. At a conservative estimate, it may cost twenty times as much for a caseworker to make one visit to an isolated elderly person as it does for a caseworker to be involved in a senior center or nutrition site, where one hour of service is purported to provide assistance to a sizable group of older persons.

In effect, it is not known how well the network "works" in relation to its directives. That it is serving a large group of older persons is well documented; however, which elderly and with what effect has not been determined. The Federal Council on the Aging has been assigned the responsibility of evaluating the policies related to the aging population and assessing the outcomes for the older people supposedly served. In its infancy, however, the council was involved primarily in a struggle to gain sufficient autonomy and financial resources to carry out its advisory role in a responsible manner. Just at the point that the council seemed to have achieved independence, its budgetary resources, as previously noted, were cut by more than half. In consequence, the one federal body empowered to evaluate the policies and programs in the field of aging has insufficient funding to accomplish even a small part of this vital effort. Accordingly, the jury on the effectiveness of the Aging Network is still out.

At the same time, it is not difficult to demonstrate that the administrative structure devised under the Older Americans Act and subsequent amendments has an impact on the delivery of services to older Americans. While the services actually implemented fall short of the specified ideal goals, they do seem attuned to the major areas of need identified through listening to a multiplicity of voices, from grassroots organizations to authorized federal bodies. The existence of a series of services, is assured. Basically, the emphasis has been on three categories covering access to services, home care services, and legal services. Beyond the specific categories of services and encompassing some of them in one way or another are the multiservice centers and the group or congregate meal sites. This array of services is indeed supportive of the informed citizen who needs help either for him- or herself or for a relative, friend, or neighbor. Yet the ambiguity over control and the ensuing fragmentation of the delivery system necessarily creates an overload of bureaucratic red tape, especially for the elderly person who is in need of multiple supports. Unless a highly informed and caring caseworker is working on the problem or dedicated intimates of the affected older person can spend the time necessary to comprehend the system, the truly disadvantaged elderly person is likely to be disappointed. The ambiguity and very deliberate division of responsibility across and between levels of government, with continual recourse to the "will of the people" all along the way, is, as we have said earlier, inherent to the American social welfare policymaking process. That the less knowledgeable and most isolated members of society lose out in the fight with the system is a cost that, to date, has been considered bearable.

The Older Americans Act has been the law of the land for roughly two decades. Its grandiose objectives remain intact, and, indeed, have been embellished slightly by the 1973 and 1978 amendments relating to transportation and living arrangements.

The governmental programs established by the Older Americans Act have grown, at first slowly, and then with increasing rapidity. Beacause of lack of funds, the Administration on Aging was at first unable to do much about actually providing social services. Its activities were thus confined largely to searching for new ways to provide assistance to the elderly. A whole new era began with the 1973 amendments and the newly established goal of providing comprehensive and coordinated service systems through area agencies under the supervision of state units on aging. The area agencies planned for the services; actual delivery was, in most instances, made possible through contracts with service providers.

The task of developing a comprehensive and coordinated service is a monumental one that in spite of considerable progress, remains elusive. What exists presently is a collection of discrete categories of services, often provided under different titles of the act, so that it is difficult to administer them as a "package." In fact, even after all these years, systems for the actual delivery of many types of service are still in their infancy. Yet the 1978 and 1981 amendments attest to the opinion of Congress that sufficient progress has been made to justify the retention of the Aging Network, although further expansion at the present time seems highly doubtful. There have been calls for the abandonment of the whole system. But the alternatives proposed have not been sufficiently precise to attract public support. The prospects are that the current network will, in large measure, be retained and that modifications will be made over time as solutions are offered to the multitude of existing problems.

III / General Financial and Retirement Programs

1. Introduction

There is no reason why everybody in the United States shouldn't be covered. I see no reason why every child from the day he is born shouldn't be a member of the social security system. When he begins to grow up, he should know he will have old-age benefits direct from the insurance system to which he will belong all his life. If he is out of work, he gets a benefit. If he is sick or crippled, he gets a benefit.[1]

Thus Franklin D. Roosevelt was heard to describe his plans for a universal, cradle-to-grave social security system after he took office in 1933. He made this declaration over and over to his closest collaborators. But the initial legislation by no means met any such standards. The system, however, has been steadily enlarged, and today it is by far the strongest pillar for financial support for the elderly. Because of the exclusionary criteria imposed on Roosevelt's initial legislative plan, when payments from the system began in 1941, only 20 percent of all people over the age of sixty-five qualified for benefits under Title II; by the 1970s the proportion had risen to 93 percent.[2] Because of its scope and profound impact on the fate of the elderly, social security figures most prominently in this chapter, although two other general programs important to the financial situation of the elderly are also described.

The United States, it was noted previously, was unusually reluctant and tardy in its entry into the welfare field. As Bremner describes it, from the value perspective of "rugged individualism," the very notion of a system of relief seemed blasphemous.[3] Yet by the time the 1932 election was approaching, many Americans had become desperate enough to question this ethos and to accept radical departures from traditional practice in the face of the apparent failure of the economic system. As Schlesinger puts it: "It was not just a matter of staving off hunger—it was a matter of seeing whether a representative democracy could conquer economic collapse. It was a matter of staving off violence, even (at least some thought) revolution."[4] The nation was beset by bankruptcies, bank failures, and staggering unemployment. According to data available from this period, the elderly were most affected by these disastrous conditions.[5] This disproportionate suffering in a climate where bank failures were wiping out savings, where personal property was virtually worthless because of market conditions, and where only a very small proportion of older people were covered by pension plans caused a number of observers to focus on the aged.[6] The catastrophe caused by the depression convincingly demonstrated that individuals could not provide adequately for old age by themselves. Society would therefore have to intervene.

The aged had by no means been completely neglected before the enactment of the Social Security Act. But as Achenbaum shows, although some concern had been expressed before that time, 1914 seems to have been a bench mark for research on older people and for the perception of the elderly as a "social problem."[7] Beginning in that year, masses of evidence were accumulated that primarily identified aging as a process of decline in health and physical vigor. As a result, old age was depicted as a period of inherent dependency and relative helplessness. Old people in general—although some exceptions were noted—were seen as not retaining the ability to keep up with the rest of society. The evidence of physical decline was also linked to deterioration of mental powers. This portrait, overdrawn to be sure, created a sense of aversion to old people in activist America.

Yet it also led to the growing recognition that aging was a critical issue that had to be addressed. The individual deficiencies and dependencies depicted in the research on older poeple were perceived to be exacerbated in a society that was rapidly industrializing and urbanizing. In many instances the new conditions robbed older poeple of social roles and traditional rural family support systems. As a result, older people were not only poor and sick but lonely and lacking in the self-esteem that goes with performing worthwhile roles. The terms "obsolescence" and "roleless role" have been used by several authors in elaborating this thesis.[8] Complicating the issue was the steady increase in the proportion of those over sixty-five.

While researchers, medical experts, and socially oriented professionals of many types were trying to find ways to help older people in the medical and social-psychological realms, economic insecurity was the focus of a number of new efforts.[9] In the 1920s a number of new retirement plans were adopted at the federal, state, and local levels for civil and municipal employees. Private employers also initiated pension plans. In addition, facilities for the care of needy older people were built by private organizations to replace the dreaded almshouses. By 1931, the public clamor over the plight of the elderly had risen to such a pitch that eighteen states had enacted old-age pension laws. A few states even enacted statutes to attempt to force children to support their elders.

Taken together, however, all of these efforts provided financial aid to only a very small proportion of the affected population, and often what assistance was provided was inadequate. Furthermore, many pension funds disappeared when companies went bankrupt, and state resources for providing relief became exhausted as the flood of needy people grew during the depression years. Nevertheless, these efforts did provide crucial precedents for the more ambitious federal old-age-relief programs of the 1930s.

In spite of growing evidence of very strong popular support and indications that many agencies and organizations were grappling with the problem, Roosevelt faced a great deal of opposition from both political sources and the private sector when he attempted to enact social security legislation.[10] At polar extremes were those who still resisted any form of federal intervention and those who felt that Roosevelt's plan did not go far enough. At first the proposed legislation received general acclaim, but then the storm clouds began to gather. Criticism, which had initially centered on the speed with which such complex and controversial legislation was being put together, later focused on social security coverage as a universal concept and on the heavy involvement of the federal government in the administration of the program.[11] Strong opposition that threatened the passage of the act developed in the Congress. Since Roosevelt and his administration thought quick passage of the bill was essential to assist the recovery of the economy, compromises and concessions were made. Individual states were given considerable latitude in determining pension eligibility, amount of pension, and methods of administration, all of which watered down the concept of universal coverage.[12] Perhaps an even more devastating blow came when the Treasury Department argued successfully that the act should be amended to eliminate farm laborers, domestic servants, and very small business establishments on the grounds, that it would be too difficult and costly to serve such workers.[13] This effectively eliminated coverage for a large segment of the poorest and neediest of the population, including the majority of black people.[14]

Thus, the act as it was finally signed by Roosevelt on August 18, 1935, was a far cry from the original dream. Yet it was a rather typical example of the political process in the United States, and also in typical fashion, the legislation has been amended and expanded over the years. Because the original legislation was rather limited, new programs to improve the financial well-being of older persons have been developed in its wake. At the same time, there exist side-by-side programs that cover special populations making the financial picture a rather complicated one.

This brief background once again illustrates the difficulties in promoting benefit programs and the caution with which they are implemented. In recent years, the serious threat to social security has excited considerable alarm among the general population, and it is easy to understand why. The nation's program of financial benefits for retired workers and their dependents and survivors far exceeds in numbers of persons benefited—as well as costs—

that of all other services to the aging combined. For well over three decades, the social security system received widespread acclaim as the classic example of a government program that pleased virtually the entire citizenry. As recently as 1971, one of the authors of the system declared that the words "social security" had become a "common and comforting expression in the American language."[15]

Within a few short years, however, soothing reassurances concerning the soundness of the system was replaced by media headlines such as "Will It Be There When You Need It?"[16] In the early months of the Reagan administration, proposals to make major changes in the legislation heightened an already serious erosion of public confidence. Elderly recipients were frightened by legislation to eliminate a number of benefits. To restore a measure of calm, the president chose not to press for further immediate changes and instead created the fifteen-member bipartisan National Commission on Social Security Reform. The function of the commission was to recommend, by the end of 1982, steps that would reestablish public confidence in the financial integrity of the system. As the deadline approached, the problem escalated to crisis proportions. In March 1983 an "accord" was reached, and an act was passed that provided answers to many questions. The president spoke for the nation when he declared "a dark cloud has been lifted."[17]

The next section of this chapter, will focus on ways in which social security plays a central economic role in the lives of older persons. The objectives and provisions of the legislation, some lingering problems or issues, and finally the current changes that are being enacted and their implications will also be discussed. Other programs intended for the general support of needy elderly, specifically Supplemental Security Income and food stamps, will also be described in this section. The final section of the chapter will analyze the ways in which the general economic programs meet the needs of the elderly. In the next chapter, a series of pension or other financial assistance programs for specific categories of elderly will be investigated.

2. General Programs to Support the Elderly

SOCIAL SECURITY

Objectives and Provisions

The popular interpretation of the term "social security" is much more narrow than the Social Security Act itself. From the moment of its passage in 1935, in the midst of the Great Depression, the act established several programs to attack the nagging insecurity caused by the lack of income. Included in the act were provisions for a national-state unemployment insurance system and for state programs for the needy aged, the blind, and sick and needy children. In the years that followed passage of the act, popular attention centered more and more upon one facet of the legislation—earnings replacement for the retiring worker. In the narrow sense, then, social security refers to cash benefits to replace earnings lost because of retirement, disability, or death.

Objectives   The main purpose of the social security system was, as Arthur J. Altmeyer, one of its first commissioners, declared, to provide "a minimum level of well-being" or, as he went on, "the minimum of income and services essential to decent human existence."[18] The "minimum level of well-being" was to be based on the worker's right to benefits. That is, instead of a flat basic grant for all persons, each individual was to receive an amount based upon his or her contributions and those of the employer.

The system, however, was not to be simply private insurance at the government level. True, the system of wage-related benefits was inspired by private insurance. But over and beyond that was the concept of weighting the benefits in favor of the low-wage earner. The words *equity* and *adequacy* were used to describe the system: equity recognized the worker's contribution; adequacy gave special advantage to the worker with a low income. The measure of social adequacy has been described as "a standard of living beneath which society feels no one should fall."[19]

Social security was meant to be a middle tier of protection. It was not to be public welfare, the first tier; nor was the benefit system meant to supplant the system of private insurance, the third tier. The individual worker and the employer were each to pay a special tax to support the worker's retirement benefits—the middle tier.[20] The amount to be contributed through taxation was small compared with contributions demanded by private or public annuity systems. For example, during the early years of the program, the individual's tax was to be 1 percent of the first three thousand dollars of income, an amount to be matched by the employer.

The original objective of establishing a "minimum of income and services essential to decent human existence" has, in considerable measure, been achieved. Although private insurance systems cover approximately 45 percent of all workers, there are many millions whose basic income stems from social security alone. It is not strange that they should emphasize the adequacy concept and expect a considerably expanded interpretation of *minimum, essential,* and *decent.* In consequence there has been pressure for ever-increasing benefits and an expanded benefit structure. Only in recent years has the tax necessary to support the benefit structure become a critical issue.

The Payroll Tax and the Earnings Base   Since its inception, the social security system has been financed by a payroll tax levied upon covered wages. The base sets a limit on the earnings taxed. It also serves to establish the maximum credit for computing subsequent benefits. Workers and employers each pay the same tax. Both the rate and the base have increased over the years in response to both the changing price structure and the inclusion of additional categories of programs and beneficiaries. The payroll tax consists of three parts. The first was initiated in 1937 to cover the basic old-age and survivors insurance (OASI); the second, initiated in 1957, covers disability; and the third, which began in 1965, covers hospital costs. The levy in 1937 was 1 percent; the maximum base was $3,000. The contribution rate in 1984 was 7.0 percent and was made up of three parts; OASI, 5.2 percent; disability insurance, .5 percent; and health insurance, 1.30 percent. In 1984, the annual maximum taxable earnings base had risen to $37,500. The tax for the employee, the employer, and the self-employed, together with the maximum base and the maximum tax for the employee and employer, are shown in table 1.

Table 1
Tax, Earnings Base and Amount, Actual and Projected

Year	% Employer and Employee each	Base	Maximum Tax	% Self-Employed
1937	1.00	$ 3,000	$ 30.00	
1950	1.50	3,000	45.00	
1955	2.00	4,200	84.00	3.00
1960	3.00	4,800	144.00	4.50
1970	4.80	7,800	374.40	6.90
1975	5.85	14,100	824.85	7.90
1980	6.13	25,900	1,587.67	8.10
1982	6.70	32,400	2,170.80	9.35
1984	7.00	37,500	2,625.00	
1985	7.05	40,500	2,855.25	
1986	7.15	43,800	3,131.70	10.00
1990	7.65	57,000	4,360.50	

Source: Social Security Oversight: Short Term Financing Issues, Hearing before the Special Committee on Aging, U.S. Senate, 97th Congress, 1st session, part 1, June 16, 1981, p. 68; *U.S. News and World Report,* April 4, 1983, p. 24.

Critics of the system maintain that the payroll tax is a steeply regressive levy upon the low- and medium-income worker. In many instances, the payroll tax takes a greater portion of the worker's pay than does the income tax. In past years, the higher-income individual escaped much of the burden of the payroll tax. The 1979 Advisory Counsel recommended unanimously that the time had come to "finance some part of social security with non-payroll tax revenues."[21] The recommendation was not new, the 1938 council having recommended that one-third of the program be funded from general revenues. The other unanimous recommendation of the 1979 council was to reject the much-touted value-added tax as a means of financing some part of social security. Not only was the tax regressive, the council declared, but "it would represent federal intrusion into a revenue source—sales taxation—customarily reserved for states and localities."[22] The payroll tax, although regressive, has the advantage of being levied on the same base used to determine social security benefits. The principle of the earned right is thus maintained.

Computing Benefits Originally, benefits were to be paid to the covered retired worker only. Since 1935, the act has been greatly broadened. For example, benefits for survivors and dependents were included in 1939; the disabled worker's dependents in 1958; and health insurance, known as Medicare, was instituted for those sixty-five and above in 1965. Of those over sixty-five, 93 percent have the protection of social security. Beneficiaries by type, as of September 1982, are as follows:[23]

Retired Workers, Spouses, Children Survivors,
September 1982

Total	31,524,728
Retired Workers	20,576,674
Wives and Husbands	3,030,844
Children	2,763,822
Widows and Widowers	4,566,066
Widowed Mothers and Fathers	508,861
Parents	12,783
Special Age Beneficiaries	65,678

To achieve "adequacy," benefits are computed in a manner that favors the low-wage earner. The procedure involves determining the AIME, or average indexed monthly earnings. The first step requires taking the earnings for each year after 1950—until the worker reaches age sixty—that were subject to the social security tax. The second step counters inflation. It requires that each year's earnings subject to the tax be indexed, that is, increased by the average increase in earnings of all workers. Thus, if over a period of, say, ten years, the average covered earnings of all workers had doubled, then the worker making four thousand dollars in covered wages in the first year would be credited with eight thousand dollars. The worker's five years of lowest indexed earnings are dropped from the calculation. The indexed earnings are then divided by the number of months. The result is the workers AIME, or average indexed monthly earnings.

Once the AIME has been determined, a formula is used to develop the primary insurance amount, or PIA. Three calculations are involved. In 1980, the first calculation required taking 90 percent of the first $230 of the average indexed monthly earnings. To that was added 32 percent of the amount above

$230 up to $1,388. To that total was added 15 percent of the remainder. The final figure was the primary insurance amount. From year to year, the percentage amounts remain constant; the dollar figures, or "bend points," increase in percentage corresponding to the rise in average wages.

The varying percentages weight the benefit in favor of the low-income worker. The end result is a replacement rate of slightly over 50 percent for a low-income worker as opposed to a rate of 42 percent for a worker with lifetime average wages. The high-income worker's replacement rate is about 30 percent.[24]

The primary insurance amount is payable at age sixty-five. However, if a worker elects to receive benefits at an earlier age—the minimum is age sixty-two—benefits are reduced permanently at the rate of .555 of a percent per month, or 20 percent for the three-year period. A worker not retiring at age sixty-five may earn a "delayed retirement credit" of .25 percent per month. At age sixty-five, the spouse of a retired worker is eligible for benefits equal to one-half that of the retiree. If a spouse elects to receive benefits between the ages of sixty-two and sixty-five, the reduction noted above applies. The average benefits of a newly retired worker in November 1982 amounted to $419.

When the decision was made in 1939 to include benefits for survivors and dependents, the original idea of social security as wage replacement was abandoned. Moreover, the wage replacement calculation was in itself meant to favor the low-income worker. In addition to the formula for determining the average monthly earnings, other features, such as the exclusion of the lowest years of earnings and the introduction of the minimum benefit (removed and then in large measure restored in 1981) and various dependent benefits, brought an aspect of welfare into the benefit structure. The weighting, or redistributive feature, is said to be a "necessary trade-off between social adequacy and individual equity."[25]

The current method of determining benefits is not without fault, according to the report of the 1979 Advisory Council. Although the council supported the principles of adequacy and equity, with low-wage earners receiving proportionately higher benefits, a majority felt that the existing plan went too far in providing benefits for those with short periods under social security. The council felt that a distinction needed to be made between workers "who have a regular attachment to full-time employment covered by social security for at least thirty years" and those who worked in covered employment for relatively short periods. The former should be "entitled to a retirement benefit that at least keeps them out of poverty."[26] The council proposed a new benefit formula that would favor the "long-service, low-wage workers while reducing the heavily weighted benefits payable to intermittent workers."[27]

Continuing Issues and Controversies

The Trust Funds When the social security system was first established, a major controversy developed over the degree to which it should follow the model of private insurance. The decision was made early that vast reserves were neither necessary nor desirable. The test of soundness was not whether sufficient reserves were on hand "to meet a test of liquidation," in the words of Robert Ball.[28] Rather, the test was whether "the provisions for financing future benefits and administrative costs are adequate to meet the obligations as they fall due."[29]

In order to assure the public of the financial integrity of the new system and also to emphasize the insurance concept, worker and employer contributions were placed in The Old Age and Survivors Insurance Trust Fund. Later, in 1957, that portion of the contributions that would cover the cost of the disability program was placed in The Disability Insurance Trust Fund. With the inauguration of Medicare, two new funds were established: The Hospital Insurance Trust Fund and The Supplementary Medical Insurance Trust Fund. The first three funds hold worker contributions; the fourth holds premiums for medical insurance coverage. Monies are invested in federal securities.

Three cabinet officers—the secretaries of the Departments of Labor, Health and Human Services, and The Treasury, and, since 1983, two public members serve as a board of trustees. The secretary of the treasury is designated by law as the managing trustee and is charged with investing funds not needed for payments to beneficiaries.

The system operates under a policy known as current-cost financing. As revenues are received from workers and employers, the monies are paid out to retirees or to those who are disabled. In reality, then, the Trust Fund Balance is a contingency reserve to meet the need for expanded benefits or to replace funds lost because of a decline in revenues. Combined OASDI trust funds in 1970 amounted to 103 percent of annual outlays. By 1981, the balance had declined to 18 percent. Although Congress, in late 1981, had provided for temporary interfund borrowing, the Congressional Budget Office warned that the ratio of trust fund levels to anticipated outlays could be as low as 7.6 percent by 1984. This was considerably below the 12 percent they recommended as an "acceptable minimum level." Either revenues must be increased or benefits decreased, the office declared, "to guarantee uninterrupted payments to beneficiaries."[30]

The Earnings or Retirement Test One of the most controversial features of the system has been the reduction of benefits for those who continue to work after reaching retirement age. Theoretically, the purpose of social security was to replace lost earnings.[31] Therefore, if the individual continued to work, there were no earnings to replace. Nor, it was feared, would jobs be available for younger people. The elderly person who continued working was required to pay a heavy penalty for so doing.

Initially, the law gave the worker almost no leeway in earnings. If earned income did not exceed fifteen dollars monthly, the worker was considered to have met the retirement test and was entitled to full benefits. But benefits were reduced if earnings rose above this sum.

Over the years, in spite of constant opposition from those affected, Congress has adhered to the original theory. The amount that the individual may earn without loss of benefits has been increased time after time. From the fifteen-dollar monthly disregard in 1939, the offset gradually grew. In 1950 a new concept was added: those seventy-five years of age and older were declared exempt from the act. In 1960, twelve hundred dollars could be earned in a year without penalty. Beyond that, however, one dollar for each two dollars of earnings between twelve hundred and fifteen hundred dollars was deducted, and one dollar for each dollar of earnings over fifteen hundred dollars up to the amount of the benefit was deducted. The policy of gradual liberalization continued, and by 1983 the earnings exemption for those sixty-five and over had been increased to sixty-six hundred dollars. Above that threshold, the reduction amounted to one dollar for each two dollars of earnings up to the total benefit. The exemption allowed for age seventy-two since 1954 was to be offered to those aged seventy in 1982. However, the reconciliation act of 1981 postponed the change for one year. The revision of 1983 provided that, beginning in 1990, the reduction would amount to one dollar for each two dollars of earnings.

Proponents of the retirement test maintain that to eliminate the test would be to change a basic feature of social security, namely, replacement of lost earnings. Whether this conclusion has been basic to congressional retention of the test is difficult to determine. It is certain that one reason for retaining the retirement test is the cost of abandoning it. According to the Congressional Budget Office, this cost would range from $400 million in 1983 to $690 million in 1987.[32]

Opponents of the test choose to ignore the philosophical basis—replacement of earnings. Instead, they put forth a different philosophy, namely, that they worked for, and thus have a right to, their benefits. However, there is little basis for the concept of an earned annuity; the benefits currently are much greater than an annuity would have produced. Nevertheless, the idea persists. A second theoretical objective is based on the "unfairness" of the test; that is, while earnings are penalized, there is no reduction for income obtained from other sources, such as interest, pension, dividends and rents. Proponents dismiss this argument as totally irrelevant to the basic purpose of the act—replacement of earnings.

A much more practical basis for eliminating the test is its damaging effect upon the incentive to work.[33] The reduction rate is not just the one dollar of benefit loss for two dollars earned. The person who continues to work after retirement will pay the normal taxes of any worker, namely, social security, state and local income, and occupational levies. On top of the normal costs, the worker then loses a portion, or all, of the social security benefits. The total loss constitutes a major disincentive to work. The percentage loss on the amount earned is incredibly high.

Women and Social Security The extensive changes in the role of women over the last several decades have inspired many proposals for revising the Social Security Act. For example, many women no longer accept the idea of dependence. Yet, under the original act, benefits for wives and widows were based on the principle that they were dependents. Economic support came from the male worker. In 1940, only 17 percent of married women were in the labor force. By 1977, the percentage had grown to 47 percent.[34] Moreover, married women increasingly wished recognition as equal economic partners. thus arises the question: how appropriate is dependency as the principle upon which women's benefits are provided?

When the Social Security Act was first passed it provided coverage only for the worker. but, by 1939, prior to the first payments, an amendment provided benefits for dependents. As of now, eligible wives—that is, women sixty-two years old or older—may receive up to 50 percent of worker benefits, and eligible widows may receive up to 100 percent, depending on age. As a consequence of various changes in the law, married persons in covered employment are now treated in substantially identical fashion. Each may be eligible for benefits either as a worker or as a dependent spouse. In 1978, roughly one-half of 1 percent of men receiving benefits were doing so as dependent spouses or widowers. In contrast, 46 percent of women receiving benefits did so as dependent spouses.[35] The married woman who works earns credits that seem to duplicate those of her husband. She has the choice, at retirement, of receiving one-half her husband's benefits or benefits based upon her own earnings, whichever is higher. Had she chosen to be a home-maker, she would have been eligible for one-half of her husband's benefits. Moreover, as a worker she had to pay the social security tax on earnings. Thus, the working women feels poorly treated in comparison with the homemaker.

There is another side to the coin, an advantage that the married woman who works may not consider. Her earnings enable her to receive benefits in her own right, without regard to the time her husband retires, becomes disabled, or dies. Moreover, her dependents are eligible for benefits in the event of her disability or death. In contrast, the woman who qualifies as a dependent does so only when her husband retires, is disabled, or dies.

Divorce has complicated the issue. Until 1979, a divorced woman had to be of appropriate age and married a full twenty years before being entitled to one-half the spouse's benefits upon his retirement or full benefits upon his death. Nineteen years and eleven months were not enough. The lowering of the marriage limit to ten years was considered to be a major step forward. Now, however, the woman (or man), divorced after ten years and of appropriate age, is entitled to benefits based upon the spouse's total earnings record. Moreover, if the spouse remarries and is again divorced after ten years, he or she is entitled to second benefits based upon the second spouse's total earnings. This regulation may seem to favor the divorced woman or man. However, another statistic alters the picture. Two-thirds of all divorces occur prior to the completion of ten years of marriage. In this event, all claim for social security coverage on the basis of marriage is lost.

One troublesome problem concerns the benefits to the person who has been widowed for several years. This problem applies to widowers as well but primarily affects women. Although she receives benefits based upon her husband's earnings, and benefits have been indexed for inflation, there is still no recognition of the wage change that may have occurred since the death of the husband. The benefit, in short, "is related to the standard of living that existed at the time of her husband's death, rather than the standard of living at the time she came on the benefit rolls."[36] This is a major reason that the benefits of two-thirds of all aged widows in 1976 were below the poverty line. The 1983 revision liberalized, to some degree, the regulation relating to widows and to divorced and disabled women.

The increasing dissatisfaction with the current law as it pertains to women has resulted in many proposals for change. Two proposals have received more attention than others. The purpose of each is to eliminate the concept of dependency.

Earnings sharing is based on the theory that each marriage partner is entitled to equal protection as a matter of right, not as a matter of dependency. Thus, half of the couple's earnings is credited to each. The portion earned by each is immaterial. This "pure earnings sharing" proposal is considered deficient, however, since benefits would be insufficient to support the survivors. The survivor normally requires more than one-half the couple's benefits. As a consequence, various modifications have been discussed. A number of these were considered at length by the 1979 Advisory Council, which observed that "earnings sharing is simple in concept but often complex in application."[37] Because of these complexities, the council was unwilling to endorse any of the plans presented for consideration.

A second proposal, known as the double-decker option, would provide two tiers of protection. The plan would provide universal protection for all recipients. The first tier would simply be a payment of the current minimum benefit to all recipients sixty-five and above or to those who were disabled. The second tier would be an earnings-related benefit amounting to 30 percent of an individual's average earnings. Additional features would provide protection for divorced women and aged widows. The Advisory Council rejected the double-decker plan as a "radical change" that "would not significantly improve the treatment of women."[38] Former Commissioner of Social Security Robert M. Ball has urged "extreme caution" in adopting what may appear to be "solutions." Rather than the hasty embrace of new proposals that may "take away important protections as well as grant new ones," he favored an "eclectic approach dealing with the specifics of the issues raised."[39]

Restoring Public Confidence

Assumptions concerning the state of the economy together with demographic assumptions relating to the number of workers and the number of retirees are key elements in determining the funding steps necessary to assure the financial solvency of the social security system. Substantial cyclical fluctuations can create havoc in plans for meeting fund obligations. Notwithstanding legislation in 1977 that promised to restore social security to "a sound financial footing for the next 40–50 years," the system deteriorated.[40] The economy did not perform the way it was supposed to. As a consequence, inflation-adjusted benefits rose. However, because of increasing unemployment and other factors, the wages supporting payroll taxes lagged behind. Year after year—indeed, since 1974—social security outlays exceeded revenues. Public confidence gradually evaporated. Sixty-eight percent of those between the ages of eighteen and fifty-four declared that they had "hardly any confidence" that funds would be available when they retired.[41]

Some Short-Range Options Proposals that would place social security on a sound basis have been wide ranging. Testimony before congressional committees has usually emphasized the need for both short-range and long-range solutions. One short-range proposal, for example, is to authorize interfund borrowing among the trust funds. Legislation enacted in late 1981 permitted this on a limited basis. The authorization expired, however, at the end of 1982.

Proposals that would increase revenues over the short term have included: (1) increasing the payroll tax, (2) increasing the wage base, (3) using general revenues, and (4) requiring coverage of all new federal, state, and local government employees. Another series of proposals that would reduce the growth of benefits includes: (1) delaying the cost of living (COLA) increases, (2) placing a percentage cap on the cost of living increase, (3) using either wages or prices, whichever is lower, to measure the increase in benefits, and (4) establishing a different, and lower, basis for the Consumer Price Index (CPI). Each of the above proposals ultimately involves a subjective judgment about the state of the economy. Whether those judgments are based on optimistic, intermediate, or pessimistic assumptions determines whether the system operates on a modest surplus or incurs a deficit of many billions of dollars.[42]

Extending the Age of Retirement The solvency of social security over the long term depends not only on the state of the economy but also on the demographics of the nation. For example, it is estimated that a population of 36 million over age sixty-five in 1980 will increase to 65 million by the year 2030. In relation to those of working age, the elderly constituted 19.5 percent in 1980. Although the number of elderly will have increased a modest percentage of 22.6 by the year 2000, it is estimated that the ratio will increase to 37.8 percent by the year 2030. This shift means that there will be but 2 covered workers for each beneficiary in contrast to the current ratio of 3.2 to 1. Raising the retirement age would lessen the burden of high taxation on the covered worker, and a proposal to this effect has received considerable attention. Workers between the ages of sixty-five and sixty-eight would continue to pay the social security tax, and, more important, they would not receive benefits unless they had chosen early retirement at a substantially reduced level of payment.

A major factor in the retirement dependency ratio has been the decrease in the birth rate since the mid 1960s. Although this decrease may result in a larger proportion of non-working older persons compared to those in the work force, it also results in fewer young dependents. Thus the total dependency ratio, including both the number of persons under the age of twenty and the number over age sixty-five, may not be markedly different from the current ratio. Whether the lower birth rate would result in decreased costs that would counteract the increased burden of social security benefits is an extremely complex question for which there can be no firm answers.

Proponents of extending the retirement age point to its positive effects. Many persons would be happier if they could continue working, especially in view of today's and tomorrow's longer life expectancy; too many are wasting away simply for lack of productive work; working beyond age sixty-five would be a practical means of countering inflation, a worrisome feature of the early 1980s; the step would be in conformity with the government's action in eliminating mandatory retirement before age seventy. These reasons have little relation to the main financial issue, namely, that an extension of the retirement age would markedly reduce the deficit projected for the early to middle decades of the next century.

Notwithstanding the arguments in favor of extending the retirement age, there is the overriding fact that early retirement has recently been preferred to normal or delayed retirement. Furthermore, early retirees frequently cite illness as the reason for leaving the labor force. To what degree, then, the trend toward early retirement could be reversed and the length of time a reversal might take are difficult to estimate. Proponents of raising the retirement age favor doing so gradually. According to their proposals, several years would elapse before the new retirement age would be in effect. Workers who are now close to retirement would not be affected. In recent years, three national advisory groups—the Advisory Council on Social Security, the National Commission on Social Security Reform, and the President's Commission on Pension Policy—have recommended an increase in the eligibility age. Their proposals differ in details such as the appropriate phase-in period. The general idea, however, is accepted by all three bodies.[43] In the Social Security Amendment Act of 1983, Congress extended the present retirement age for two years. Retirement at age sixty-six would be achieved in the year 2009, following a two-month increase for each of six years beginning in 2003. Retirement at age sixty-seven would be effective in 2027, following a similar six-year procedure starting in 2020.

Changing the Method of Computing Initial Benefits Another proposal to relieve the financial burden of social security that has received considerable attention concerns the benefit formula. This is a highly technical area involving the weighting method, which, over the years, has operated in favor of the low-wage earner. The basic procedure, described briefly in the section on computing benefits, might be altered. For example, the specific percentages used in determining the primary benefit formula might be changed. Another approach might be to modify the indexing method.[44] Through changes in the formula, the benefit structure could be altered to produce substantial reductions in the level of income replacement. In the 1983 revision, Congress chose not to alter the benefit formula. It did, however, delay the cost-of-living increase for six months to January 1, 1984.

Taxing Social Security Benefits One suggestion that would introduce a greater measure of equity into the system and, at the same time, bolster the funding base is the proposal to tax the social security income of middle- and upper-income beneficiaries.[45] For years, the degree of public indignation aroused when this suggestion has been made has frightened off both the president and the Congress. Opponents sharply attack the suggestion that benefits be taxed. They argue that it would constitute a breach of faith on the part of the government. In reality, however, there would be no breach of faith. The often-heard argument that "I paid my social security tax; therefore I am entitled to the benefits" assumes that the benefits are based strictly on the amount paid in. This assumption is faulty, however, for it ignores the weighting system favoring lower paid workers. Current beneficiaries actually receive sums that far exceed those paid to recipients of private pension systems, given an equal salary base and time span.

Suggestions for a change in policy vary. One proposal would include all social security benefits in the individual's taxable income. A second would include only the benefits attributable to the employer, since the employer's contribution has not been taxed. A third proposal would place a tax on benefits attributable to the employer and to the interest on the contributions of both employer and employee. A majority of the 1979 Advisory Council recommended a fourth approach, namely, making half of the benefits taxable. This, they declared, would provide "rough justice."[46]

In 1982, one of the suggestions of the Congressional Budget Office for reducing the deficit was to tax half of the social security benefits of couples with incomes of $25,000 and above and of single persons with incomes above $20,000. This step, the CBO stated, would affect only those with the greatest ability to pay and would result in a five-year savings of $11.6 billion for the period 1983–93. This system would make social security somewhat comparable to private pension systems. Indeed, the CBO reported, "if Social Security were taxed like private pensions, about 83 percent of retirement benefits would be taxable."[47]

The Report of the National Commission on Social Security Reform also proposed a tax on benefits for recipients having a substantial income. In the 1983 amendments, Congress adopted the commission's basic principle. The act provided that a single person with an adjusted gross income that combined with one-half of social security benefits, exceeded twenty-five thousand dollars would pay income tax on the total. The threshold for a couple filing a joint return would be thirty-five thousand dollars. Any tax-exempt interest income would be included in determining the twenty-five thousand dollar or thirty-two thousand dollar threshold.

The National Commission and the 1983 Amendments The preceding somewhat extended review of several of the more difficult problems awaiting solution in early 1983 demonstrates the nature of the task that faced both the National Commission on Social Security Reform and the Congress. For months, the bipartisan body appointed by President Reagan in December 1981 seemed to be hopelessly divided.[48] Although the commission had been scheduled to submit a final report by the end of 1982, the deadline and life of the commission had to be extended by the president. The crisis caused by the social security problem resulted in an unusual approach to a solution. The commission did not arrive at a series of recommendations on its own. Rather, the chairman, Dr. Alan Greenspan, involved the president and congressional leaders, especially Speaker Thomas O'Neill, in the negotiating process. Thus, the final report had the backing not only of a substantial majority of the commission but also of the principals in the executive and legislative branches. The Accord, as the final report was called, served as the basis for bills prepared by the Ways and Means Committee of each house. In slightly over a month, a "compromise rescue plan" moved through Congress and was adopted by a 58–14 vote in the Senate and by a 243–102 vote in the House. The measure signed by the president on April 20, 1983, was to take effect January 1, 1984.

The legislation resulted in many changes in the social security system. Although some of these have already been mentioned, they will be highlighted a second time in order that a summary of all the principal features of the 1983 act be included in this section.

The major provisions follow:

1. The tax rate will increase in stages from 6.7 percent of the earnings base in 1983 to 7.65 percent in 1990.
2. The retirement age will be raised. Beginning in 2003 the eligibility age will be raised two months each year for six years. As a consequence, in 2009 the retirement age will be sixty-six. A similar procedure will follow beginning in 2020. In 2027, the retirement age will be sixty-seven. A person will still be fully eligible for Medicare at age sixty-five. Early retirement at age sixty-two will be retained. However, benefits will be reduced from 80 to 75 percent in 2009 and to 70 percent in 2027.
3. Coverage will be required of new federal employees as of January 1, 1984. Also, the president and vice president, members of Congress, federal judges, and employees of nonprofit corporations will be required to participate.
4. State and local governments and nonprofit organizations may no longer withdraw from the system.
5. Some benefits will be taxed. Single persons with adjusted gross incomes, including half of social security benefits, exceeding $25,000 will pay income tax on the total. The threshold for a married couple is $32,000. Tax-exempt interest will be included in determining the threshold.
6. Self-employed persons will be required to pay the tax now paid by employees and employers. However, tax credits will offset much of the increase through 1989.
7. Cost-of-living increases were postponed for six months to January 1, 1984.
8. The earnings or retirement test will be further liberalized. Beginning in 1990, benefits for those under seventy will be reduced by one dollar for each three dollars earned over $6,600.
9. Beginning in 1990, the bonus for delaying retirement will rise one-quarter of a percent per year, from 3 percent of benefits in 1983 to 8 percent in 2008.[49]

The Stake in Social Security The continuance of a strong social security system is of extreme importance to millions of old people. For many, social security is the principal source of income. The benefits for the low-income worker have been pitifully small. Yet they have often been sufficient to make any recourse to welfare unnecessary. The system has enabled the recipient to feel he can "make it on his own." The importance of this feeling of self-sufficiency can scarcely be overestimated.

For millions of other old people—those with larger incomes who have been able to build at least limited resources for this stage of life—the monthly social security check or deposit has been a welcome addition. The percentage of individuals whose incomes are so large that the benefits mean virtually nothing is extremely small.

But the elderly and those nearing retirement are not the only ones who have a major stake in social security. For the younger worker, the prospect of retirement some thirty or more years hence is so remote that the value of the system may be only dimly perceived. However, two aspects of the program that affect the younger worker provide a sense of immediacy and enhance greatly the meaning and purpose of social security. These are the survivorship and disability provisions, which provide family benefits that no private insurance program can approach.

There is a price attached to social security. Unless the price is paid, the system will not survive. The price is the revenue necessary to meet promised benefits. No one can predict with assurance the point at which payment of the tax may arouse deep hostility. In theory, the government's power to tax is unlimited. In fact, however, without widespread public support, the theory becomes untenable.

One of the greatest dangers to the system lies in the overextension of expectations. Individuals must be willing to assume a fair share of the costs and to ask no more than an appropriate share of the benefits. For their own safety, and for that of generations to follow, the elderly should insist upon universal adherence to this policy. "Fairness" as it applies to social security, however, involves a complex set of considerations, and many persons who receive or are about to receive benefits are quite at a loss when it comes to understanding the workings of the system.

SUPPLEMENTAL SECURITY INCOME

In 1974, a major shift occurred in the federal provision of financial assistance for the elderly needy. Old Age Assistance, a grant-in-aid program, administered through the states for almost four decades, was eliminated. The Supplemental Security Income program (SSI) funded from federal general tax revenues, took its place. Authorized by the 1972 amendments to the Social Security Act, the new program removed operating control from the states and placed full responsibility with the Social Security Administration.[50] In December 1980, 2,226,000 aged, blind, and disabled persons—8.7 percent of those over age sixty-five—were receiving cash assistance payments through the SSI program. Other age groups of blind and disabled persons receiving SSI payments brought the total to 4,141,000.[51]

The principal objective of SSI is to assure a minimum income to aged, blind, and disabled persons. Achievement of this objective depends upon eligibility and standards of payment that are uniform throughout the nation. The new legislation does not prohibit the participation of the states. Instead, each state is permitted to add to the national cash assistance payment any amount it might choose.

Fundamentally, the SSI Program, as it developed, is little different from the Old Age Assistance Program. In each instance, the basic criterion is need. Old Age Assistance had been one of the key features of the Social Security Act in 1935. The program depended upon states initiative. At first, if a state chose to comply with specified federal requirements, the federal government would pay one-half of the assistance payment up to fifteen dollars per month. Over the years, the matching formula changed and so did the regulations, but the basic division of responsibility remained. In some states the program was administered entirely by the central state government; in others the administration was shared by both state and local governments.[52] All states participated, but the monthly payments varied widely. At the time the Old Age Assistance Program was terminated in 1973, average monthly payments to individuals ranged from $56 to $121. In six states, average payments were below $60 monthly; nine states had payments above $100.[53] Under SSI, the individual without income or resources, as determined by federal standards, was initially eligible for a maximum federal payment of $130 monthly. Before the program actually began, on January 1, 1974, this figure was raised to $140. Six months later it went to $146. From July 1982 to June 1983, the maximum was $285.50 for an individual and $426.40 for a couple. In 1975, automatic cost-of-living increases were incorporated into the payment system.

Eligibility

Eligibility under the new program, as under the old, is based upon income and resources. In determining the level of payment, federal regulations provide that not all income shall be counted. A number of "income disregards" or "exclusions" apply to both earned and unearned income. For example, there is a monthly unearned-income disregard of twenty dollars and an earned-income disregard of sixty-five dollars, plus one-half of earnings above sixty-five dollars. Similarly, there are limitations on resources. Thus, an individual may have assets of no more than $1,500 and a couple of no more than $2,250. Again, the regulations provide leeway in determining the cash value of a particular resource. Initially, the reasonable value of a home was excluded, the maximum exclusion being $25,000 on the mainland and $35,000 in

Alaska and Hawaii. Currently, the home is entirely excluded. So is a car, if the market value is $4,500 or less. Household goods and personal effects are excluded up to a limit of $2,000.

The complexities in determining an individual's income and resources were explained to the Senate Special Committee on Aging by the commissioner of the Social Security Administration in 1974:

In determining SSI eligibility, we start with the question of the person's resources and the amount of his earned or unearned income, including his Social Security benefit.

But, we don't depend on him to tell us all the information in order to determine SSI eligibility. If he otherwise appears to be eligible, his case is then teletyped into Baltimore and the computer checks the Social Security number. If he is receiving the Social Security benefits, $20 in Social Security benefits is not counted against his SSI eligiblity. Anything over the $20 is deducted from the standard SSI payment amount on a dollar-for-dollar basis, and anything remaining would be paid to him as his SSI benefit. The matter, however, that must be determined locally in the district offices, relates to the man's other sources of earned and unearned income. This then becomes, I'm sorry to say, very complex. I wish it weren't so complex, but we have to go into the question of whether he works, whether he owns a home, whether he owns an automobile, whether he has a bank account, and things of that sort, or whether he has received any other form of State assistance during the period for which his eligibility is being determined.[54]

SSI payment levels vary. Payment is reduced by one-third for the recipient who lives in the household of another person. Reductions are applied, also, to those who receive in-kind support. Unfortunately, regulations of this nature quickly become "hairsplitting," as a 1976 study reported, making "uniform interpretations . . . difficult to achieve."[55]

Eligibility for Medicaid is intertwined with SSI. In thirty-five states, SSI recipients are eligible for Medicaid. The SSI monthly benefit is limited to twenty-five dollars for beneficiaries in public and private institutions who receive over 50 percent of the cost of their care from Medicaid. However, those in private institutions receive the standard payment, providing the cost of care is not met by Medicaid.

SSI recipients are eligible for food stamps. For various reasons—lack of awareness, inability to get to food stamp offices, the perception that food stamps are a form of welfare, and others—perhaps as many as one million of those eligible do not participate in the Food Stamp Program.[56]

Optional State Supplementation

When the SSI Program began, the states were required to supplement federal payments in order that persons eligible for SSI payments would not be adversely affected by the transition. In addition, the states were authorized and encouraged to supplement the federal payment. A state may choose to administer its own supplement. This choice enables the state to establish both eligibility criteria and the amount of payment. Administrative costs are borne by the state. About half of the states providing supplementary payments have elected federal administration. In making this choice, the state agrees to accept rules that provide the most "efficient and effective administration of both the SSI payments and the state supplementary payments."[57] An incentive for electing federal administration is the absorption by the federal government of the administrative expense.

The states vary in their standards for determining basic needs. All include consumable items such as food, clothing, shelter, fuel, and utilities. Some allow telephones, transportation, household supplies, and other items. A few states also provide funds for "special needs" like moving expenses, burials, and emergencies.[58] However, financial pressures may not permit the payment of the state-determined needs. Some set maximum payments, others may apply a percentage reduction to the payment standard. A few states require that in order to qualify for a supplementary payment, a lien be placed upon the individual's property. Enforcement of a lien is the responsibility of the state. Provisions for liens are not included in the federal SSI regulations.

Special Problems

The Supplemental Security Income Program has provided a federally determined minimum income for the elderly poor. The program has been a step toward the reduction of extreme poverty for many thousands of old people. The extent of this achievement is blunted, however, by the emergence of a number of problems, some arising from the program itself and others from the administration of it. A summary of some of these problems follows.

1. The passage of the SSI legislation resulted in the addition of a new and heavy administrative load to the responsibility of the Social Security Administration. Although Old Age Assistance recipients were "grandfathered in," there were many new eligibles. For many months following the beginning of the new program, the Social Security Administration was subjected to criticism for failure to publicize adequately the new law, for delays in processing applications, and for overpayment or underpayment of beneficiaries. One critic declared that "lack of information about SSI, fear, emotional problems, language and cultural barriers, transiency and the like should not stand between the doors of SSA offices and individuals in need."[59] More than any other income maintenance program, SSI, to be of maximum effectiveness, requires a high degree of administrative cooperation among federal agencies and between national and state administrative bodies.

2. The cash payment will not of itself solve the problem of the aging poor. Of great significance is the necessity for coordinating the money needs of the

aged individual with his social service needs. This function belongs to the state, although the state's program is supported in large measure by federal funds and operates under federal guidelines. As a consequence, the individual may be forced to go from office to office, a process that "oftentimes results in the older person 'giving up' in frustration and despair."[60]

3. The system has been criticized for failure to take into account the emergency situation or special need that may suddenly arise. The recipient whose refrigerator or hot water heater fails to function currently cannot be helped, although a number of states help solve problems like these through the optional state supplement for special needs.

4. The process of appeal for one denied eligibility has been attacked as being unnecessarily complex and by its nature geared to the upholding of the Social Security Administration.[61]

5. The act setting up SSI permitted recipients to be excuded from Medicaid. Sixteen states chose this option. The provision has been described as "a tremendous step backward from any concept of social insurance."[62]

Proposals for the Future

Except for the first two years following its inception, the net expansion of SSI has been remarkably small. Indeed, over the period from 1974 to 1980, although the number of aged, blind, and disabled over age sixty-five increased from 1,952,000 to 2,226,000, the percentage of the aged in relation to the total number of SSI recipients decreased from 61 percent to 54 percent. The decrease was in part due to the increase in the number of disabled children. However, a second factor was the decrease in the number of eligible elderly. This factor has been the subject of much speculation. How many of the elderly might have been eligible but were not fully informed about SSI? How many were reluctant to apply because of the welfare stigma, the complexity of the application process, or the low payment levels that those who were recipients of social security or other income would receive?[63]

Specific proposals by the 1979 Advisory Council on Social Security touched on a number of current issues. The council recommended that the income of all SSI recipients be brought up to the poverty level as soon as possible. The combination of social security, SSI, a state SSI supplement, and other sources may fail to achieve this objective. The council recommended that federal matching funds be supplied to states whose supplementary payments would elevate recipients' incomes to the poverty level. Other recommendations included revising and indexing the asset levels, modifying the income disregards, providing benefits for dependent children, and liberalizing the stipulation requiring the reduction of benefits by one-third for the recipient living in the home of another person.[64]

Similar recommendations were made by the National Commission on

Social Security in its final report of March 1981. The commission members came down especially hard on the asset test, which, they declared, disqualified persons with small savings accounts producing "an insignificant amount of income."[65] The commission declared that SSI, as a means-tested program, had "a proper place alongside Social Security to provide a safety net of minimal protection." The commission supported the 1979 Advisory Council on Social Security, which recommended an increase in payments that would bring the incomes of recipients to the poverty threshold. The net result of the recommendations of both commissions would have meant a substantial increase in the annual cost of the SSI program. Legislation in 1982 left the program substantially intact, although minor cutbacks effected some savings. For example, recognition of the asset-test problem was demonstrated by the authorization of specifically segregated burial funds in the amount of fifteen hundred dollars each for an individual and spouse.[66] In general, however, the recommendations of the commissions have been ignored by a Congress and a chief executive concerned with stemming further expansion.

THE FOOD STAMP PROGRAM

One observer has declared that the Food Stamp Program "represents the most important change in public welfare policy since the passage of the Social Security Act in 1935."[67] Others less favorably disposed have used harsh language to criticize the program, one former cabinet officer attacking it as a "haven for the chislers and rip-off artists."[68] It was estimated that in November 1982, 20.3 million persons of all ages were participating in the Food Stamp Program. Roughly 10 percent of this number, or 2 million persons, were believed to be elderly—a participation rate "in excess of 50 percent" of those eligible.[69] However, fewer than 6 percent of total food stamp dollars went to those sixty years old and older.[70]

Origins

The Food Stamp Program dates from May 1939, when an experimental operation was begun by the Department of Agriculture in Rochester, New York. The program served a dual objective: (1) to assist in disposing of surplus farm commodities, and (2) to help low-income families obtain additional supplies of food. Orange-colored stamps were purchased by families on relief in an amount equal to their normal food expenditures. The postage-size stamps were issued in denominations of twenty-five cents and one dollar and could be used to buy any food. Blue stamps amounting to half the value of the orange stamps were then given to the families for the purchase of surplus commodities. At the height of the program in 1942, 1,941 counties and eighty-eight cities were serving 4 million persons.[71] World War II resulted in a quick reduction of both agricultural surplus and unemployment. As a consequence, the program was terminated in 1943.

In his first executive order, President Kennedy established a pilot food stamp program. The initial project began in McDowell County, West Virginia, in May 1961. Additional pilot projects were started during the next three years until by May 1964 there were forty-three in operation in twenty-two states. Both the early program and the pilot projects were based on one section of the Agricultural Adjustment Act of 1935. Specific and detailed legislative authorization did not come until the passage of the Food Stamp Act of 1964.[72]

The enactment of permanent legislation did not result in a sudden expansion of the program to all parts of the nation. On the contrary, the first year's expenditures were held to the cost of the pilot operation—about $50 million. The act did, however, signal a major shift in policy. For many years, the Department of Agriculture had been operating a direct distribution program to dispose of surplus foods. For example, in 1964, families in over fifteen hundred counties received a billion-and-a-half pounds of food. However, the system of direct distribution had serious weaknesses. The number of commodities that could be distributed was limited to about ten. The distribution system itself was cumbersome, with bulk foods being turned over to the states at specified locations. The designation of recipients was a state responsibility.

As a consequence of the various problems arising out of the direct-distribution system, a gradual movement to phase out this method was begun. However, the prewar food stamp program was not adopted as the model for the new system. "In most respects," former secretary of agriculture Orville L. Freeman observed, "what we have done is to lift up the radiator cap and drive a whole new machine under it."[73]

As late as 1969, fewer than one-half of the nation's counties had Food Stamp Programs. Participation amounted to 2.9 million in the Food Stamp Program and 3.8 million in the food distribution program. The growth of the Food Stamp Program accelerated in 1971 with the nationalization of eligibility requirements and the expansion of benefits. In 1973, Congress mandated a nationwide program under the direction of the Food and Nutrition Service of the Department of Agriculture.[74] The administration of the program at the local level was made the responsibility of the states, which were charged with certifying applicants, issuing coupons, developing complaint procedures, and carrying out other functions in accordance with plans approved by the Department of Agriculture.

By April 1975, participation in the food distribution system was limited mostly to a few Indian reservations and had declined to 86,000. In contrast, by June 1975, 19.2 million persons were participating in the Food Stamp

Program, which was operating in virtually all of the United States, as well as Guam, Puerto Rico, and the Virgin Islands.[75]

Difficulties with the Monthly Purchase Requirement

The purpose of the program was to enable families to increase their ability to buy food. The family was required to purchase coupons. The cost, called the *monthly purchase requirement*, was related to the household income and the number of persons in the household. The number of coupons received, *the allotment*, was greater than the monthly purchase requirement. The difference constituted the *bonus*. Basic to the system was the set of standards used to establish the monthly allotment of coupons and the monthly purchase requirement. The allotment standards were related to the cost of an adequate family diet—the Economy Food Plan and later the Thrifty Food Plan—established by the Department of Agriculture.

The purchase requirement was limited to 30 percent of the household's net income. For example, at one time the monthly purchase requirement for a family of four with a net income between $310.00 and $329.99 was $89.00. With this purchase, stamps were allotted amounting to $162.00, a bonus of $73.00. Provision was made for the coupon allotment to be adjusted semi-annually to compensate for inflation.

With the passage of years, there was increasing evidence that the program was not meeting the original objectives. There was almost universal acceptance of the principle that the "deserving poor" should not go hungry. But at that point agreement ceased. One group criticized the Department of Agriculture for its failure to seek out those in need. Another group deplored the extensive regulations, which were degrading to the applicant and difficult to administer. One unhappy state official testified before a Senate committee that "the program is humiliating, often nonproductive, cost ineffective, and dominated by a nonresponsive, elephantine bureaucracy."[76] Other groups attacked the department for its inability to stop abuses by individuals and because it interpreted the regulations in such a manner that stamps could be used by strikers and college students.

Rising turmoil brought government response at several levels. In the Senate, the Committee on Nutrition and Human Needs and the Committee on Agriculture and Forestry conducted extensive hearings. Similarly active were the House Committee on Agriculture and the Joint Economic Committee of the Congress. The Food and Nutrition Service of the Department of Agriculture prepared special reports and the comptroller general conducted a management study of the total operation.[77]

Among the troublesome issues discovered was the participation rate of the elderly, which was no more than 40 to 50 percent of those eligible. Some elderly people felt the stigma of a welfare program. But there were other reasons for nonparticipation. It took cash to pay for the monthly purchase requirements, the only way of obtaining bonus stamps. Moreover, many old people apparently were unaware of the program. Others were repelled by the red tape involved in becoming certified and by the seemingly large effort that had to be expended for a comparatively small return. Of all the barriers to be overcome, the assistant secretary of the department declared, "the most important was the food stamp purchase requirement."[78]

The 1977 Revision and Current Practice

Attempts to overhaul the program finally met with success in 1977. "The 1977 revisions were incorporated in the omnibus farm bill and had an easy trip through Congress, ushered by an urban rural coalition. Farmbelt congressmen sought the help of their city colleagues to pass higher crop price supports and urban representatives needed rural members' votes to push through the food stamp revision."[79]

In addition to the elimination of the monthly purchase requirement, there was a number of other changes, some of which were of particular help to the elderly. For example, the certification period, that is, the amount of time during which those eligible for stamps could participate in the program without review, was extended to one year for the elderly. Also, the work registration age requirement was lowered from sixty-five to sixty.

Eligibility for participation was limited to those whose net income was at or below the poverty line. At the time the act was passed, the poverty line established by the Office of Management and Budget for a nonfarm family of four was $5,850 ($9,300 in 1983). In defining income, several of the deductions formerly allowed were eliminated. Instead, a standard monthly deduction of $60 ($85 in 1983) was authorized. Shelter expenses exceeding 50 percent of household income less deductions were to be waived up to $75 monthly ($115 in 1983), and an annual adjustment was made to reflect changes in the housing component of the Consumer Price Index. Currently, the elderly may disregard all shelter costs that exceed 50 percent of income after other deductions have been made.

The 1977 revision provided that families with assets of more than $1,750 were excluded from participation. This figure was reduced to $1,500 by the Food Stamp Act Amendments of 1980. The pre-1977 exclusion level of $3,000 was retained for families of two or more, providing one person was sixty years old or older. Again, items such as a home, household goods, personal effects, and the cash value of life insurance were not be counted as assets. That portion of an automobile's fair market value over $4,500 was to be counted, providing the car was not "exempt as an income producer or as a home."[80]

Initially, SSI recipients were automatically eligible for food stamps. A few states had increased SSI supplementary payments specifically to cover food stamp benefits. Under these circumstances, the recipients were declared ineligible for further food stamps. This provision was retained in the 1977 revision. An approach slightly different than the "cash out" procedure is currently being used in demonstration projects in several states. A separate check is distributed to SSI recipients to cover the value of the food stamps. This procedure is meant to remove "participation barriers" such as the "welfare stigma" associated with the use of food stamps.[81]

Usage of Stamps

Households that have met the eligibility requirements are certified for participation. Each month they then receive an ATP card, or *authorization to participate,* from the state agency. Families deliberately transferring assets to achieve eligibility are disqualified.

The stamps may be used for most food purchases. However, they may not be used to buy alcoholic beverages, tobacco, and hot food products. Nor may they be used for household supplies or other nonfood items. Stamps may be used by persons over the age of sixty and other specified groups such as the mentally handicapped to participate in a home-delivered Meals-on-Wheels Program or to purchase meals served in senior centers. Any person denied the benefits of the food program may appeal to the state welfare office for a hearing. A final administrative decision, based on a review of the hearing record, must be made within sixty days.

The power to issue coupons may be delegated by the state agency to banks, post offices, community action agencies, or others. Federal regulations also authorize a "direct coupon mailout system" as well as other systems that meet "accountability requirements."[82]

On a per person basis, the number of stamps issued is reduced as the size of the household increases. The decline has been explained as a "rough measure of economics of scale that exists in food purchasing and preparation for larger sized households and allows for differences in sex-age composition.[83] In setting up the program, the Food and Nutrition Service declared that "equity is carefully considered to make the benefit uniform among people with equal needs and to taper benefits as income rises to preserve work incentives and not provide artificial incentives to stay on the Program."[84]

Equity is not easily achieved. Coupon allotments, for example, are based on cash income after deductions rather than on cash and in-kind income. A Medicare benefit is classified as in-kind rather than cash. So also is a rent subsidy. Thus, one individual has an advantage over another with equal cash income. The determination of legitimate deductions even under the 1977 revision has proved to be an area affecting individual equity; caseworkers working with the same set of facts may reach different conclusions.

So far as the elderly are concerned, the revision of 1977, which became effective in 1979, seems to have improved considerably the degree of participation by those eligible. According to the Food and Nutrition Service, the greatest gains were scored by the rural poor and the elderly.[85]

The elimination of the purchase requirement made possible the adoption of simplified operational procedures. The system for issuing coupons,for example, has been adapted to the particular circumstances of the participants. In many parts of the country, food stamps are distributed partly or entirely by mail, thus eliminating the possibly difficult trip to the welfare office or the stamp distribution center. The advantages of the mailing system developed in New Hampshire were described as follows: "Sixty-five people spend one work day a month putting food stamps for 15,000 households in envelopes and into the mail. The time involved seems minimal compared to 15,000 individual trips participants would have to made to 75 banks and 21 welfare offices throughout the states."[86] Because of the elimination of the purchase requirement, issuance agencies handle fewer stamps and no cash. Thus the volume of work has been reduced and the security problem has greatly improved. Experiments in the distribution system include a project in the District of Columbia in which the elderly obtain stamps in their public housing complexes.[87]

Since its establishment in 1964, the Food Stamp program has gone through the throes of an identity crisis. Initially intended to aid in the disposition of surplus farm commodities and to raise the level of nutrition among low-income families, the program has become almost totally a tansfer payment device. Indeed, in 1975 the secretary of agriculture, Earl Butz, declared that since the program had become "essentially a welfare program," it should be transferred to the Department of Health, Education, and Welfare.[88]

So far as the elderly are concerned, the future of the program is not altogether clear. At one point the Reagan administration declared that beginning in 1984, responsibility for the Food Stamp Program would be turned over the states. The proposal was not quickly embraced by the Congress. A prominent scholar of welfare policy declared the proposal to be a "big, historic step backward."[89] The Congress did, however, accept a number of the president's suggestions for reducing costs. The 1981 Omnibus Reconciliation Act spared the elderly from some restrictions that would have resulted from the tightening of eligibility requirements. However, all participants were affected by a provision delaying the adjustment for food-price inflation from January to October 1981. Additional reductions in the 1983 budget proposal would have: (1) eliminated energy assistance payments as income in determining eligibility and monthly benefits, (2) provided for the rounding off of adjustments in benefit paid, dropping any amount over a whole dollar, (3) eliminated monthly benefits of less than ten dollars, (4) combined federally financed food stamp administrative funds with other welfare funds, and (5) refused to share the cost of payments found to have been made in error.[90]

Proposed presidential changes aimed at achieving a substantial reduction in the program must be balanced with favorable attitudes of congressional leaders. For example, Senator Robert Dole declared the Food Stamp Program to be "the greatest social program since Social Security."[91] In time food stamps may be superseded by modernized technology, but the basic idea that government must help the poor will almost certainly remain.

3. Summary Analysis

From relatively modest beginnings, social security coverage has extended to the point that it provides almost universal coverage for older persons. In addition to increasing the number of older people covered, the upgrading of benefits by various means has succeeded in bringing the large majority, although not all, of the older population above the poverty line. The concept of "adequacy" in addition to "equity" has helped in this respect, since it benefits lower-income people, although it has led to very complex formulas for calculating the benefits to be received by any given recipient. This accomplishment does not signify that social security has ever been problem-free. As has been discussed, continuing controversies that seem impossible to solve to the satisfaction of all have plagued the system.

Whether they wish to or not, almost all American workers must contribute to social security. The latest federal legislation will, in fact, bring some of the remaining "outsiders" into the fold. This development will be discussed in the next chapter. Although social security affects not only the aged, it is by far the largest and most widespread program providing benefits to older people. Under social security almost all old people receive payments on one basis or another. The benefits vary widely, however, and some recipients receive a substantial monthly sum while others get quite small amounts. Part of the source of this variation lies in the formulas by which benefits are calculated.

The original plans for funding social security leaned heavily on a "pay-as-you-go" concept borrowed from the private sector. The "insuree" and the employer would each contribute to a fund, which would then be available to the worker upon retirement. In fact, however, this idea was flawed from the outset, because the adequacy provision required some redistribution in favor of lower-income workers. It became even more inaccurate when the coverage was extended to include dependents and survivors of workers. Since increases in benefits structures occurred in the face of rising wages and inflation, social security payments in reality largely represented transfers of money from those still working to those who were not working. The payments that workers made to social security, in other words, were used to support the system. It is for this reason that there is so much concern with the changing ratios between workers and nonworkers, especially as these reflect the ever-increasing proportions of aged persons in this society.

The older persons eligible for social security benefits cannot expect earnings replacement, although the formula to ensure adequacy brings replacement somewhat closer for the lower-income worker. The purpose of social security was to provide a financial floor, which the recipient was expected to supplement by other means. To recapitulate briefly what was discussed earlier in this chapter, the calculation of benefits incorporates two major principles. Equity refers to the principle that there should be some relationship between what the worker paid in and what the worker will receive after retirement. To calculate the equity value, the number of quarters, in which the worker contributed to social security, the worker's salary during that time, and the indexing to increase the benefits by the average increase in earnings of all workers must be considered. This formula constitutes the average indexed monthly eranings, or AIME. Adequacy refers to the attempt to bring all benefits up to some minimum standard by favoring lower-income workers. A three-step process applied to the AIME figure allows 90 percent of the first $230 of allowable monthly wages and then very substantially reduces the percentage permitted over each of two succeeding steps. At this point the primary insurance amount, or PIA, the recipient will receive has been determined.

Special circumstances change the procedure by which payments are determined. If, for example, a person retires before age sixty-five, payments will be reduced; conversely, a person retiring at a later age may earn an increment. Determining benefits for dependents and survivors also require additional figuring, although this may not be very complex: a dependent spouse, for instance, will receive up to 50 percent of the retiring worker's benefit; a surviving widow up to 100 percent. Even the still highly controversial policy that applies to the two-worker family is relatively simple to work out since it operates essentially along the same lines as the policy that applies to one retiring worker and one dependent spouse. Finally, the person who claims social security benefits but still continues to work faces downward adjustments that depend on the amount of income earned.

Social security has meant a very great deal to older people. With increases in coverage over the years and with indexing to compensate for inflation, the system has been quite successful in raising the incomes of those over the age of sixty-five out of the poverty bracket. For example, in 1959, approximately 35 percent of those over age sixty-five had incomes below the poverty level, but by 1975 this proportion had declined to 15 percent.[92] Nevertheless, the threat of poverty has not been completely banished in old age, by any means. While one of the purposes of other programs such as SSI and the Food Stamp

Program is to ameliorate or prevent poverty among old people whose social security payment are very low or who somehow fall through the cracks in the system, evidence suggests that this goal is not being achieved, as we have discussed before, and as has been documented by several investigators.[93]

Supplementary Security Income replaced the Old Age Assistance (Title I) provisions of the original act through legislation enacted in 1972. Basically, a grant-in-aid program administered through the states was replaced by a program funded from federal general tax revenues and administered by the Social Security Administration. The rationale for the change was to equalize payments among the states and provide a minimum income for the elderly poor. However, the continuing requirement for demonstration of need makes the program unwieldy to administer; also, the individual states still have considerable input in determining "need." Accordingly, the new program, although it has helped thousands of elderly poor, has fallen far short of its goals. The "means" tests for eligibility, the failure to reach many impoverished elderly, and the resistance to allocating sufficient funds to truly provide a basic minimum income have been strongly criticized. However, it is difficult to anticipate any major changes in the current budgetary climate. The Food Stamp Program has waxed and waned, depending on social attitudes. Although benefits can and to some extent do provide extra financial supoort to the elderly, this program suffers from many of the problems inherent in SSI. In short, there are several systems intended to prevent need in old age, and while much has been accomplished, a significant proportion of our elderly, especially the very old, the widowed, and minority group members, are still in want.

Because of social security's popularity, any discussion about dismantling or even significantly reducing its benefits causes a tremendous uproar. The recent legislative changes finally agreed upon under the Reagan administration seem relatively minor, although their actual impact has yet to be assessed. Even very small changes in benefits could have the effect of pushing the incomes of more older people below the poverty line. Also, many fear that the current changes are but the "tip of the iceberg" and that other changes are yet to come. The purpose of one part of the new legislation is to integrate under social security some of the retirement programs to be discussed in the next chapter. If successful, this approach could both reduce the complexity of public retirement and produce more equal treatment across groups.

IV / Other Selected Financial and Retirement Programs

1. Introduction

Social security is the centerpiece of financial support programs for persons in the older population. It was born, however, as was discussed in the previous chapter, rather tardily, and there was already a plethora of private and public programs to provide pensions or some other type of financial assistance to older people. Some of these programs have continued to exist side by side with social security, some have merged with that system to a greater or lesser extent, and many have, at least to some degree, been subject to federal scrutiny. A few new public programs to directly and indirectly afford special kinds of additional financial help or at least help alleviate certain financial burdens have also been spawned in social security's wake. Although most of the programs that fit this description affect relatively small proportions of the aged population, they provide some key pieces to the mosaic of public policies for the aging.

At first glance it may seem surprising to begin a discussion of these programs with private pension plans. Such plans have a very long history. Since the federal government did not exist as a social welfare entity in the first third of the twentieth century, the United States relied heavily on other groups to conceptualize and implement procedures in this area. Business, as well as state and local governments, played an important role, and its influence still lingers. In fact, Berkowitz and McQuaid argue that, contrary to popular opinion, business was on the cutting edge of this development.[1] For it was business firms and corporations that were the most affected by the labor unrest that occurred with increasing industrialization and the development of national markets in the early twentieth century. Thus, private pension plans long predated social security, and they have continued to grow in number and scope, especially since the 1950s. The U.S. Bureau of the Census estimated that the percentage of the aged drawing private pensions had risen to 39 percent in 1976, and the proportion continues to rise.[2] Median yearly payments are rather modest, but there is no doubt that the added income is welcome.[3] Drawing a private pension should be in no way incompatible with

85

receiving social security benefits, since the latter were not intended to provide more than a floor of financial support. But the assumption that private pensions are independent from federal programs has become largely a myth, as we shall see in the next section.

If originally business was in the forefront in developing pension plans, the shoe seems to be largely on the other foot now. Private pensions might at best be considered "semipublic" since the federal government now looms large in their regulation, and many have in fact become integrated in some fashion with the social security system. But the failure of the federal government to mandate that every worker be eligible for a private pension, causing many workers, usually those who will also draw the least from social security, to be deprived of this coverage, has been highly criticized by Crystal.[4] It is his thesis that from the "irrational patchwork of private and public policies" there has emerged a number of special benefit programs that favor those who are already at least fairly well-to-do while discriminating against the truly needy.

This censure does not apply only to private pensions. As Crandall also notes, there are a number of public pension programs—for example, those for federal civil-service retirees, railroad retirees, and military retirees—that provide substantially higher benefits to their recipients.[5] Although the material to be presented in the next section will show that some reservations must be made to this last statement, these plans offer advantages that cannot be brushed away. It is not, however, that all of these pension programs have so many inherent advantages; rather they allow the pensioner to "double-dip" into social security by contributing to that system for at least a minimum period.[6] Pension plans at the state and local levels, however, offer far less financial security for the retiree, although coordination of these plans with social security has made many workers less vulnerable to future financial stress.

In the next section all the pension plans referred to above will be described, as well as the Black Lung Program, whose purpose is to compensate miners who contract lung disease as a result of continuous exposure to hazardous materials. This special compensation program applies mostly to elderly persons, since it takes many years for the results of exposure to be realized. The program is also worth considering since other health issues are developing in industry and elsewhere that may have to be similarly dealt with. Eventually, then, programs of this type may have consequences for a much larger proportion of the aged population. The third section of this chapter contains a brief discussion of three programs that benefit older people financially but are not related to pensions or retirement. They are included, however, because they do augment the incomes of at least some elderly persons. The fourth and final section is a summary analysis of all the programs that addresses the question of who is affected and how.

2. Pension Plans

THE REGULATION OF PRIVATE PENSION PLANS

Over 33 million persons are active or retired members of private pension plans.[7] Developed in the latter part of the nineteenth century, the concept of pension plans had its most rapid growth after the 1950s. Large and small businesses established employee pension plans as a means of attracting and holding employees or in response to labor demands made through the collective bargaining process. Some of the plans were integrated with social security; others were totally separate.

For a host of reasons, such as fraud, mismanagement, and restrictive rules of operation, many of the plans failed to provide the income protection that workers anticipated. Early corrective legislation proved to be ineffective. The private pension often proved to be a delusion. In testimony before Congress an official of the Department of Labor declared: "If you remain in good health and stay with the same company until you are 65 years old, and if the company is still in business, and if your department has not been abolished, and if you haven't been laid off for too long a period, and if there is enough money in the fund, and if that has been prudently managed, you will get a pension."[8]

Extensive public concern over the failure of many private pension plans led to the enactment in 1974 of the Employee Retirement Income Security Act (ERISA).[9] The act, which was ten years in the making, attacked two principal deficiencies of private plans. The first deficiency related to the inability of the employer or the employer's pension fund to meet the promised payments. Bad management of the company or mismanagement of the pension plan assets might result in a catastrophe for the employee. There would then be no money available for retirement payments. The second deficiency related to the employee's inability to qualify for the pension. For example, there might have been a break in the continuity of service. Whether the break in service was the fault of the employee or the employer was of small consequence; the fine print in the plan was controlling. Upon retirement, the employee discovered to his horror, that, notwithstanding a long work record, he was ineligible for a pension.

THE EMPLOYEE RETIREMENT INCOME SECURITY ACT[10]

The purpose of ERISA was to protect the worker covered by a private pension plan. The act did not require the employer to have a plan. However, if a plan was established, certain protections were required.

Participation-Eligibility In general, an employee qualifies for membership in the plan providing he is twenty-five years of age and has completed one year of service. There are exceptions to these requirements. For example, one thousand hours of work during a twelve-month period constitutes a year of service. However, in a seasonal industry, the secretary of labor may, by regulation, establish the minimum number of hours constituting a year's service. Similarly, educational institutions may, under certain conditions, require an employee to be thirty years old before becoming a "participant" in the plan.

An employee may not be excluded because of advanced age. Nevertheless, participation may be denied in instances where the employee is within five years of normal retirement and the plan is classified as a defined benefit plan.[11]

Earning Retirement Credits Participation in the retirement plan enables the employee to earn, or "accrue," credits toward retirement. Under the defined benefit plan, the process of accrual may be delayed to two years after initial employment. Under a defined contribution plan, an individual account must be established immediately.

One of the practices curbed by ERISA is "backloading," or establishing a much higher rate of accrual in later work years than in the early years of employment. The act limits the credit for a later year of service to $1\frac{1}{3}$ times that of an earlier year. Special formulas apply to credits for employment prior to ERISA.

Vesting One of the principal contributions of ERISA was the nailing down of the employees' nonforfeitable *right* to receive accrued benefits upon retirement. This is known as vesting. An individual may change jobs, but if he has met the vesting requirement of the first employer's pension plan, the individual will, upon retirement, receive a pension based upon the accrued benefits earned during that first period of employment.

In plans where the accrued benefits are due in whole or in part to the employee's own contributions, these contributions are vested immediately and in full. Accrued benefits based on employer contributions must vest in accordance with one of several schedules. In one schedule, called cliff vesting, there is no vesting prior to the completion of ten years of service. However, upon completion of the tenth year, the plan is fully vested. A second schedule, graded vesting, provides 25 percent vesting after five years with full vesting after fifteen years. A third schedule, the rule of forty-five, is based on age and service. When an employee has five years of service and his age and service add up to forty-five, vesting amounts to 50 percent. The employee receives an additional 10 percent for each succeeding year until full vesting is achieved.

Prior to ERISA, a break in employment, no matter how small, often resulted in the loss of all pension credits. ERISA does not recognize a break in service of less than one year. The break-in-service topic is a complex one and is surrounded by numerous regulations.[12]

Standards for Fiduciaries   In order to prevent the misuse of assets, ERISA established guidelines for the trustees, officers, and those responsible for administering pension plans—the fiduciaries. The act spells out four duties of fiduciaries:

1. "Discharge his or her duties solely in the interest of plan participants and beneficiaries and for the exclusive purpose of providing plan benefits to them and defraying the reasonable expenses of administering the plan."

2. "Act with the care, skill, prudence, and diligence under the circumstances then prevailing that a 'prudent man' acting in like capacity and familiar with such matters would use in the conduct of an enterprise of a like character and with like aims."

3. "Diversify plan investments in order to minimize the risk of large losses unless it is clearly prudent not to do so."

4. "Operate in accordance with plan documents and instruments." [13] The fiduciary provisions include requirements whose purpose is to prevent conflicts of interest on the part of those responsible for handling funds. For example, the fiduciary is subject to court removal and is personally liable for prohibited transactions.

Funding   One of the most important features of a pension plan, obviously, is the ability to finance promised benefits. Thus, ERISA is concerned with fund accumulation practices. The act endeavors to promote the establishment of orderly arrangements for amortizing past service liabilities and for meeting future costs. The problem of estimating future funding costs is especially difficult. The actuarial specialist must make many assumptions relating to mortality figures, employee turnover, interest rates on pension fund investments, and other factors, no one of which is constant over a short period, not to mention a lifetime. For example, assumptions relating to life span may require correction not only because of the differences between men and women but also because of the impact of increasing percentages of women workers.

Survivor Benefits   Many early pension plans made no provision for benefits to the spouse upon death of the retiree. Some, by reducing the benefits to the retiree, enabled the spouse to receive a pension upon the retiree's death. This type of plan, called a joint and survivor annuity, required certain positive steps on the part of the retiree. Otherwise, the spouse was left without protection.

ERISA reverses the previous practice. Under the new act, the joint and survivor annuity is automatic unless the retiree takes positive steps in writing to reject it. Thus, if the plan is classified as a qualified joint and survivor annuity, upon the death of the retiree the annuity provides benefits to the spouse for life. The amount of the annuity may not be less than one-half the benefit received by the retiree and the spouse. The employee is not required to notify the spouse of the rejection of the joint and survivor option. Remarriage of the spouse does not terminate the annuity payments.

Plan Information In order to help participants understand the terms of the pension plan to which they belong, the act requires that certain kinds of information be made available automatically and that other kinds be made available upon request. For example, a summary description of the plan must be supplied within a specified period after a person becomes a participant or a beneficiary. Upon written request, the participant must be furnished a statement of accrued benefits. Other more detailed information must be supplied at reasonable cost or made available at the office of the administrator. For plans covering more than twenty-five participants, copies of documents are required to be filed with the Department of Labor. Copies are available for public inspection and may be purchased.

The plan administrator is entitled by law to receive certified information from banks, insurance carriers, and others who may have custody of plan assets. The administrator, in turn, is required to supply information to appropriate federal departments and agencies.

Plan Termination Prior to the enactment of ERISA, the threat of plan termination was a source of worry to many participants in private pension plans. Lack of funding, plant closing, mergers—these and other factors contributed to an increasingly troublesome problem. In an effort to eliminate plan terminations, the act established a wholly new government agency, the Pension Benefit Guaranty Corporation.

Help for the Self-Employed and Those without Private Pensions ERISA endeavors also to assist the self-employed and workers not covered by private pensions. As early as 1962, the Self-Employed Individuals Tax Retirement Act—the Keogh Act—had enabled individuals to establish what was, in effect, a pension. Each year until retirement a portion of one's earned income could be put into a fund that was tax free and which accrued tax-free interest. Under ERISA, larger amounts of earned income can be set aside—15 percent in 1983, up to fifteen thousand dollars annually. The self-employed person who employs others can obtain even greater tax concessions, providing a plan is arranged to include employees with three years of service.

ERISA makes provisions, too, for the individual who is not covered by any employer pension. The act provides for Individual Retirement Accounts, called IRA's. The worker may deposit up to 15 percent of his annual compensation, not to exceed $2,000, into a tax-sheltered IRA. If a nonemployed spouse is included in the plan, the maxium percentage remains at 15 percent, but the maximum deposit is raised to $2,250. A self-employed person may also utilize the IRA.

In theory, the IRA is a device to assist the rank-and-file employee. Opponents of the IRA contend that, in practice, it "provides a tax-sheltered arrangement for people who are in the middle-income and upper-income brackets."[14] This is especially relevant when one considers that persons covered by employer pensions may now also invest in IRA's.

THE PENSION BENEFIT GUARANTY CORPORATION

The subject of private pensions is extraordinarily complex. The complexity was not lessened by the passage of the Employee Retirement Income Security Act in 1974. The supervision of the roughly 500,000 private plans is distributed among three agencies—the Department of Labor, the Internal Revenue Service of the Department of the Treasury, and the newly created Pension Benefit Guaranty Corporation, (PBGC). The Department of Labor is charged with responsibility for protecting the rights of the pension participant through various reporting and disclosure requirements. The Internal Revenue Service, again by means of reporting requirements, is charged with assuring that scheduled pension funds are set aside under appropriate safeguards for pension purposes and that plan sponsors are given proper tax deductions. The Pension Benefit Guaranty Corporation is responsible for operating an insurance system. Participants in deferred benefit plans receive promised benefits through the corporation in the event of plan failure.

PBGC is a self-sustaining corporation. A principal source revenue is an annual premium to be paid by each plan. Initially, the premium was fifty cents. Later, it was raised to $1.00 per participant in single employer plans and, over a period of several years to $2.60 per participant in multiemployer plans.[15] These and other resources such as assets acquired from terminated plans constitute the insurance base from which payments are made. PBGC becomes the trustee of the plan and in that capacity administers the distribution of benefits. The agency may initiate action to terminate a plan when substantial long-run losses appear inevitable.[16]

One pension authority characterized the termination insurance features of the act as a "vast innovation," a "leap in the dark."[17] An evidence of uncertainty was the provision that the operation of automatic insurance in multiemployer plans be delayed until January 1, 1978. This was later extended to 1979 and then to 1980. The argument was advanced that the multiemployer plans would not terminate, since more than one employer was involved. However, within a short period, PBGC was forced to guarantee the pensions of persons in millinery multiemployer plans in New Jersey. Declining business threatened other multiemployer plans in the maritime, apparel, shoe and leather, and other industries. It became evident that pension benefits were in danger whenever the ratio of active workers to pensioners was markedly reduced. The government was threatened with having to assume enormous pension payments unless corporations could be persuaded to continue rather than to terminate plans. The government's potential liability was eased with the passage of legislation in 1980 requiring employers to pay a portion of the cost of future benefits if they withdraw from a multiemployer plan. Those persons already receiving benefits are assured the full level of payments through the guaranty of PBGC.[18]

Troublesome Issues

At the time of its enactment, ERISA was considered to be a legislative milestone. A study of 131 plans by the Bureau of Labor Statistics in 1978 showed a number of significant changes as a consequence of ERISA. Since 1974, 94 had liberalized the normal retirement benefit formula. The most common formula, "dollar amount times years of service," averaged $10.70 per month. The highest formula was that of plumbers' union in San Francisco—$30.00 per month—and the lowest was that of a shoe corporation in New Hampshire—$3.50 per month. One of three plans was integrated with social security, a device that, as social security expanded its benefits, often decreased the benefits received from the private plan. Nearly all plans made provision for retirement at age fifty-five, or earlier, provided the service requirement—usually thirty years—had been met.[19] Notwithstanding a number of accomplishments, the act has come under increasing criticism. The charge has been made repeatedly that the complexities of the act and the extensive reporting required have discouraged employers from establishing new plans and resulted in the cancellation of many already existing plans. However, a study by the General Accounting Office declared that ERISA had acted to "prune away" many pension plans that "would not have been able to deliver on their promises."[20]

Among the troubling issues in most private plans is the absence of any provision for compensating for inflation.[21] A few plans subject to collective bargaining contain machinery for making cost-of-living-adjustments. The courts have held, however, that employers are not required to bargain over the issue of increased benefits for those receiving pensions. Thus, for participants in plans having no provision for compensating for inflation, pension income quickly becomes eroded.

Another issue concerns the question of fairness to that portion of the working force—almost half—not covered by a pension plan. Both business and employee contributions to pension plans, as well as earnings, are tax deductible. These tax breaks amounted to an estimated federal tax loss of $12.9 billion for fiscal 1980, a subsidy that must be made up by all tax payers.

The issue of women's rights is also not to be overlooked. The charge has been made that only 10 percent of retired women workers in the private labor forces receive pensions. To correct this condition, women's rights advocates contend, the ten-year vesting provision must be reduced and pension credits once vested must be portable.

At the time of its passage ERISA contained no provision for portability, that is, enabling a worker with vested pension credits to transfer them to another employer. The lack of any portability clause means that many workers under private pension plans will never receive a pension.

A recent issue concerns the manner of managing private pension fund assets. In the last decade, attention has shifted from the previous practice of concentrating exclusively on earning additional moneys for the pension fund. Now the question is heard frequently as to whether fund assets should be invested chiefly in businesses whose end product or whose mode of operation is approved by the workers in the corporation supplying the pension fund assets. Also in question is who should vote the shares of stock held by the pension fund—the corporation which supplied the money or the worker, who may claim that the money in the fund belongs to him.

The greatest single issue awaiting resolution is the relationship of private pensions to social security. Meshing the two systems in a manner that recognizes both corporate and individual needs as well as the needs of society as a whole presents a problem that has extraordinary ramifications. If the objective of a total retirement system is an adequate income, what portion should be supplied by social security and what portion by a private pension? If a solution is reached for the worker with monies from both sources, where does this leave the almost 50 percent of the labor force that does not participate in private pension plans? The solution is not simple. Rather, the problem requires continuous patient study and incremental action by corporate and public representatives dedicated to the public weal.

The recent study by the President's Commission on Pension Policy recommended the introduction of a totally new concept—MUPS, or Minimum Universal Pension System. The system would be funded by employers (through a 3 percent payroll tax) and would be applicable to employees aged twenty-five or over. Vesting would be immediate. The employer would be eligible for a tax credit of 46 percent of the contribution. Funds would be maintained in employer pension trusts or in financial insurance institutions. Employers not wishing to administer the plan would have the option of transferring contributions to a MUPS portability fund. Favorable tax treatment would be provided for voluntary employee contributions to MUPS or other employee pension plans. MUPS would be entirely separate from social security. Current private plans, however, would be amended to provide at least the MUPS equivalent.[22] Immediate reaction to the new proposal was not enthusiastic. One pension industry executive used the expression "overkill" to describe the plan.[23] Whether the proposal will capture the imagination of the public and ultimately become the law of the land remains to be seen.

In summary, ERISA is a major step forward in protecting workers. The legal responsibility of corporations for the well-being of their employees during retirement is substantially increased. Pensions are "serious commitments."[24] However, if workers become further burdened by inflation and unemployment, the cry will surely increase for government action to provide additional protection to current and prospective retirees.[25]

PUBLIC RETIREMENT SYSTEMS:
FEDERAL CIVILIAN EMPLOYEES RETIREMENT

Over the years, legislation has been enacted that establishes retirement systems for several categories of federal employees. Some systems are for individual positions, others are for relatively small groups such as the judiciary or the Federal Reserve Board. Larger systems include the Foreign Service, the Tennessee Valley Authority, and the Central Intelligence Agency. The District of Columbia has one system for its judges, another for its teachers, and still another for its police force and firefighters. Each system was created for a specific group with little regard for other existing plans. The responsibility for establishing policy for thirty-eight federal retirement systems is divided among roughly half of the standing House and Senate committees.[26]

By far the majority of federal employees are members of the United States Civil Service Retirement and Disability System (CSR). Roughly 90 percent of all federal civilian employees, about 2.7 million workers, are covered by this one system. Retired federal employees and their survivors numbered 1.7 million in 1981. Total outlays in 1981 amounted to $17.7 billion, of which $15 billion went to retirees and $2.2 billion to survivors.[27] From 1981 through 1986, an estimated 92,500 employees each year will join the 1.8 million persons currently receiving CSR retirement, disability, or survivor benefits.[28]

Established in 1920, CSR provided for retirement at age seventy. The original act provided that for those with thirty or more years of service, the annuity would amount to 60 percent of the average salary during the final ten years. The minimum annual benefit was $360, the maximum $720. There were no survivor benefits.[29]

From its inception, the system was contributory. Initially, the contribution rate was 2½ percent of basic pay, an amount matched by the employing agency. The employee contribution rate was increased periodically, but for a number of years the agency matching rate was not. The consequence was a large unfunded liability. A major revision of the law in 1969 provided for the current employee contribution rate of 7 percent, to be matched by the employer.[30] The act also provided for transfers from the U.S. Treasury to the Civil Service Retirement and Disability Fund, a practice meant to stem the increase in the unfunded liability. Future deficiencies resulting from salary increases ot other benefits were to be fully funded over a period of thirty years. In practice, pressures to modify the system have resulted in new costs, with the result that the unfunded liability has increased substantially.

The major portion of the annual income of CSR comes from general fund appropriations. In 1980, 46.5 percent of the income came from this one source. The contributions of the employee and of the agency for which the employee worked amounted to 26.5 percent. Interest, 20.7 percent, and contributions from so called "off-budget" agencies such as the Post Office, 6.2 percent, accounted for the remainder.[31]

Projections of substantially rising federal costs over the next years have made CSR a target for change. One feature, the cost-of-living adjustment, was altered by legislation in 1981.[32] As of 1982, inflation adjustments are to be made once each year rather than semiannually.

Retirement Ages and Benefits   Most civilian federal employees automatically become members of CSR. Some, for example, those in the executive branch serving under indefinite or temporary appointments, are excluded by law or administrative regulation. As previously indicated, others may have membership in separate plans, such as the Foreign Service Retirement System.

Under the provisions of CSR, retirement is possible at various ages. An employee may take voluntary retirement after thirty years of service at age fifty-five. Law enforcement offices or firefighters may retire at age fifty. If involuntarily separated, but not for misconduct or delinquency, the employee with twenty-five years of service may retire regardless of age. A disabled employee with five years of service may retire. The requirement of mandatory retirement at age seventy was abolished in 1978.[33]

The level of retirement benefits follows the "high three" principle. The base is the average of the three years of highest earnings. The percentage of the base to be received as a pension varies with the number of years of employment. For example, after ten years of service, the employee is entitled to 16.25 percent of the base. The percentage then increases 2 percent per year to a maximum of 80 percent. Credit for military service favorably affects the element of time and the amount of the benefit.

Survivor Benefits for Retirees   The principle of protection for the survivors of retired federal employees has been in effect since 1940. At that time, by electing to take a reduced annuity, the employee could provide for the spouse. The survivor was to receive one-half of the reduced annuity. In 1984, the plan was enlarged to include surviving children. The survivor's benefit was raised to 55 percent of the retiree's annuity in 1962, and the benefit was made automatic unless the employee specifically elected in writing to provide no survivor benefits or benefits limited to a small portion of the base. The annual cost to the employee for coverage of a spouse is 2½ percent of the first $3600 of the retirement pay and 10 percent of the remainder.

Life Insurance and Health Benefits   Most federal employees have group life insurance and health benefits. The Federal Employees Group Life Insurance Program, authorized in 1954, is made available automatically, although the employee has the right to waive the coverage.[34] The amount of the insurance is related to annual pay and as of 1977 ranged from a minimum of ten thousand dollars to a maximum of sixty thousand dollars. Two-thirds of the cost is borne by the employee and one-third by the government. Additional optional insurance in the amount of ten thousand dollars may be obtained, although all of this cost is borne by the employee. After retirement and upon reaching age sixty-five, the insurance is free, although the amount is reduced by 2 percent a month until the balance in force is 25 percent of the original.[35]

The Federal Employees Health Benefits Program, authorized in 1959, encompasses several plans on a contract basis with private carriers.[36] In each instance, the cost is shared by the government and the employee, with the government normally assuming 60 percent of the premium. Upon retirement, enrollment continues and the annuitant is entitled to the same benefits and is obligated for the same costs.[37] The separate Retired Federal Employees Health Benefit Program provides protection for annuitants retired before 1960 and their dependents.

CSR: Strengths and Deficiencies   The provision of full pension benefits for those aged fifty-five who have worked for thirty years tends to place the federal employee in an extremely favorable position in contrast to workers in private pension plans who retire at much later ages. The substantial advantages of CSR on this point is not without its drawbacks. The cost to the government is extremely high, for it involves the payment of benefits over a greatly extended period. Moreover, it removes a larger number of employees from their positions at a time when they are highly productive. Again, the cost to the government, this time the cost of replacement, is high.

CSR has come under attack in recent years for various deficiencies. In a number of areas, it compares unfavorably with both private systems and social security. One complaint concerns the large number of federal workers who leave their positions before qualifying for pension benefits. Those who leave will not receive social security coverage for their years with the government. Another related complaint concerns the lack of pension portability. After five years, the employee becomes vested, but to leave before that is to forego all pension credit. The employee who leaves receives back the amount contributed, but without interest.

The formula for paying CSR benefits is skewed in favor of the employee who remains in service for more than ten years. Thus, the short-stay worker receives a relatively small percentage of his final salary at the time of retirement. In contrast, a worker retiring at age sixty-five with forty years of service receives 72 percent of final pay. However, he must pay income tax on this income in contrast to the retiree whose social security is or at least has been up to now free. Other deficiencies of CSR relate to the disability and survivor protection features, which are inferior to those of social security.[38]

CSR and Social Security   A growing public issue concerns the relationship of the CSR system to social security. The two systems are separate. CSR was established almost two decades before social security became operational. At that time federal employees had little interest in the system since they had their own retirement plan, which was at first far superior. In recent years, however, social security benefits have been greatly expanded. Retirees who had low incomes receive proportionally higher benefits than those who had larger incomes. The redistribution aspect of social security has resulted in minimum benefits levels, which have proved attractive to federal employees. Two principal avenues have been open that have enabled the federal employee to qualify for social security. One has been a part-time job in the private sector, in additional to regular government employment. The second has been private employment following early retirement from governmental service. As a consequence, roughly two-thirds of those retiring from the federal service will, upon reaching age sixty-two, be eligible for social security benefits. Indeed, in 1979, only 9 percent of those retiring from CSR were without any employment covered by social security.[39]

At first glance, the dual beneficiary is no different from the corporate pensioner who receives funds from both the corporation's plan and social security. But, in fact, there is a considerable difference. CSR may be considered a substitute system for a combination of social security and a private pension plan. Combining CSR and social security, as they now exist, results in an entirely new and costly set of benefits for the government employee. The question thus arises of whether some modification is in order. From the standpoint of the worker, CSR is in certain respects considerably superior to social security. As previously indicated, government employees with thirty years of serivce can retire at age fifty-five. At that time, their level of retirement benefits is 56.25 percent of "high three" average earnings. This level of replacement earnings is unobtainable at that age under almost all private plans; they are geared to retirement at age sixty-five in conjuction with social security. Indeed, benefits are reduced for those seeking early retirement.

Various proposals to reduce the substantial costs of CSR and to make its benefit system comparable to private pension plans have been advanced. One proposal, for example, would reduce the annuities for early retirement. The pay-out system would be made comparable to that of representative corporate plans that are integrated with social security. Another proposal would require that the federal employee's contribution be raised, thus reducing the annual payroll cost to the government and making it more nearly equal to that of private firms. A third proposal would extend social security to cover federal employees in combination with a representative private pension plan. This plan would be phased in gradually with the objective of achieving an equitable system at a substantially reduced cost.

A three-tiered system has also been proposed. Social security would serve as tier one, an agency contribution would constitute tier two, and a savings plan in which limited amounts deposited by the employee would be matched by the employing agency would make up tier three.[40] An initial step toward ultimate integration occurred when 1983 amendments to the Social Security Act required all federal workers hired after January 1, 1984, to join CSR. At the time the bill was before Congress, the Senate, responding to pressures from federal unions, favored delaying entry of new workers pending the development of a supplemental system applicable to all federal employees. However, the conference committee ruled otherwise. The act required not only new federal employees to become members, but also the president, the cabinet, federal judges, and members of Congress. Thus, the new act side-stepped a number of issues of major concern to current members of CSR.

Despite the host of proposals advanced to alter the existing system, little progress has been made. Although federal employees and retirees may be aware that ballooning costs must somehow be held in check, they are naturally suspicious of suggestions that seem to affect them alone. The time is ripe for a major effort to integrate CSR and other federal retirement systems with social security. But the process will be an extremely complex one.

PUBLIC RETIREMENT SYSTEMS:
STATE AND LOCAL RETIREMENT SYSTEMS

In 1977, there were 2,271,000 persons receiving an average of $298 in monthly benefits from state and local retirement systems. Over 1,660,000 of these were members of 197 state systems; 610,000 belonged to 2,878 locally administered systems. Cash and security holdings of the systems amounted to over $123 billion.[41]

Public pension legislation has a long history. The policemen of New York City were the first to benefit. A law enacted in 1857 covered policemen injured in the line of duty. In 1878, the incapacity requirement was eliminated in favor of a measure providing half pay at age fifty-five for those with twenty-five years of service.[42] In that same year, Boston policemen were recipients of a noncontributory plan providing an amount equal to one-third of a year's salary after only fifteen years of service. The Massachusetts Commission on Old Age Pensions, Annuities, and Insurance issued a report in 1910 favoring pensions for "superannuated" employees. According to one authority, "The 1910 report achieved national significance. It gave the country as a whole a sober and reasoned recommendation from a prestigious commission, based on detailed study of pension provisions for public employees throughout the United States and Europe."[43]

Over the next decades, many hundreds of pension laws were enacted throughout the country. Some established state-wide systems for particular categories of employees. Other laws applying to counties and municipalities were seemingly general in nature but upon analysis were often found to apply to one person. Gradually, but ever so gradually, a degree of order was introduced.

State employees generally are covered by a retirement system administered by the state. Nebraska is the one exception. Its state employees are covered by a privately administered plan. Public school teachers are under state administered plans in all fifty states. Municipal and county employees in some instances are covered by a state-administered plan; in other instances they are covered by a system operated by the municipality or county. Special retirement systems often cover police, firefighters, and other public officials.

Characteristics of Plans

The variety among the hundreds of state and local plans makes it difficult to give brief but realistic descriptions of their principal characteristics. The age of retirement, the years of service required, the basis upon which benefits are calculated, the vesting provisions, the amount of the employee contribution, the relationship to social security, the funding arrangements—these and other features vary from state to state, from county to county, and from municipality to municipality.

The following summary of the practice of one state—Wisconsin—is presented as a means of touching on various typical characteristics of state retirement plans. The Wisconsin Retirement System is new, having been created in 1976 to bring together three already existing state-administered systems. In 1978 the system had 187,427 active members and 48,232 beneficiaries. Coverage is mandatory for employees of the state and county, teachers, and most police and firefighters. Local governing bodies can request coverage for their employees. Over one thousand units contribute to the system, including counties, cities, villages, towns, and school districts. Two notable exceptions are Milwaukee city and Milwaukee County, each of which has its own system.

Vesting is immediate; there is no requirement of a minimum service credit. "Final average salary," meaning the average of three years of highest earnings, is used to determine the monthly annuity. Normal retirement is at age sixty-five; retirement between the ages of sixty-five and sixty causes a benefit reduction of 5.5 percent per year. Those in "protective service occupations"—sheriffs, deputies, conservation wardens, police, firefighters—normally retire at age fifty-five. A "formula factor" built into the system reflects the period of service of a given group.

Funding is complicated because the three major systems that merged into the new system were not fully funded. Thus, the employee's contribution not only covers current costs but must also amortize previous liabilities.

An unusual feature concerns the so-called "pickup" of employee contributions. The employee contribution rate is 5 percent. However, the employer may pick up as much as 4 percent of this amount. As a consequence, state workers pay only 1 percent. Most local governing bodies provide some pickup. Various options enable the retiree to elect a lower benefit rate in order to provide for designated beneficiaries. The employee must also elect a variable annuity plan; up to 50 percent may be invested in an equities fund and the remainder in a fixed annuity fund. Social security coverage has been required for all new employees since 1972.[44]

Funding

One factor that determines the fiscal soundness of any governmental unit is the condition of its pension plan. Funding provisions have too often received insufficient attention, with the consequence that unbelievably large liabilities have been incurred. The benefits provided for in legislating a pension system are its future costs. Too often the future costs are not considered at the time the system is put into effect. The efforts of the governing body may be centered on meeting the demands of a particular employee group; future cost may seem a minor consideration deserving of little attention. Years later, a new body of officials may be reluctant to raise taxes to meet the obligations its predecessors blithely assumed. A Michigan legislator has described the problem as follows: "Right now we have what amounts to a porkbarrel and piecemeal approach to (state/local) pension modification. We modify one system without regard for fiscal consequences and then other systems want the same. This takes place in a totally political atmosphere without any regard for how the bill will be paid, by whom, and when. There is a total absence of logical structure. Employees had better get concerned that there is enough cash on hand to meet requirement needs and taxpayers had better get concerned with these massive and increasing debt obligations. We simply cannot continue in this helter-skelter fashion."[45]

Planning a system of retirement benefits normally involves taking into account actuarial assumptions, that is, estimates of such factors as life expectancy, job retention, and investment yield on pension assets. If the actuarial assumptions are unrealistic, the retirement system's liabilities may increase dramatically. The assumptions built into the system may, of course, cancel each other out. For example, a rising wage base may increase costs; however, a rising interest rate on pension funds may decrease costs. Lamentably, many retirement systems, especially those of local governments, face dismayingly large deficits in the immediate future.

Most state and local systems are contributory. Two systems in Michigan and two in New York are major exceptions. In 1979 to 1980, employee contributions in state-administered systems amounted to 18.5 percent of total system receipts. Government contributions amounted to 45.5 percent and investment earnings to 36.0 percent.[46]

Portability

In the early 1960s, a municipal study commission reported that in most states and cities "retirement credits have turned into an anchor."[47] This condition is still widespread, especially for administrative, professional, and technical personnel. The fear of pension forfeiture caused by moving to another position has been eased by various arrangements. However, the lack of portability remains a frustrating problem for many employees at the state and local levels.

Intrastate portability is often made possible by reciprocal agreements. Reserve funds may be shifted between systems. However, when there are differences in the systems, meshing the two may present problems. Hawaii is said to have the one "all inclusive" system providing "complete intrastate portability for public employees."[48]

Interstate portability is relatively rare. Most public school teachers are able to purchase transfer credits for teaching service performed in another state. Fewer than 10 percent of other state and local employees have this option.[49] Some reciprocal state agreements have been worked out. However, there is a considerable reluctance to permit transfers, especially on the part of states whose compensation scales are not competitive. Nor are transfers between states and the federal government common. Indeed, in a study for the National Planning Association Munnell and Connolly declare that "transfers between states and the federal government are generally impossible."[50]

Relationship with Social Security

Initially, all state and local employees were excluded from the social security program. The exclusion was based on the constitutional theory that the national government could not tax state or municipalities. However, a series of amendments in the 1950s made social security coverage possible if both employers and employees approved in effect making the tax voluntary. As a consequence, many states and local governments developed plans to permit employee membership in social security. For some, social security was the "integrated" or "coodinated" plan whereby the employee's benefits were reduced by some portion of the social security benefit.

Of the 12.9 million jobs in state and local government in March 1978, 9.2 million were covered by social security. Coverage exceeded 95 percent in fifteen states. All jobs were covered in Pennsylvania, New Jersey, Maryland, Louisiana, and Alabama. None were covered in Ohio amd Massachusetts.[51] All told, 30 percent of state and local employees do not have social security coverage. Moreover, higher tax costs apparently have persuaded some jurisdictions to take steps toward withdrawal. In 1976, for example, New York City signaled its intention to withdraw. Persuaded that any savings were illusory it subsequently reversed its decision.[52]

Not so Alaska. On January 1, 1980, Alaska terminated coverage for all its employees. The state gave the required two-year advance notice of termination, to be effective January 1, 1978. However, the notice was later withdrawn. Notice was given a second time, to become effective 1980. A state law was enacted in 1979 providing for a preference vote of the employees. Fewer than 25 percent favored withdrawal, but that was more than the 19 percent who wished to remain. Over 50 percent of the 14,451 state employees did not vote. The result is reported to have precipitated a turning point in the "hands off" policy of the Social Security Administration. Now they are said to take a "vigorous approach to informing the public of the advantages of social security."[53] Alaska's action was attributed in part to "sentiment against the federal government as a whole."[54] In the last two decades, groups of state and local employees numbering one hundred thirty thousand, or 1 percent of the total have withdrawn.[55] The 1981 Social Security Act Amendments prohibit further terminations and permit previously terminated groups to elect coverage.

PERISA

The extensive effort by Congress, through ERISA, to establish a measure of order in private sector pension plans has not been matched with respect to pension plans for public employees. Particularly at the local level, the absence of funding standards has resulted in grandiose promises that have virtually no prospect of being fulfilled. In an effort to bring ERISA-type remedies into the area of public pensions, the Public Employee Retirement Income Security Act (PERISA) was introduced to Congress in 1978. The proposal was not approved. In 1979, a joint survey of the Advisory Commission on Governmental Relations and the National Conference of State Legislatures showed that "many state and local governments are making great strides in an effort to improve their public plans." An important factor in the reform process undoubtedly was the "threat of PERISA," which would have meant federal regulation.[56] In its final report the President's Commission on Pension Policy opted for PERISA on the grounds that "state and local government employees deserve the same protection as employees in the private sector.[57] Certainly, the inadequate retirement provisions of many systems and the total absence of any system in many local governments place many thousands of employees in a most unenviable financial position.

RAILROAD RETIREMENT: A HYBIRD

Nearly 1 million individuals received monthly benefits from the U.S. Railroad Retirement Board in 1982. Two-thirds of this number were retired railroad employees and their wives. The survivors of deceased employees made up the remainder. Of those receiving benefits, 81 percent were sixty-five years old or older. Benefit payments amounted to $5.7 billion.[58]

Initially, the railroad retirement system was entirely separate from the social security system. Over the years, however, changing concepts of the role of a retirement system, the decline of the railroads, and financial necessity resulted in a linking together of the two. The words *coordination, merger, unification* are partially descriptive of existing arrangements. Yet the separation continues. A staff report in 1972 characterized the system as a "hybrid."[59]

In the early decades of the twentieth century, the railroad industry was an extremely important segment of the total economy. At the industry's peak in 1920, railroad employees constituted 5.2 percent of the total number of employed in the United States. The percentage declined to 2.5 during the Great Depression and continued downward to .7 percent in 1970. Nationally, railroad labor was a potent political force. Indeed, since the Railway Labor Act of 1888, Congress had been alert to the problems of the railroad worker. For over half a century, efforts by railroad management and by unions to provide pension plans had proved unsuccessful. In the mid-thirties, an overriding concern of the unions was the development of a pension plan that would be attractive to older railroad employees, thus enabling these to retire and younger workers to move into more secure positions. As a consequence of this concern, Congress passed the Railroad Retirement Act of 1934. Quickly challenged in the courts, the act was declared unconstitutional. In somewhat modified form, the proposal was reintroduced. The result was the Railroad Retirement Act of 1935 and the Carriers' Taxing Act of 1935. Congress appropriated funds—to be repaid by taxes on carriers and employees—in order that benefits could be paid immediately. Railway workers were thus excluded from coverage under the Social Security Act which was passed at about the same time, but which did not envision paying benefits until 1942.

Administration of the new system was to be the responsibility of the Railroad Retirement Board, a three-member body in the executive branch representing the public, railway labor, and management. Amending legislation in 1937 established the Railroad Retirement Account in the U.S. Treasury, from which retirement benefits were to be paid.

Benefits were centered upon the retired and disabled worker, with number of years of service in railroading a determining factor. Survivors received little. Indeed, until 1946, 95 percent of all benefits went to the employee.[60] Benefits were considerably higher than those of social security recipients. But so also were the supporting contributions. In 1940, for example, the retired railroad employee received an average monthly benefit of sixty-six dollars. The retired worker under social security received twenty-three dollars. The contribution rate was 3 percent on earnings up to three hundred dollars monthly for the railroad worker, but only 1 percent up to three thousand dollars annually for the worker under social security. These sums in each instance were matched by the employer.

There was much dissatisfaction over survivorship provisions: benefits were smaller for railroad workers than for those under social security. New legislation enacted in 1946 altered the conditions for survivorship insurance and increased the benefits. Disability provisions were also liberalized.

Financial Interchange

A process known as financial interchange developed with the passage of the Railroad Retirement Act of 1951. As the scope of benefits under social security increased, railroad workers insisted that their benefits be equal and indeed better. These demands resulted in the financial interchange system. The Railroad Retirement Account was to have paid the social security trust fund for taxes since 1936 had the railroads been covered by social security. By a reverse step, social security was to have paid the Railroad Retirement Account for any additional benefits railroad workers would have received has they been covered by social security. The act also guaranteed that a surviving annuitant would receive 100 percent (raised to 110 percent in 1959) of any benefits made available under social security. Railroad workers with fewer than ten years of service who retired or died were to be covered by social security only.

The net result of the financial interchange was the payment by the Social Security Administration of large sums annually to the Railroad Retirement Board. In 1980, $244,280 million was transferred from the Railroad Retirement Account to social security trust funds, while $1,429,879 billion was transferred from social security tax receipts to the Railroad Retirement Account.[61] These sums included the cost of health insurance (Medicare), which was made applicable to railroad workers when the system was established in 1965. By legislation enacted in 1973, whenever social security benefits was increased, the increase was immediately "passed through" to the railroad annuitants.

The complexities of the railroad retirement system coupled with those of social security led to much difficulty in computing benefits. The result was described as a "claim examiner's nightmare."[62] Moreover, inequities developed between the worker who had been employed only by the railroads and the one who by virtue of a split career qualified for the dual benefits of social security and a railroad pension. The latter's dollar benefits approached, and in some instances exceeded, the preretirement income of the former.[63]

Eliminating individual inequities was but one facet of the total problem. The solvency of the Railroad Retirement Account was threatened by the "windfall" payments to workers who qualified under both systems. In extensive negotiations over proposed corrective legislation, neither employee unions nor management representatives were willing to assume, through additional taxation, an estimated total liability of $7 billion. The impasse was thought to be resolved in 1974 when, over the president's veto, legislation was enacted that required an annual payment of $285 million from the general tax funds to the Railroad Retirement Trust Fund for twenty-five years.

The Two-Tiered System

In an effort to simplify the benefit structure,[69] the 1974 legislation established a two-tiered system.[64] In the first tier, benefits were to be related to employment credits earned in the railroad industry and in nonrailraod employment. These would represent the social security component of the total benefit. Thus, tier one was to be financed by a tax on covered earnings, to be paid by both employer and employee in the same manner as the social security tax. The second tier—the railroad retirement component—was to be based on railroad earnings and years of service. It was, in effect, a private industrial pension.

Calculations for the second tier were complicated. There was a "past service part," a "bonus part," and a part based on railroad service after 1974. In addition to tier one and tier two, there was a third component called the "dual benefit windfall" for those with vested rights at the time the new system was adopted in 1974. Finally, there were "supplemental annuities" for those with a minimum of twenty-five years of service.[65] The tax on tier two was to be paid solely by the employer. Collective bargaining was to determine the actual amount of monthly earnings on which the tier two tax was levied. The supplemental annuity for long-term service was to be paid by the employer as well.

The individual employee was entitled to an annuity at age sixty-five, providing he had completed ten years of "creditable" railroad service. An employee retiring after June 1974 with thirty years of railroad service was entitled to an annuity at ages sixty to sixty-four. It was possible to retire at age sixty-two with less than thirty years of service, but the benefit was reduced by 20 percent, as in social security.

A two-tiered formula was also provided for the spouse. One feature was a guarantee of an annuity 10 percent above "the highest possible spouse's benefit under social security."[66] Survivor annuities were also made up of tier one and tier two components and could amount to about 30 percent more than social security benefits.[67]

Recent Legislation

The anticipation of a sound financial base resulting from the Railroad Retirement Act of 1974 proved to be groundless. Railroad employment continued to decline, sliding from an average of 600,000 in 1974 to 510,000 in early 1981. Moreover, the cost-of-living increases were higher than expected.

Finally, the "windfall" benefits proved to be improperly financed. Corrective legislation was again necessary.

Changes affecting the railroad retirement system were included in the Economic Recovery Tax Act of 1981 and the Omnibus Reconciliation Act of 1981. The payroll tax on employers to finance tier two benefits was increased from 9.5 percent to 11.75 percent. Employees were required to pay an additional 2 percent payroll tax, for a total of 8.7 percent. The benefit structure for tier two was considerably simplified. The new formula provided that the average monthly compensation for the sixty months of greatest earnings was to be multiplied by .7 percent times the number of years of service. The cost-of-living increase was limited to 32.5 percent of the increase in social security. Adjustments were made to reduce somewhat the "windfall" benefits and spouse and survivor benefits. Persons previously denied tier one benefits, such as divorced wives and remarried widows, were given the same status as those same categories of persons covered by social security.

The modifications made in 1981 were expected to solve the Railroad Retirement Board's immediate financial problems. Unfortunately, the projected employment assumptions of 500,000 workers proved to be much too optimistic. By January 1983, the employment level had fallen to 388,000. Moreover, the pension fund was reduced by loans to cover jobless benefits. The retirement board warned of the necessity for extensive cuts in benefits unless steps were taken once again to shore up the system's finances.[68]

Proposals for change took many forms, from bills to provide full funding to recommendations that the tier two structure be removed from the federal budget. More modest proposals suggested eliminating the special advantages railroad retirees enjoyed, such as (1) retirement at age sixty with thirty years of railroad service, (2) more generous spouse provisions than were common in the private sector, and (3) the absence of any taxation of benefits that were over and above those stemming directly from the social security portion of the monthly benefit.[69]

Facing the Railroad Retirement Board's threat that on September 1, 1983, 1 million retirees would be notified of substantial benefit reductions to take effect at the beginning of the 1984 fiscal year, the Congress passed a bill in early August. The act was all-inclusive in that it provided for, increased taxes, reduced benefits, and a major appropriation from general revenues.[70] Upon signing the measure, President Reagan declared that it would assure the solvency of the rail pension system at least until the end of the decade.[71]

Employee taxes were to be increased 1 percent annually from 11.75 percent in 1983 to 14.75 percent in 1986. Employee tier-two taxes were to increase gradually from 2 percent in 1983 to 4.25 percent in 1986. Employee tier-two benefits and windfall benefits were, for the first time, to be taxed as income. Scheduled cost-of-living benefits were deferred for six months and future tier-two cost-of-living benefits were slightly reduced. After July 1, 1984, individuals with thirty years of service who retired between the ages of sixty and sixty-two would receive a cut in benefits. The Railroad Retirement Board was instructed to honor court orders classifying tier-two benefits as property in divorce proceedings and thus subject to division. Finally, the act provided $1.7 billion from the general revenue fund.[72]

In summary, the complexities of the system remain extensive. The effort to integrate what was, in effect, a private system into social security and to achieve a full measure of equity for all participants resulted in a series of regulations only a specialist could comprehend. In time, retirees will be unaffected by "supplemental" and "windfall" benefits. At that point, only tier-one and tier-two benefits will require explanation. That time is far distant, however: substantial windfall payments are expected to continue well into the twenty-first century.[73]

The railroad retirement system is still the only industrial plan whose pension is administered by the federal government. Initially, there were firm declarations by both unions and management that the financial soundness of the system was assured through the contribution structure; government subsidy was neither necessary nor wanted. The establishment and subsquent expansion to the social security system put tremendous pressures upon the railroad retirement system to match, or to exceed, the kinds of benefits available to workers generally. With a rapidly declining work force, the only viable solution was a financial tie-in with social security. The arrangements to carry out this interlinkage have been modified repeatedly. The 1974 legislation was a major effort to preserve the equities of railroad employees; the revisions in 1981 were expected to assure solvency for a decade. However, the higher than anticipated unemployment during the recession brought on a new financial crisis. Salvaging the system once again depended upon congressional action.

MILITARY RETIREMENT: A VERY SPECIAL CASE

The complex issues surrounding private, and most public, pension systems are relatively simple when compared with those affecting the military retirement system. In the former, the emphasis is upon the individual. In the latter, the welfare of the individual constitutes one element only, in the determination of public policy. In ERISA, for example, primary concern is focused upon assuring an income to the retired worker. The welfare of the corporation is by no means ignored, but it does not occupy center stage. In contrast, when the Department of Defense reviews the retirement systems for military personnel, a major element receiving intense scrutiny is the impact of any proposed revision upon "force management objectives." In short, the mission of the Department of Defense must be taken fully into account.

The expression "retirement system," to most people, refers to a plan for providing income to those who are approaching the final years of their life span. Thus, it is difficult to accept the fact that a military retiree may be under forty years of age. Elderly retirees constitute a small fraction of the total. Of 1,192,000 military personnel receiving retirement pay in September 1978, only 146,000, or 12.2 percent, were over the age of sixty-five.[74]

Most members of the military retire between the ages of forty and forty-five. Having completed twenty years of service, they are eligible to receive an inflation-protected pension for the rest of their lives. That the system is not quite as idyllic as it may appear becomes apparent from statistics contained in the *Report of the President's Commission on Military Compensation in 1978.* During the period 1973–1979, only 11 percent of enlisted persons and 29 percent of officers completed twenty years of service. Only 1.7 percent of the enlisted persons and 5.3 percent of officers completed thirty years of military service.[75] Notwithstanding the small ratio of those who reach military retirement, the numbers resulted in a retirement budget of an estimated $16.8 billion for 1984, which is projected to increase to $20.1 billion in 1988.[76]

The Nondisability Retirement System

In the early years of the nation's history, government pensions were granted only for wartime service. However, in 1855, provision was made for payments to retired naval officers. Six years later, benefits were provided for retired army officers. "Piecemeal modifications" were made during the next two decades until World War II, when the large numbers of military personnel focused attention upon retirement issues.[77]

The current system provides that, upon completing twenty years of service, military personnel will receive an annuity for life. The annuity amounts to 2.5 percent of final basic pay multiplied by the number of years of service. The resulting figure of 50 percent, however, needs further explanation. Basic pay cannot be equated with a civilian salary. The military uses the expression "regular military compensation," or RMC, in making comparisons. RMC includes not only basic pay but also basic allowances for quarters and subsistance, together with the amount of the tax advantage resulting from the exemption of those allowances from federal income taxation. Thus, after twenty years of service, the annuity amounts roughly to 35 percent of regular military compensation. After thirty years of service, the figure rises to 57 percent.[78] Annuities are increased automatically as the Consumer Price Index rises.

No annuity is paid for service under twenty years. Vesting, in short, is nonexistent prior to twenty years of service. There is virtually universal agreement that this feature of the system is wrong. Attrition occurs principally in very early years. Eighty-two percent of enlisted personnel and 80 percent of officers who have served ten years stay on to retirement. Some form of vesting prior to the twentieth year would be advantageous to the military person who wishes to pull out of the service before twenty years of service but who cannot afford to in light of the annuity at the twentieth year.

At ages sixty-two to sixty-five, the military retirees receive social security benefits. That portion of the benefit based on military service stems from equal contributions from the retiree and the Department of Defense. The President's Commission on Military Compensation estimated that the social security benefit added to the retirement benefit after taxes equaled 95.9 percent of the final year's military income for the retiree with twenty years of service and 97.7 percent for the thirty-year retirees.[79] This percentage is considerably higher than that allowed by most private or public retirement systems. Military retirees, old and young, receive other benefits also, such as the use of commissaries. Military medical facilities provide free medical care on a space-available basis to retirees and their dependents.

The military retirement system is unfunded. No monies whatever are set aside to meet future liabilities. Nor does the military employee pay any portion of his salary to meet the later costs of the annuity. Thus, the system is unlike that of a private company, which must meet ERISA's demands for appropriate funding; and it is unlike social security, which requires annual contribution from both employer and employee.

The system has come under constant attack as being overgenerous and excessively costly. The overgenerous indictment is caused by two features: the time required in the service—only twenty years—and the sizable amount of the annuity. The total cost of the system, as a percentage of the defense budget, will continue to increase. Assuming an inflation rate not to exceed 6 percent, the 1978 outlay of $9.1 billion will increase to $37.5 billion in the year 2000. In constant 1978 dollars, however, the projected outlay will be $12.4 billion.[80] The chief argument for retaining the twenty-years-of-service requirement relates to the need for a military force able to do combat. Under normal circumstances, most personnel are not engaged in physically demanding jobs. One recent study declared that "of all enlisted retirees, 80 percent never spent any time at all" in jobs demanding physical stamina.[81] That finding can scarcely be considered a conclusive argument for eliminating the twenty-year retirement feature, since it does not address the question of need for combat readiness.

Notwithstanding a number of major inquiries about retirement policy, the military services have been reluctant to alter the nondisability retirement system. Five recent studies have all agreed that annuities should be reduced for those retiring with fewer than thirty years of service.[82]

In 1979, the Department of Defense, in response to the findings of the President's Commission on Military Compensation, introduced a plan that was purported to focus on equity and force management.[83] Any one in the service at the time had the option of choosing the then-current system or the proposed plan. The administration's proposal provided a two-level system of annuities: pre-old-age benefits and old-age benefits. The military employee who served from ten to twenty years would be eligible at the age of sixty for an old-age annuity based upon the length of service. In addition, the employee who had served ten or more years could withdraw cash sums against these benefits. The maximum withdrawal would amount to twenty months of basic pay for the employee who had served fifteen years. The annuity could be restored, providing the amount withdrawn was repaid within five years. Those completing twenty years of service were to have the option of a reduced annuity to compensate for the early withdrawal.

The employee who completed twenty years of service would be eligible immediately for a pre-old-age benefit based upon an average of the highest two years of basic pay multiplied by varying percentages for length of service: for example, 1.75 percent for the first ten years and 2 percent for the next ten. Upon reaching age sixty, the old age benefit rate would apply. For example, the annuity would be 2.75 percent for years of service over ten, with a maximum of 76.25 percent. When social security payments began, there would be an offset of 1¼ percent per year of military service. The new plan also provided severance pay for both officers and enlisted men involuntarily separated from the service after five years.

Benefit levels of the proposed system would be lower than those provided under the system existing in 1979. No one serving at the time of the new plan went into effect would necessarily receive a decreased pension. The system was touted as meeting societal pressure for a reduction in military pensions while at the same time providing an increase in compensation for a considerable number of service personnel. Moreover, the plan was said to improve the distribution of the career force and at the same time provide greater flexibility for management purposes.

A separate legislative proposal was developed to meet the criticism directed at the lack of funding for the military retirement system. However, significant savings would not begin until the year 2000. At that time, the estimated costs were expected to be 26 percent below 1979 costs.[84]

Survivor Benefits

The provision of appropriate military-retiree survivor benefits has been the subject of much legislation in recent decades. In 1953, the Uniform Services Contingency Option Act established a plan whereby members of the military could, by receiving reduced retirement benefits, provide an annuity for their widows and eligible children. The decision to participate in the plan had to be made before the beginning of the eighteenth year of service. The plan was set up on an actuarial basis, with the participant electing to establish an annuity of

½, ¼, or ⅛ of retirement pay. There were many uncertainties about the system. Moreover, the costs were high. The net result was a participation rate of only 15 percent.[85]

The plan was liberalized to some degree in 1961 with the passage of the Retired Servicemen's Family Protection Plan.[86] The costs continued to be high, however, and, notwithstanding additional legislative changes, the participation rate remained at a low level. The system was terminated in 1972 with the passage of the Survivor Benefit Plan, modeled after the plan for the civil service.[87]

A major feature of the new act was federal cost-sharing. Enrollment in the program was automatic for military members with eligible dependents, unless the member, prior to retirement, elected not to be covered or to be covered at less than the maximum level. The normal survivor annuity was to be 55 percent of the member's retirement pay, called the base amount. For spouse coverage, for example, the cost to the member was 2½ percent of the first three hundred dollars of the base amount plus 10 percent of the base amount remainder. In 1979, the participation rate for new retirees was 58 percent.

The Survivor Benefit Plan is linked in part to social security. Under certain circumstances, the annuity of the dependent is reduced to take account of that portion of the social security benefit attributed to the member's military service. In other circumstances, the plan and social security are considered completely independent. By the Uniform Services Survivors Benefits Amendments Act of 1978, members of military reserves were extended the privileges of Survivor Benefit Plan.[88]

Following the enactment of the plan in 1972, the system placed an increasing percentage of the cost on the participant. Indeed, the portion paid by the participant, especially recently retired enlisted members, was much higher than originally contemplated.[89] In 1980 the Congress amended the act to eliminate the inequity. A study by the Congressional Budget Office declares, however, that by the year 2000 the contribution formula will need further revision if the original intent—federal sharing of the cost of survivors' benefits—is to be retained.[90]

In summary, the studies of the President's Commission on Military Compensation served to call attention to those features of the military retirement system that tend to set it apart from other pension systems. One major negative feature concerns the total absence of benefits for the individual with fewer than twenty years of service. In contrast, those serving twenty years have an unusually liberal pension program. A military pension plus social security provides an annual wage replacement feature substantially greater than that provided by most other public and private systems. Moreover, military retirees receive pensions, on average, for thirty-three years—double the benefit years in private industry.

Thus far, proposals to improve the military retirement sytem, treat individuals within and without the military system with a greater degree of fairness, and attack the problem of severely burgeoning costs have failed to meet legislative acceptance. The President's Commission on Pension Policy, in its final report in 1981, did, however, declare its opposition to the use of pension plans as "recruitment, retention and separation devices." Instead, it favored the development of other tools to serve these ends and declared that the pension program should be used "solely to provide retirement income."[91]

BLACK LUNG: A UNIQUE CASE

Black lung benefits, it may be argued, are outside the scope of a discussion of public policy and the aging. It may appear that the topic is more properly related to a discussion of occupational health or workmen's compensation than to one of retirement or survivor benefits. However, almost three-fourths of black lung beneficiaries were elderly when they first began to receive benefits. The program is unique among federal benefit programs, and its special relevance to older people will be made clear later in this discussion.

Coal miners who are adjudged to be victims of black lung disease, or pneumoconiosis, receive monthly cash benefits. The disease may develop as a consequence of prolonged inhalation of coal dust. There are two principal categories of pneumoconiosis—simple and complicated. Miners with the latter may have lung impairment so severe as to result in total disability or premature death. Of the 120,000 miners and widows whose claims were approved at the end of the first year of the program's operation, 71.1 percent were over sixty-five years of age.[92]

The program was initiated with the passage of the Federal Coal Mine Health and Safety Act of 1969.[93] The act provided lifetime benefits from general tax funds for underground miners totally disabled by the disease and for widows of miners who had died from the disease. By subsequent amendments in 1972 and 1977, the definition of miner was broadened to include surface miners and the provisions relating to dependents were liberalized.

Initially, the black lung section of the safety act was opposed by the administration as an intrusion into the role of the states in the area of workmen's compensation. The leadership of the United Mine Workers Association also opposed the measure.[94] However, public sentiment was aroused following a major mine explosion that killed seventy-eight workers near Farmington, West Virginia, in October 1968, and the vigorous efforts of a number of congressional leaders resulted in passage of a measure that President Nixon signed, reportedly with "a great deal of reluctance."[95]

The Social Security Administration was charged with the responsibility for putting the program into operation. However, the benefit provisions were tied, not to the social security system, but to the Federal Employees Compensation Act. The basic monthly benefit amounted to 50 percent of the minimum amount payable to a federal employee in Grade GS-2 who was totally disabled. The benefit increased to 100 percent for those with three or more dependents. When federal salaries increased, benefits were automatically increased.[96]

The act made benefits dependent upon a finding of total disability as a consequence of black lung disease. The criteria for determining total disability were not to be more restrictive than those used in the social security disability program. By their nature, however, the two sets of criteria had to be widely divergent. Social security disability was not necessarily related to employment. Workers could become totally disabled for any one of a host of reasons. On the other hand, the miner could obtain benefits under the Black Lung Program only if there was a finding of complicated pneumoconiosis.

The Social Security Administration was severely criticized for the high rejection rate that was in effect in the first months of the program. Moreover, the rejection rate varied substantially from state to state. Early denials amounted to 46 percent in Kentucky, 31 percent in West Virginia, and 22 percent in Pennsylvania. Initially, the X-ray examination was the only basis for determining the presence of the disease, a practice "never intended by this Congress" and "a disgraceful situation insofar as justice is concerned to the coal miners in this country."[97]

Benefits for widows were complicated by the absence of adequate records. Claims were filed for deaths occurring many years or even decades prior to the passage of the act. "Doctors did not recoginze it as a disease. It was originally thought of as an occupational hazard. . . . What the miners had was described as miners' consumption. Well, after certain of the doctors out in our area made some discoveries that it was not tuberculosis from which the men were suffering, they began to give it a new name, and they called it miners' asthma. They then decided that it was not asthma, and they called it silicosis. They got to the next stage, and called it anthrasilicosis, and now the doctors have come along and given it the final and fancy name of pneumoconiosis."[98]

By April 1971, over 286,000 claims had been filed and the processing completed on 245,000. Claims were allowed for 120,000, but for 125,000 others claims were denied.[99] The high rate of denial brought renewed demands for liberalization of the act and revision of the standards for determining total disability. The following year, Congress passed the Black Lung Benefits Act of 1972.[100]

The Act Liberalized

The changes were significant. First, the definition of "dependent" was broadened. For example, one acknowledged deficiency in the original act concerned the "double orphan." The child who had lost both parents was not eligible for benefits. Under the new act, dependents were also determined to be eligible if the miner at the time of his death was totally disabled, regardless of cause.

The second major change related to the definition of black lung. No longer was the X-ray to be the sole determination. The X-ray could be negative, but if there was other evidence of "a totally disabling respiratory or pulmonary impairment then there shall be a rebuttable presumption that such miner is totally disabled due to pneumoconiosis."[101] This provision applied to those who had had fifteen years or more of employment in the mines. Moreover, the new act no longer limited eligibility to the underground worker, thus enabling the surface miner to apply for benefits.

A third significant feature of the act related to the recognition by Congress of the burgeoning costs of the program and of the necessity for the states and the coal operators to share in meeting those costs. When the act was adopted in 1969, proponents of the measure asserted that the program was a "one-shot effort" to correct the injustices arising from a critical occupational health problem. The act was not intended to establish a federal workmen's compensation precedent.[102] On the contrary, passage of the act and the payment of benefits for previous cases out of general revenues, it was argued, would eliminate the past and make possible the assumption of payments for future cases by state workmen's compensation plans. Moreover, as working conditions in the mines improved, the disease would be eliminated.

Not surprisingly, the states moved slowly. Black lung was a major problem in only a few. If a state failed to meet the criteria established by the federal government, the law placed the responsibility upon the coal mine operator. When the operator could not be located—as happened in 50 percent of the cases—approved claims were to be met from federal funds.[103]

The 1972 amendments provided that claims filed after December 31, 1973, would be administered by the Department of Labor. Regulations, however, regarding medical standards and standards of evidence were the responsibility of the Social Security Administration. This division of authority led to a considerable amount of bickering at the federal level.[104] A representative of the United Mine Workers Association declared that the "dual system promotes confusion, overlap, inconsistency, and buckpassing."[105]

The program was beset by much unhappiness on the part of individual miners and the association representing them. A principal complaint was that the Social Security Administration, through various stratagems, unjustly denied many claims. For example, following the 1972 act, the cases of previously denied claimants were reviewed. At the same time, the liberalization of the act resulted in thousands of new claims. To eliminate abuses, the administration contracted with firms of radiologists to review the positive findings of physicians operating in the geographical area of the claimants. The second review often resulted in a denial of benefits. "The rereading of x-rays has contributed greatly to the distrust miners now feel for the black lung program. They see the process as one in which Social Security is fishing for evidence to defeat their claim. Social Security, on the other hand, contends that the rereading of x-rays is necessary because there are many coalfield doctors who gave fraudulent interpretations."[106] The president of the West Virginia Black Lung Association asserted that during the year 1973–1974 over 95 percent of the claims had been denied.[107]

An appeals procedure for those whose claims were denied was similarly attacked. The unsuccessful claimant could appeal to a government-designated administrative law judge. However, a favorable ruling by the judge could be appealed by the government to the Appeals Council, an agency of the Social Security Administration, and beyond this body to a federal court. In 1974, reversals of administrative-law-judge rulings in cases that the government appealed approached 90 percent.[108]

The often-extended delay and ultimate disappointment experienced by potential recipients were brought to public attention through the hearings of the Subcommittee on Labor Standards of the House Committee on Education and Labor. Proposals to eliminate various areas of controversy were debated yearly. The assumption that the states would modernize their workmen's compensation laws and assume responsibility with the operators for new cases, thus eliminating the liability of the federal government, proved to be totally erroneous. The states were in no hurry to alter their workmen's compensation status. Moreover, the operators were not about to assume any financial obligations they could avoid. As a consequence, federal financial responsibility continued to mount. In addition, the hostility of many miners and their dependents who had been deprived of benefits—unjustly, they felt—resulted in continuing heavy pressure upon Congress to bring about a further liberalization of the program. The result was the Black Lung Benefits Reform Act of 1977 and the Black Lung Benefits Revenue Act of 1977.[109]

The 1977 Revision

The definition of the term *miner* was broadened to include individuals who were working or had worked "in or around a coal mine or coal preparation facility."[110] Transportation and construction workers were covered by the act provided they could establish exposure to coal dust. The definition of pneumoconiosis was enlarged to include not only chronic disease but "respiratory and pulmonary impairments, arising out of coal mine employment." Survivors of a miner who had died prior to the 1977 act were entitled to benefits, provided the miner had been employed for twenty-five years before June 30, 1971, "unless it is established that at the time of the miner's death, such miner was not partially or totally disabled due to pneumoconiosis."[111]

The medical evidence to support a claim was expanded to include the chest

X-ray, breathing test, blood-gas test, and physical examination. A negative X-ray alone was in no sense final. The miner adjudged to have black lung disease was eligible for medical treatment and medications. Identification cards were to be made available for presentation to participating physicians and clinics. Bills for services were to be sent by the physicans to the Department of Labor.

The new act provided that an attorney or other representative of a miner could not be paid a fee unless an award was made. Moreover, the amount of the fee was subject to government approval. This provision was in sharp contrast to early experience when many miners were charged large sums for legal services. Provisions for vocational rehabilitation training and relocation allowances made possible transfers to other employment.

The benefit base in the 1977 revision was not disturbed. It remained one-half of the minimum paid to a disabled federal employee in Grade GS-2. As of September 1980 a miner or one survivor was entitled to $254 monthly. The maximum to be paid a miner or survivor with three or more dependents was $508.

Pending claims and those previously denied were to be reviewed. If approved, payments were to be made retroactive to January 1, 1974. Payments were to cease only if eligibility ceased. For example, a surviving widow who remarried was declared to be no longer eligible, a provision in direct contrast to a provision in the Social Security Act passed two months previously.

During the early years of the Black Lung Program, coal producers were largely free of financial obligations. Until 1974, the federal government paid all benefits. Claims filed after December 31, 1983, were to be paid by the operators or by the government if the "responsible" operator could not be determined. Of approximately 125,000 claims processed by the Department of Labor after December 31, 1973, only about 6,000 were declared eligible.[112] Proposals to revise the act and to require coal operators to share a greater portion of the financial burden were stalled in Congress for many months over the method of taxation. A flat assessment on each ton produced, favored by the House Conference Committee, was unacceptable to the Senate Conference, which argued that this solution penalized the strip-mine operator whose coal sold for less and whose employees were less subject to black lung disease. The end result to the Black Lung Benefits Revenue Act of 1977 was a tax of fifty cents per ton upon underground coal and twenty-five cents per ton for strip-mined coal. In either case, the limit was not to exceed 2 percent of the sales price. These monies would support a Black Lung Disability Trust Fund, which would pay claims of miners whose last employment preceded January 1, 1970. The fund would also pay if an operator responsible for the miner's disability could not be determined. Coal companies were given the option of obtaining private insurance or of establishing tax-exempt funds to support payments of claims in which responsibility could not be determined.

The liberalization resulting from the 1977 law meant that thousands of claims previously denied were reexamined. The process proceeded at a pace that once again aggravated potential recipients by its slowness. Heavy pressure from miners' advocacy groups resulted in a substantial speedup of the number of cases reviewed monthly. Unfortunately the newly established fund did not take in sufficient monies to pay for the many claims approved under the liberalized act. A New England congressman declared that "everyone who has ever seen a coal mine is now entitled to collect black lung payments."[113] Each year the fund paid out more than it took in, the balance coming from general revenues. In December 1981, an act whose purpose was to eliminate a deficit of $1.5 billion was passed. The tax rate was doubled to fifty cents a ton for surface-mined coal and one dollar a ton for underground coal. Eligibility standards were again tightened.

The 1972 amendments had provided for the termination of the program in 1981. The theory was that except for the payment of benefits already determined, no further federal administrative action would be required. New dust standards would virtually eliminate the disease, and state workmen's compensation laws would provide for new victims. Neither of these theories materialized. The 1977 revision set no termination date for the program. In September 1982, there were 359,400 beneficiaries, including 104,246 miners, 145,159 widows, and 109,995 spouses and children. Average monthly family benefits amounted to $354.20.[114]

The assumption by the federal government in 1969 of a special obligation with respect to victims of pneumoconiosis has not been repeated. The black lung experience, however, has alerted other groups of older workers and retirees to the possibility of similar compensation for work-related diseases not apparent until decades have elapsed. Moreover, the recent emphasis upon ferreting out possible disease-bearing chemical waste dumps may result in demands to provide special benefits programs for victims of enviroment-related illnesses.

The Department of Labor is reported to have estimated that eighty-five thousand textile workers are victims of "brown lung," or byssinosis, resulting from exposure to cotton dust.[115] Employees have been unable to deal with the limitations of state workmen's compensation statutes and the evasive actions of corporations. Workers in a number of states contend with "white bug," or talicosis, brought about by the inhalation of dust in talc mines and mills.[116] The Department of Labor has estimated that 60,000 of over 1 million workers exposed to silica dust have silicosis.[117] Veterans exposed to Agent Orange in Vietnam claim that the chemical has been responsible for a variety of health disorders, including birth defects in their children.[118] One of the most wide-spread threats to health may be asbestosis, described in a Pittsburgh law suit as a "progressive, irreversible, and often fatal chest and lung disease" that carries the risk of "one of several types of cancer."[119] The problem of assist-ing individuals who are victims of diseases, whether work-related, war-related, or arising from the use of a consumer product adjudged years later to contain a disease-causing substance, is beyond the scope of the state or local decision making. They must be attacked nationally. The nation's action in grappling with the problems arising from pneumoconiosis serves as one model for the future.

In summary, the Black Lung Program is unique in that it is a federally administered program that provides compensation for workers exposed to long-term health hazards in a particular industry. Its history is a turbulent one, and the eventual expansion in coverage and resulting overall costs cannot be anticipated. It is especially worthy of mention, however, because it may well be a precedent-setting case. As has been mentioned there are many other situations in occupational and other settings that may be hazardous to health over the long run. People exposed to such hazards are beginning to mobilize themselves for compensatory action on their own behalf. The precedent of the Black Lung Program will almost certainly make such claims far more difficult to deny. And, as with the Black Lung Program, most beneficiaries will be elderly since the effects of exposure are usually determined only after many years.

CONCLUSION

This section has reviewed some of the plans that are available to workers in addition to social security. It is not possible to cover all of them, but the major plans have been described. Most of them predate social security, and some continue to coexist with social security. Linkages have been formed with social security in many instances, however. These linkages are by no means uniform. The uniform, integrated systems that many perceive as optimal is by no means close at hand. At present, juggling the various programs constitutes a bureaucratic nightmare, and the system contains many inequities. In the final section of this chapter, a more complete summary analysis will be offered.

3. Financial Programs Affecting Older People

The federal government has instituted several programs that benefit the elderly. The purpose of these is to augment the financial resources of older persons either directly or indirectly. The most comprehensive plan is the tax structure that makes special provisions for those over age sixty-five, resulting in lower tax payment, or in the case of poorer older persons, often no tax payments at all. Other programs to be covered are the energy conservation program, which offers persons with low incomes assistance in paying their energy bills and in reducing energy costs in other ways. The third program, legal services, which provides free legal assistance to lower-imcome persons, may be regarded as a financial program in two senses. First, it offers legal advice to persons, including older persons, who otherwise would not be able to afford it. Second, the legal advice it offers might well enable older persons to secure financial benefits that otherwise would have been denied them. This program has not so far been used extensively by the elderly poor, although some special efforts are now being made to encourage their participation.

TAX BENEFITS FOR THE ELDERLY

Attainment of the magic age of sixty-five carries with it a significant, and often underestimated, lessening of the federal tax burden. The reduction takes several forms.[120] For example, the income level at which a tax form must be filled is higher for the person over age sixty-five than for the person under that age. Moreover, an extra exemption of one thousand dollars is applicable to all persons on the day before their sixty-fifth birthday. A third type of reduction is dependent upon a particular circumstance such as the sale of a home; the gain may be excluded from the seller's income. A fourth category is the tax credit for the elderly person whose income is below specified limits. Finally, the burden of taxation is lessened simply by "tax expenditures" such as the total absence of a tax on social security income and the basic railroad retirement income.

Filing Requirements   The filing requirements are more generous for the person over age sixty-five. For example, in 1982 the married couple over the age of sixty-five was not required to file an income tax return unless their gross income amounted to $7,400. If only one spouse was aged sixty-five, the filing figure was $6,400. For the couple under the age of sixty-five, the figure was $5,400. Single persons over sixty-five were required to file if their gross income amounted to $4,300; for those under sixty-five, the figure was $3,000.

Exemptions   Effective in 1979, the personal exemption is increased from $750 to $1,000 for each taxpayer. The person over sixty-five retains a double benefit previously authorized by Congress. As a consequence, the elderly couple is entitled to personal exemptions totaling $4,000. The blind person over sixty-five receives an additional $1,000 exemption. The age exemption, however, is not applicable to the elderly dependent person. Thus, the son who lists his eighty-year-old father as a dependent is limited to one exemption for the father. Similarly, if the father were blind, the son would be limited to one exemption in addition to his own.

Sale of a Home   A major benefit effective in 1981 provides for the exclusion of as much as $125,000 of the gain on the sale or exchange of a home. This benefit, to be utilized on a one-time basis only, is applicable to those over age fifty-five who have used the property as their principal residence for three of the five years preceding the sale. The exclusion was first introduced in 1964 and amounted to $20,000. This was increased to $35,000 in 1976 and to $100,000 in 1978, when the age limit was lowered to fifty-five.

The purpose of the one-time forgiveness of the capital gains tax liability on residence sales is to assist the elderly who might wish to rent or obtain a smaller home. The Congressional Budget Office has indicated that the distribution effect of the exclusion upon various income groups of the elderly is uncertain because of lack of data. It is estimated, however, that the revenue loss to the government, will range from $590 million in 1981 to $950 million in 1986.[121]

Credit for the Elderly   A credit toward the amount of the tax may be obtained by those aged sixty-five and over who qualify by reason of limited income. For example, a couple filing a joint return is eligible for credit if their adjusted gross income is below $17,500 or if their income from nontaxable pensions and annuities does not exceed $3,750. Comparable limits for the single person were $12,500 and $2,500.

Tax Expenditures   Tax expenditures are of several kinds. There may be exemptions or deductions; there may be special exclusions. All have the same result—revenue losses. The Congressional Budget Office defines tax expenditures as "revenue losses that arise from provisions of the tax code that give special or selective tax relief to certain groups of taxpayers." The budget office further explains that "just as a forgiveness of debt is equivalent to a payment, so a remission of tax liability is equivalent to an expenditure."[122] Tax expenditure is simply one form of subsidy.

Illustrations of tax expenditures abound. Business, for example, is encouraged by investment tax credits. Individuals purchase tax-exempt state and local government bonds. They may also benefit from the exclusion of taxes on a high percentage of capital gains. The elderly and the blind benefit from additional exemptions, as previously noted.

The prime example of a tax expenditure for the elderly is the absence of a tax on social security. For those in the middle- and upper-income brackets, the absence of any tax on social security income amounts to a substantial windfall since, as has been discussed, there is little relation between the amount originally paid into the system and the amount received.

There are a number of sources of nontaxable income for corporations and individuals. Some are of special importance to the elderly, since the percentage of old people affected is much greater than the number affected in the population as a whole. Included among these sources of income are basic railroad retirement benefits, certain mortgage assistance payments, energy assistance payments, food benefits, veterans benefits, and black lung benefits.[123]

ENERGY CONSERVATION

Energy Assistance

The low-income elderly have been victimized by a series of unforeseen developments in recent years. One of these, rising energy prices, has been especially difficult to overcome. The increase in the price of oil has been a phenomenon of worldwide significance. The efforts of the United States to counter that development by decontrolling domestic prices of energy-producing resources have resulted in additional price increases. Inflation has also had a devastating effect upon the price structure. Efforts on the part of the federal government to assist those suffering the greatest hardship have taken several forms.

One of the most important steps has been the establishment of cash payments to meet the costs of home heating—and, in some areas, cooling. At first, because of severe winters in both 1976 and 1977 and 1977 and 1978, special appropriations were made by the Congress amounting to $200 million each winter for so-called "energy crisis intervention" procedures to be administered by the Community Services Administration. A formula for distributing the monies to states was established. The number of low-income households, the severity of the weather, heating fuel costs, and other factors entered into the formula. The low-income elderly were to receive special priority. A maximum of $250 per household was to be paid directly to the fuel suppliers and utility companies.[124] The pattern established in 1976 shifted somewhat from year to year, but the appropriation of about $200 million continued until 1981, when it was reduced to $87.5 million.

A major expansion of the whole concept of energy assistance occurred following the passage in November 1979 of an amendment to the Interior Appropriations Bill. A special one-time direct payment was provided for SSI recipients. Monies were also made available, to low-income persons not receiving SSI payments. The Crisis Intervention—renamed Crisis Assistance—program was also enlarged. Funding was provided for an array of goods such as heaters and blankets as well as for supportive services for those who qualified. The total cost rose to $1.6 billion.[125]

Still further modifications occurred with the passage of the Home Energy Assistance Act of 1980.[126] Administered by the Department of Health and Human Services, the law provided that "priority be given to households with lowest incomes and to eligible households with at least one elderly or handicapped individual." Subsequent regulations required that state plans specify "how priority will be given to eligible households with elderly or handicapped persons."[127] The act declared that energy assistance payments were to be disregarded in determining eligibility for other programs.

The states were given greater leeway than formerly in determining the amount of each household's benefits. Although the federal guidelines established the maximum income eligibility, the states were free to set income limits below the maximum. In 1981, thirty-seven did so.[128] The states could also determine the types of assistance, such as cash or vender payments.

The program has not been easy to implement. A study by the staff of the Senate Special Committee on Aging found that there was "an overwhelming need for long range planning." Reporting requirements and demands for data were said to be excessive. Despite various technical difficulties, the program was considered to be "consistently targeted to those most in need."[129] The Leadership Council on Aging Organziations has declared that the Low-Income Home Energy Assistance Program (LIHEAP), as it is now designed, "is a significant source of support for older people who are over burdened by the high cost of energy."[130]

Weatherization Assistance

During the last decade, thousands of low-income elderly have benefited through federally financed weatherization programs. Services have included activities to make homes more comfortable as well as more energy-efficient. The principal activity has been the installation of insulating materials including storm doors and windows.

The word "erratic" has been used to describe the history of the weatherization programs.[131] Begun on an experimental basis in 1973 by community action agencies, weatherization activities for low-incomed persons were authorized by the Economic Opportunity Act of 1975. Financing was provided by the Community Services Administration. The following year Congress authorized the Federal Energy Administration, later the Department of Energy, to operate a similar program. In 1977 and 1978, both Community Services Administration and the Department of Energy were engaged in weatherization activities. Many community action agencies at local levels operated the programs concurrently, notwithstanding the fact that the two programs were separately funded and regulated. Both programs were criticized for mismanagement and poor performance. Critics charged, for example, that undue emphasis was placed on materials and not enough attention was given to supplying skilled labor. Program administration was also said to be inadequate. Moreover, insufficient attention was given to renters.[132]

The principal weatherization appropriation for fiscal year 1979 was limited by Congress to the Department of Energy. Funded at approximately $200 million annually, the program was continued through 1983 at a reduced level.

Grants were made to the states, which then provided funds for local organizations to perform the services. Labor was supplied principally by CETA workers, that is, persons employed under the Comprehensive Employment and Training Act, a program under the Department of Labor. To be eligible for assistance, a household had to have an income no greater than 125 percent of the poverty guidelines established by the Office of Management and Budget. Exceptions to this general regulation applied to families receiving aid for dependent children, general assistance, and supplemental security income. Also, priority was to be given to the elderly and the handicapped. As of October 1981, under the programs of both the Community Services Administration and the Department of Energy, over 900,000 homes had been weatherized; "most were occupied by the elderly."[133]

In addition to the weatherization assistance noted above, under the National Energy Act of 1978 homeowners may receive tax credits amounting to 15 percent of the first two thousand dollars expended for energy conservation improvements, such as storm doors and windows and furnace modifications.[134] This program remains in effect to January 1986 and can be extended two additional years in cases where the credits exceed the amount of tax owed. Tax credits to 1986 are also available for those installing residential solar equipment.[135]

The administration proposed the elimination of the weatherization program in fiscal year 1982 and again in 1983. The argument was advanced that an energy and emergency block grant would provide limited funding for a state choosing to continue weatherization activities. Congress rejected the proposal each year with the result that continued, although reduced, funding was available through 1983.

These rebuffs did not deter the administration from omitting the program from its 1984 budget proposal. In brief, the future of the weatherization program continues to be uncertain.

LEGAL SERVICES

Obtaining "equal justice under the law" is not easy for the poor, especially the elderly poor. Although for many years the federal government has sponsored legal service programs, the number of persons receiving help has been extremely limited. A 1976 estimate indicated that although possibly 200,000 persons received legal aid in that year, there may have been as many as 5.8 million "without access to essential legal representation."[136]

The first federally sponsored programs providing legal services for the poor were initiated in 1965. Under the authority of the Economic Opportunity Act, neighborhood legal-service offices were established in many communities. Not until 1972 was any special emphasis placed upon services for the elderly.

At that time, the National Senior Citizens Law Center (NSCLC) was created to serve as a "backup center" for the various neighborhood offices. NSCLC thus provided a special focus on the problems of the elderly.[137]

First introduced in 1971, proposals to establish a legal services corporation became bogged down over the issue of authority of the president to appoint the members of the governing board. Legislation was enacted three years later with the passage of the Legal Services Corporation Act of 1974.[138] The structure of the corporation reflects congressional effort to isolate the new entity entirely from political pressure.

The corporation is independent; neither officers nor staff are federal employees. Ultimate authority resides with an eleven-member board appointed by the president with the advice and consent of the Senate. No more than six members are from the same political party. A majority are members of the bar, although at least two are "eligible clients." The board selects a president who serves as chief executive officer.

The corporation does not represent clients. It is responsible for the distribution of funds appropriated by Congress to over three hundred legal service programs that in 1982, were operating roughly twelve hundred neighborhood offices. At the state level, the governor is responsible for the appointment of a nine-member advisory council. Each program "recipient" reports to a locally selected board, one-third of whom must consist of "eligible clients." One major client guideline established by the corporation pertains to a maximum financial eligibility standard, namely, 125 percent of the poverty level as determined by the Federal Office of Management and Budget.[139]

Although the corporation itself does not represent clients, it has funded units that advise legal-services offices throughout the country. For example, in 1982, NSCLC with offices in Washington and Los Angeles, developed manuals on nursing home care and on civil legal problems of importance to the rural elderly. Other offices funded by LSC are the legal Council for the Elderly in New York.[140]

Eligible Client Problems

A major stumbling block for the elderly poor is in the area of public benefits. The person who feels aggrieved over the ruling of a clerk in, say, the office concerned with Supplementary Security Income may wish to appeal. In communities where public legal aid is available, the aggrieved person may quickly obtain help at little or no cost. Questions pertaining to interpretations of the law and administrative regulations may arise in virtually every public benefit area, including social security, veterans' benefits, Medicare, Medicaid, public housing, and food stamps. Other types of problems requiring legal assistance pertain to housing, merchandising, wills, the rights of patients in hospitals and nursing homes, the securing of guardians, and the acceptance or rejection of commitment procedures.[141]

In 1981, Community Legal Services Inc. of Philadelphia, for example, supervised a number of legal service centers. With fifty-seven lawyers and forty-seven paralegals, Community Legal Services had twenty-four thousand clients. Family problems, such as child or spouse abuse and divorce matters, constituted 23 percent of the caseload. The second largest category, 20 percent, consist of public assistance cases. Housing problems accounted for the third largest number. These estimates relate to the entire range of cases coming before the Philadelphia agency.[142] A recent nationwide study conducted by the Legal Services Corporation estimated that elderly clients constituted 13.9 percent of the median caseload.[143]

The Legal Services Corporation and the Administration on Aging

An especially interesting feature of the expansion of legal services for the elderly concerns the role of the Administration on Aging. The 1975 amendments to the Older Americans Act identified legal services as one of four priorities to receive funds under Title III. A special agreement to encourage cooperative projects was arrived at. Joint efforts were launched to inform elderly persons of the existence of legal aid services. Funds were made available for the training of lawyers and paraprofessionals. A major objective was to make legal assistance available in every planning and service area.[144]

The Legal Services Corporation in 1982 was the "principle delivery mechanism" for legal services funded by the Older Americans Act. Title III of the act requires that Area Agencies on Aging use a portion of social service monies for legal services. Contracts are made with legal service providers. In some cases, the providers are financed by service block grants and by local government funds. In most cases, however, the providers are linked to the Legal Services Corporation. Older Americans Act Title IV funds are, in part, allocated to state aging agencies to support the development of legal service activities benefiting older persons.[145]

Uncertainties Ahead

Notwithstanding the substantial growth of legal services for low-income persons, the future of the corporation has become clouded. The agency was criticized by some in the early eighties for the types of legal actions taken, for example, class action suits against federal, state, and local offices. There was objection, also, to lobbying activities of LSC personnel. Moreover, the president had endeavored to eliminate the LSC from the federal budget, arguing that the function was one that should be performed at the state level. If federal funds were to be involved, the state could utilize social service block grant monies. The Congress, with strong backing from the American Bar Association, refused to abolish the agency, although appropriations were reduced about 25 percent, from $321 million in 1981 to $241 million in 1982 and again in 1983. Another complication concerned appointments to the eleven-member governing board. The *Senior Citizen News* declared that the president had "packed the Legal Services Board with conservatives who, he hoped, would succeed in dismantling the agency from within."[146]

The reductions in staff, the closing of offices, and the continued efforts to eliminate the agency do not bode well for the future of the corporation. The Leadership Council of Aging Organizations has declared the "if LSC is eliminated, the most fundamental of safety nets, equal justice under law, will be totally out of reach for virtually all poor and many older people."[147] In support of its position, the council quoted David Brink, a past president of the American Bar Association: "Equal access to justice is a national goal and a public responsibility. With all our best efforts, private lawyers cannot meet the goal alone."[148]

CONCLUSION

The financial status of the elderly is enhanced or potentially enhanced by the three programs just discussed. The special tax advantages given to those over age sixty-five are, for the most part, available to all persons of that age. The other two programs are intended to help the poor, although elderly persons are in fact those who have benefited most from energy subsidies as well as from weatherization efforts. Free or at least very-low-cost legal services are also intended primarily for the poor. The elderly poor do not seem to have made very great use of these services to date, although there are many potential financial benefits. Efforts to specifically engage the poor among older people have begun only quite recently. Both weatherization and legal services, however, are endangered species under the Reagan administration.

4. Summary Analysis

The web of the federal government spreads over an amazing number of pension plans. It has been possible to cover only the more important ones in this chapter. Some of the plans are quite independent of social security; others are linked to it but in highly inconsistent ways. Long before social security came into being, private pension plans sprouted and then multiplied without support—or interference—from the federal government. It was discovered, however, that private plans in general offered very little security to workers who were supposedly covered. For any number of reasons the worker might well find himself or herself without a pension when retirement time came around. As a result, the federal government began to get involved. In the seventies, the federal government assumed a heavy role in regulating pension plans, primarily to protect the rights of workers. Since that time some private plans have become integrated with social security; others remain totally separate. All are subject to federal regulations. No rule, however, specifies any type of linkage with social security. When private plans do become tied into social security, there is usually some diminishment in private benefits, but this is often more than offset by what social security has to offer in benefits and guarantees.

Just over half of all workers are now covered by private pension plans of one kind or another. Although private pension income is often quite small and diminished in worth because there is no mechanism that allows it to keep pace with inflation, there is no doubt that the retiring person is at least somewhat better off when covered by both social security and a private pension. The federal government, however, does not require that private organizations offer pensions or that pensions be offered to all workers in a given company. That "extra piece of income" is therefore denied to a very large proportion of retirees, including those who could use it most. Given social security's intentional limitations in replacing earnings or indeed providing anything above minimal income sufficiency, some pressure has been exerted to make private pensions a general feature of employment. So far the federal government has chosen instead to provide the option of Individual Retirement Accounts, or IRA's, for the uncovered worker. Over time this option has been extended as well to some workers already covered. For this and other reasons the IRA option has come under criticism of late.

Some federal employees receive in several ways what amounts to social security plus private pension plan benefits. Even the retirement system for federal civilian employees, which has so far been quite separate from social security, allows room for adding social security to the regular pension. Federal civil servants, whose pension system was in place well before social security, initially had no desire to be included in that system. Their benefits were, and remain, greater in amount, relatively speaking. But as social security benefits increased, the superiority of the federal pension system was reduced. In fact, the federal employee plan had distinct drawbacks, especially in relation to benefits for survivors and dependents. Most federal retirees are now also covered by the social security system, since eligibility for social security can be acquired by working part-time in the private sector while holding a full-time federal job or by holding a postretirement job.

Those covered by public retirement systems at the state and local levels have been less fortunate, although gradually integrated or coordinated plans with social security have improved the situation for most workers. Still, state and local pension plans tend to be a hodgepodge of conditions and benefits that leave many workers in poor shape financially and also make movement from one locality to another very difficult. In spite of attempts to reduce this problem, the fear of forfeiting pensions because of a change in jobs for whatever reason remains a problem. When, and this is true for about 70 percent of state and local employees at the present time, a combination of social security and a public pension exists, more secure pension rights are attained. Most of these combinations, at the same time, cannot be equated with social security plus pension, which is the optimal retirement situation. Not only do the integrated or coordinated plans require some reduction in social security benefits, but the employee must also pay higher taxes to be in both plans. For the state or especially the local worker who is covered only by public pension, the situation is far worse. Many such pensions have very precarious financing, and the danger of losing the benefits through default is ever present. Also, again, the employee who changes jobs, whether by choice or by force, may well lose all.

Not so the railroad retiree, in whose behalf an advantageous "interchange" system has been worked out with social security. Originally the railroads had their own independent system, again predating social security. But as the railroads fell on hard times, the federal government intervened. The railroad industry is the only one whose pension plan is administered by the federal government. The program for railroad retirees operates like a combination of social security plus a private pension plan. Calculating the benefits is tricky, and the entire enterprise has proved very costly. Railroad workers have managed to keep "ahead of the game" by demanding and getting more than they could under social security alone, eventually even achieving benefits for survivors and dependents.

More advantaged still, providing he or she acquires the necessary twenty years of service, is the retiring military person. Because the mission of the Department of Defense and its "force management objectives" take precedence, military personnel may retire after twenty years and have an inflation-proof pension for the rest of their lives. In addition, between the ages of sixty-two and sixty-five, the military retiree will also become eligible for social security benefits. All in all, the financial benefits add up to well over 90 percent of the after-tax income of the final year of service. No other pension plan provides such a return. It exceeds even the most generous of returns from the "private pension plus social security" programs. Even though only a minority of military personnel actually stay the course for the required twenty years, it is not surprising that the costs to the government are enormous. Indeed, the military establishment is a very special case, providing many additional benefits to the retiree.

Taking all the programs mentioned above together, it is clear that there are a number of ways that retirees can reach the enviable position of having "social security plus private pension" income status. Since few persons are able to amass savings and investments that will provide any substantial income in old age, these arrangements are the most common means of achieving a comfortable old age. There are exceptions, of course. Not all private pensions yield very much in the way of retirement income, and neither do many state and local pension plans that have been tied into social security. Nevertheless, the existence of so many pension entities, all in some way included under the federal umbrella, is prohibitively costly to administrate and helps to create a highly unequal distribution of income in old age. Congressional committees and other bodies are making efforts to chip away at some of the costs, but little progress seems to have been made toward a truly integrated system that has social security as the standard for all public pension benefits and promotes "social security plus" as an ideal for all older Americans.

We would not, given the circumstances, consider the victim of black lung disease privileged because he or she gets extra income from the federal government. Although benefit levels are tied into the Federal Employees Compensation Act, the Black Lung program is in a class by itself. It provides compensation for a specific industrial group: miners who have contracted severe lung disease through long-term exposure to hazardous materials. Black lung legislation and compensation have affected primarily older persons, and this is one reason it has been included in this chapter. It is also, however, worthwhile to consider this program in juxtaposition with the plethora of federally administered or at least federally regulated pension plans just discussed. It has been noted that the uncoordinated nature of the various enterprises creates administrative and budgetary havoc. If, as seems likely given all the evidence being presented about exposure to other hazardous materials, the history of the Black Lung Program is an example of others to follow, there is a quagmire ahead. If the federal government, which will in all probability be forced to take the responsibility, cannot effect a reasonably coordinated and evenhanded pension system, how can it possibly cope with a series of new claimants in the hazardous materials arena?

By contrast, taxation legislation favoring the elderly seems to follow quite logical rules. As a group, those over age sixty-five do not have to file returns until income reaches a higher level than that of those under age sixty-five. They are entitled to double exemptions and have until the present time been exempted from paying taxes on social security and basic railroad retirement. While the tax breaks benefit all old people, those with low incomes may far more often be exempted from paying any tax at all or may even receive tax credits. It is possible that the provision allowing a one-time exclusion for any gains made through the sale of a home favors older persons with higher incomes. On the other hand, better-off older persons will now have to include social security benefits in their tax calculations.

The other two programs, Energy Conservation and Legal Services, are specifically intended to assist lower-income persons, including older persons. The Energy Conservation Program has in fact served primarily the elderly poor, while the Legal Services Program has helped at least some small proportion of this group. While any financial help must be counted as a blessing for older persons with low incomes, none of these programs offers more than either a small amount of money (or goods) or possible assistance in being accepted into a public program offering financial benefits. All three financial assistance programs must surely be considered as federal largesse to older persons, but in fact the tax program is the only one with major impact. The two that overtly favor the older person with lower income offer only minor assistance and, in fact, may well be slated for the axe in the near future.

V / Major Medical Programs

1. Introduction

For many decades there have been proponents of a national health care program in the United States. Leading politicians, indeed presidents of the United States from Theodore Roosevelt to Harry Truman, have supported such a program. And public opinion polls over many years have demonstrated that the majority of all adult age groups in the United States have favored a national plan for medical care and medical insurance.[1] Other western countries, some considerably poorer than our own, offer viable medical plans for all their citizens.[2] Yet in the United States this has been a subject of long and often acrimonious debate. When it was finally accepted that a comprehensive plan in any form would not be approved by either the Senate or the House of Representatives, let alone both, a compromise was reached. According to the incremental approach adopted, the first group to be covered would be the elderly. Experience with covering medical expenses for this group so that adequate care would be ensured would eventually be used to extend the coverage to other age groups. From this compromise the major programs, Medicare and Medicaid, were born in the mid-sixties. Developments around implementing these programs, as will be described, have probably pushed the "eventually" of a comprehensive medical program off into the distant future.

The rationale for beginning with the elderly—since no more than a beginning was feasible—certainly seemed to be sound. As age increases, so do medical care costs. The elderly have more chronic illnesses and are hospitalized more frequently and for longer periods than those sixty-four and under.[3] And, as has been discussed earlier, the incomes of older persons decrease substantially so that more persons aged sixty-five and older are living at, near, or below the poverty line. Older Americans spend about three times as much on medical care as younger age groups.[4] Even with the health programs in effect, larger sums still come out of their own pockets. In 1977, for example, Medicare benefits paid only 43 percent of all the health expenses of the aged.[5] Before the programs were put into effect, the burden on the elderly was obviously enormous, especially for persons with lower incomes,

131

who had to use up large proportions of their incomes for medical care or remain unserved or at least grossly underserved. Medicare was intended to provide universal health benefits for the elderly. Medicaid was to provide health benefits to several categories of the needy, including the needy elderly. The successes and limitations of these programs will be recounted in the next section of this chapter.

Medicare and Medicaid will occupy most of our attention since they are the giants among the federal efforts to improve the health of the elderly. However, federal efforts to attack health problems of the elderly take many forms. They range from these two huge programs costing billions of dollars and affecting millions of aging persons to one academic person using a modest research grant to pursue the solution to one perplexing question. The administration of some of the benefit plans is extraordinarily complicated as federal laws and regulations pursue goals to aid the elderly and at the same time attempt to accommodate the desires of the medical and health service professions.

The two programs stemming from legislation enacted in 1965 constitute the most important elements of the federal effort. The Medicare program was established especially for the elderly; the Medicaid program, although applicable to all age groups, has been especially valuable to the aged poor, particularly those in nursing homes. The federal government has become involved in assisting in the building of nursing homes and in regulating them. This involvement will also be discussed as it ties in with other aspects of medical care for the elderly. Additionally, the federal government expresses concern for the medical needs of the elderly through a relatively small but growing system that provides financial support for research on aging and through a series of service programs for target groups likely to be unserved or underserved, some of whose members are elderly. All of these programs will be discussed in the next section. The third and final section of the chapter will be devoted to a summary analysis on the medical programs described.

2. The Programs

MEDICARE

In 1965 health insurance was made an integral feature of the federal government's program of aid to the elderly. For three decades there had been sporadic controversy over the establishment of some form of government-sponsored health protection for all persons. Although the end result, Medicare, is a program intended to aid the elderly, it has had strong repercussions for the entire nation in the whole area of delivery of health services. Today Medicare "is the most universal of all Federal health programs for the elderly, servicing essentially the entire elderly population."[6]

Compulsory health insurance had been advocated by Theodore Roosevelt and the Progressive Party in 1912. Initially the proposal was approved by the American Medical Association.[7] However, in 1920 the AMA reversed its position and for the next decades vehemently opposed any suggestion of government-sponsored health insurance. In 1934, one reference to health insurance in the social security bill caused such a violent reaction that the Ways and Means Committee deleted it.[8] During succeeding years, legislative supporters of a national system were too few in number to achieve passage in either house. President Truman's vigorous support in the early 1950s was without effect.

Failure brought a search for alternatives, and subsequently a new proposal was born: "An incremental approach was substituted for a comprehensive one."[9] The concept of health insurance for the entire population was narrowed to one of a program for the aged; they were the ones with the largest medical expenses and were the least able to pay. A proposal was developed whereby hospital insurance would be financed through the increasingly popular Old Age and Survivors Insurance system. In order to lessen AMA opposition, there was to be no interference with the normal means of payment for the services of physicians.

Congressional interest in the new proposal developed slowly. However, beginning in 1958, in the waning years of the Eisenhower administration, annual hearings were begun. In theory, health costs of the poor aged were provided for in 1960 by the enactment of the Kerr-Mills Bill, a needs-based approach that required participation and partial financing by state governments. In practice, many of the states refused to participate. Five states with 32 percent of the aged population obtained almost 90 percent of the funds. Notwithstanding this sorry record, the proponents of the new proposal— Medicare, as it is now called—were unable to produce the votes in Congress for its passage. Nor was President Kennedy's support sufficient.

The national elections of 1964 were crucial to the future of Medicare. President Johnson had campaigned for improved health care for the aged. His landslide election brought almost immediate results. Medicare was given the congressional symbols indicating highest priority, HR 1 and S 1. Congressman Wilbur Mills, chairman of the Ways and Means Committee and a previous opponent of the administration proposal, assumed leadership in molding several bills into a new and expanded measure. After some modification by the Senate and the resolution of over five hundred differences in conference, the bill was passed by large majorities in each house and signed by President Johnson on July 30, 1965.[10]

The 1965 act, a "strange mixture, brewed by adept political alchemists," consists of three parts.[11] Part A is a compulsory hospital insurance program linked directly to social security and financed by a separate payroll tax. Part B is a voluntary medical insurance program financed in part by monthly premiums. The third part, Medicaid, a joint federal-state operation, is an assistance program aimed at providing for the medical needs of the eligible aged and others.

The new act provided a grace period of eleven months before health insurance for the aged was to take effect nationwide on July 1, 1966. Implementation of the program involved establishing standards of quality for institutions desiring to participate. Hundreds of hospitals were required to upgrade their facilities and the care they provided. Within ten months after the start of operations, over 6,800 hospitals were participating. In that same time about 4,000 extended-care facilities with half of the skilled nursing beds in the nation were approved for participation, together with 1,800 home health agencies and 2,800 independent laboratories. A new day was beginning to dawn for at least half of the nation's elderly who previously had no health insurance protection whatever.[12]

Once enacted and put into operation, Medicare was well received by the public. Indeed, the popular acceptance of the new program resulted in a rapid expansion of hospital admissions. Costs also increased rapidly, and the management of the program became a burden. The 1965 enactment of a health insurance system for the aging proved to be not just one increment in a soon-to-be-developed health plan for the nation. Instead, a decade and a half later, the country was searching for ways to establish reasonable controls over a system that had undergone unprecedented growth and had produced a seemingly endless series of difficult issues.

Part A—Hospital Insurance (HI)

The purpose of Part A of Medicare is to cover the costs of medical services (as distinguishable from physicians' services) in institutional settings. Hospitals are the principal recipients of funds, with lesser sums going to skilled-nursing facilities. Services for home health care are also included. The purpose of the Part B of Medicare is to cover physicians' and certain other services and equipment. Parts A and B are financed separately.

Part A pays for up to 90 days of inpatient hospital care in any benefit period. A benefit period may be as long as 90 days, covering one or more hospital admissions. The deductible is paid only once in each benefit period. However, in 1983 the insured had to pay the first $304; after 60 days and up to 90 days the patient paid the daily rate of $76. If a stay longer than 90 days was required, the insured paid all costs. However, a lifetime reserve of 60 days may be drawn upon by the patient's payment of $156 per day. There are also related benefits; for example, entitlement to 100 days in a skilled nursing home, providing the treatment pertains to the condition that required hospitalization, that is, for post-hospital care. After 20 days, the insured had to pay

$38 per day. Home health services, such as visiting nurse and various therapy services, may also be included, providing the treatment relates to the condition requiring hospitalization.

To finance Part A, the employee and the employer are required to pay a tax, just as in social security. In 1966, each was to pay .35 percent on annual taxable wages not exceeding $6,600. These monies were to be deposited in the Hospital Insurance Trust Fund. The rate in 1983 had risen to 1.3 percent on wages not exceeding $35,700. Persons over age sixty-five not eligible for social security may obtain Medicare hospital insurance protection by paying a monthly premium.

Eligibility for Medicare is not automatic for anyone reaching the age of sixty-five. The program is tied into social security. Just as a specified number of quarters of coverage is necessary to obtain retired worker benefits, eligibility for Medicare benefits is contingent upon a similar arrangement. Approximately 1 million persons in 1976 were outside the Medicare system. Civil service annuitants constituted the largest single group of those excluded. Annuitants with the requisite quarters of social security coverage are included, as are those who participate through the payment of premiums.[13]

The administrative mechanisms that operated Part A differed significantly from those that operated basic social security. It was initially under the general supervision of the Social Security Administration; the government was not the direct operator. Instead, providers of services, that is, hospitals, extended-care facilities, and home-health agencies, were to select "fiscal intermediaries" approved by the Department of Health, Education, and Welfare. These intermediaries, or third parties, were organizations with which the hospitals were familiar, such as the Blue Cross Association and commercial insurance companies. The intermediary was paid by the government not only for contracting with service providers such as hospitals but also for performing a host of administrative services in connection with the program.[14] The intermediary was reimbursed for administrative costs. Benefit payments under the program were covered in full by the federal government. In 1980 there were seventy-five intermediaries, sixty-seven of them Blue Cross plans.[15]

Medical Hospital Insurance, 1981 (in thousands)[16]

Number of Bills: Persons aged 65 and over	13,162
Amount Reimbursed	$24,171,267
Inpatient Hospital	23,190,190
Home Health	613,175
Skilled Nursing Facility	367,902

In 1977 the Health Care Financing Administration (HCFA) was created by combining personnel from the Social Security Administration and other units.

HCFA has general supervision of both Medicare and Medicaid. Service providers choosing not to work with an intermediary are serviced by HCFA's Office of Direct Reimbursement.

Part B—Supplementary Medical Insurance (SMI)

Doctors' services are paid through Medicare's medical insurance program. Individuals eligible for enrollment in Medicare may elect to obtain medical insurance. Once the insured has paid out seventy-five dollars for expenses in a year—the medical insurance deductible—the program will pay 80 percent of reasonable charges for additional covered services—in effect, co-insurance. Part B also provides other benefits such as covered outpatient hospital and home health-care services. Enrollment in Part B, or SMI, is not contingent upon entitlement to Part A, or HI.

To finance Part B, the enrollee pays a monthly premium rather than a tax. This sum is matched by the federal government from general revenues. Initially, the premium was $3.00 monthly. In 1983, it was $13.70 and is scheduled to rise to $15.30 in July 1984. The premium is deducted from the individual's social security payment and placed in the Federal Supplementary Medical Insurance Trust Fund.

As in Part A, HCFA supervises but does not operate the program. Carriers, principally Blue Shield but sometimes commercial insurance companies, enter into contracts with the secretary of the Department of Health and Human Services to process claims and to make payments for services. The carrier also serves as the channel of communication between the government and those supplying the services. In 1980 there were forty-three carriers operating in sixty areas; twenty-nine were Blue Shield associations.

There are two methods of paying the physician, or supplier. Payment covering 80 percent of the reasonable charges as determined by the carrier may be made directly to the insured. The doctor's or supplier's charges are not confined to the reasonable charge. Payment may also be made by the "assignment" method. By accepting assignment, the physician agrees to receive as full payment the amount determined to be reasonable by the insurance carrier. Medicare pays 80 percent of the reasonable charge. The remaining 20 percent is paid by the patient. If the physician does not accept assignment, the patient must pay the difference between the physician's charge and the amount of reimbursement permitted by Medicare.[17]

A study of assignment practices in 1975 revealed that physicians were more inclined to accept assignment for persons aged eighty-five and over. The authors of the study were unable to determine whether acceptance of assignment for the older person was due to recognition of the decreasing assets of the aged or whether many of the patients were Medicaid participants, for whom acceptance of assignment was mandatory for the physicians who treated them. Acceptance of assignment for aged beneficiaries was found to vary from Oregon's 18 percent to Rhode Island's 80.6 percent. The study found no geographic pattern. Indeed, the rates in states next to each other sometimes differed greatly.[18] In recent years the assignment method has decreased in acceptance among physicians. In 1969, 38.5 percent refused to accept the assignment method. In 1978, 49.6 percent refused.[19] One obvious consequence of this growing refusal to participate has been the increasing lack of protection for the Medicare beneficiaries who must pay the roughly 50 percent of unassigned claims. A recent study declared that physicians' charges in excess of Medicare reasonable charges increased nationally from $81 million in 1969 to $699 million in 1977.[20] Overall costs for Part B in 1981 were as follows:[21]

Medicare Supplementary Medical Insurance, 1981

Number of Bills: Persons aged 65 and over	136,558
Amount Reimbursed	$8,608,990
Physicians	6,724,177
Outpatient Hospital	1,240,324
Independent Laboratory	137,942
Home Health	135,284
All Others	723,093

Soaring Costs

No sooner was Medicare established than a series of difficult financial and administrative problems developed. One of the most persistent was that of soaring costs. Actuarial estimates were repeatedly short of actual expenditures. Within the last decade, also, hospital costs have risen dramatically, not only because of inflation but also because of expenses for capital and equipment, specialized services, and ancillary services such as laboratory work.[22]

Payments to hospitals, extended-care facilities, and home-health agencies were to be made on the basis of reasonable costs. The notion "reasonable" was open to many interpretations. For a time, reimbursement was on a cost-plus basis, but this method was dropped in 1969 because it "created an unhealthy economic incentive to maximize operating costs."[23] Moreover, the initial assumption that the fiscal intermediaries would exercise extensive cost controls proved to be in error. As a consequence, abuses were frequent.

Congressional concern with spiraling health costs took a new turn in the early eighties. Attention was focused on Medicare's Federal Health Insurance Trust Fund, in which revenues were dependent upon one portion of social security payroll deductions. Reports of the social security trustees and the Congressional Budget Office warned that program expenditures would substantially exceed revenues to the end of the decade. Hospital costs attributable to Medicare beneficiaries were projected to increase 13.2 percent annually, a rate more than double the projected increase in income. The end result was estimated to be a deficit of over $400 billion by 1995.

The major overhaul of social security in early 1983 included a number of changes aimed at exerting increased control over Medicare costs. Instead of continuing the practice of reimbursing providers on a "retrospective, cost-based system," the act provided for a "prospective" payment system. This plan was not developed overnight nor was it to be put into effect immediately. The Tax Equity and Fiscal Responsibility Act of 1982 had required the secretary of Health and Human Services to develop a prospective payment plan. The act required the Senate Finance Committee and the House Ways and Means Committee to participate in the process of development. Borrowing from plans in effect in a number of states, particularly New Jersey, and making use of a patient classification system developed at Yale University, the new payment plan enacted in 1983 provides for 467 "diagnostic related groups," or DRG's. Each of the 467 DRG's has a different payment rate. Briefly stated, the patient's rate is set in advance according to the circumstances of the case. Adjustments are made in the rate also depending on the location of the hospital—that is, whether it is in an urban or rural area or in an area where higher or lower wage and labor costs prevail. Beginning in 1986 and every four years thereafter, the secretary of Health and Human Services, together with an advisory group, is required to consider needed adjustments in treatment and payment patterns. The program is to be phased in initially over a period of three years.[24]

Another approach to controlling costs is to increase competition. A voluntary Medicare voucher system, for example, was suggested in the administration's 1984 budget as one means of furthering competition. The voucher would enable the Medicare beneficiary to shop around and thus, it is hoped, obtain the precise health service needed and at a reasonable cost.[25] Among the unknowns in the procompetition approach are such questions as whether low-cost insurance options might result in individuals underinsuring themselves and to what degree quality of care would be affected. A Congressional Budget Office study has pointed out that the voucher system would alter greatly the Medicare entitlement from one providing "a defined set of medical services when needed" to one providing money "to be applied toward the premiums of qualified private health plans."[26] The difference is substantial.

Professional Standards Review Organizations and PRO's

When Medicare was first initiated in 1965, participating hospitals were required to establish procedures for determining that patients were receiving appropriate care. The process was known as "utilization review." The review could encompass one or many areas of inquiry. For example: Is surgery necessary in this case? Should a second opinion be required? Is hospital admission necessary or could the patient be treated as an outpatient? Is the patient, once admitted, receiving unnecessary services?

In order to formalize the machinery for utilization review and at the same time to check rapidly escalating costs, the Social Security Amendments of 1972 provided for the establishment of Professional Standards Review Organizations (PSRO's).[27] The nation was divided into 203 PSRO areas. Any physician was free to become affiliated with the local PSRO. State Professional Standards Review Councils were set up in areas where there were three or more local PSRO's. At the top, a National Professional Standards Review Council advised the secretary of HEW and developed regional standards.

In the years since the PSRO's were established, they have been concerned to a large degree with what is called "concurrent review," that is, questions relating to admissions and length of stay. The expectation was that the process would reduce both. For example, if a decision was made by the peer group of physician examiners within a hospital that continued stay was unnecessary, both patient and attending physician had a right to appeal. A denial, however, resulted in the prohibition of reimbursement by Medicare or Medicaid. Most hospitals performed their own review under contract with the local PSRO.

PSRO's also conducted "medical case evaluations" to uncover medical-care practices of poor quality. A third, although relatively little used, activity was "profile analysis." This involved statistical studies of large numbers of cases in order to identify areas requiring special attention.

The effectiveness of PSRO's eventually came under intense scrutiny. Indeed, one authority observed that "the PSRO program has been subjected to a greater evaluation effort than any federal program in history."[28] A 1979 study of the Congressional Budget Office declared that the utilization review process had effected only minor cost savings.[29] The nature of the system itself worked against the achievement of the large results anticipated when the PSRO's were established. Most hospitals, for example, perform their own reviews. A local review team is placed in the uncomfortable position of working against the long-range interest of its own physicians and hospital administrators by making findings of unnecessary admissions and overextended stays. This factor becomes especially important in periods of low occupancy. The study recommended changes in the PSRO program to make it more cost effective as well as an examination of other options aimed at lowering health care expenditures.[30]

Increasing dissatisfaction with the PSRO's, and, indeed, efforts by the administration to eliminate them completely, led to a change in name and a reorganization of the review structure. In 1982, Congress created the Peer Review Organization (PRO) Program, to become effective in 1984. One hundred and forty-three PSRO's are to be consolidated into fifty-two PRO's.

Although the new organization has the same basic function as the old, various changes in the Medicare reimbursement system have "diminished," according to the administration, the need for the newly created PRO's.[31] The 1983 Social Security Act revisions, however, require hospitals to contract with the PRO's for review of topics such as admissions, quality of care, and other matters.

Hospices

One recent step to correct the imbalance in the overall system of health care has been the extension of Medicare reimbursement to hospices. The goal of hospices is to care for the terminally ill, not to cure the patient—that stage is passed. Rather, hospice programs emphasize helping the patient—whether at home or in an institutional setting—to approach death as free as possible from pain and stress.

The first hospice program was established in the United States in 1971. After a decade of relatively slow growth, the "hospice movement" suddenly caught on, and by July 1981 there were four hundred hospices in operation and another four hundred planned. Legislation in 1982 resulted in the authorization of Medicare payments to persons under hospice care. Nationwide, an estimated 50–70 percent of hospice patients are over age sixty-five.[32]

Equality of Treatment

Administering Medicare uniformly throughout the country has been a recurrent problem. In theory, for example, every person covered has access to the same benefits. In actuality, there are striking differences. Studies indicate that families with incomes of over fifteen thousand dollars receive through Part B greater benefits than do those with lower incomes. It is quite possible that persons with higher incomes go to the specialist more quickly. However, it is apparent that the annual deductible fee and the 20 percent co-insurance requirements restrain lower-income persons from seeking medical help. There are inequalities according to race and region as well: "the groups with the poorest health—blacks, rural residents, and people living in the South—receive the lowest benefits from the program."[33]

In addition to the problem of achieving uniform treatment of beneficiaries, there is also the problem of achieving internal administrative uniformity. One major proposal under consideration would combine Parts A and B under a single contractor. Administrative costs, it is argued, could be greatly reduced. Moreover, this development would have the beneficial effect of eliminating confusion among beneficiaries who do not understand the necessity for dealing with two organizations: one for hospital benefits and another for doctors' bills. The initial reason for this separation, namely, the delicate negotiations with representatives of the medical profession, would seem to be no longer a valid basis for continuing a cumbersome and confusing system.[34]

Relationships with the medical profession, indeed, are an important though largely untouched element of cost control. One authority has declared that "the solution to a Medicare shortfall lies . . . in examining the forces driving the medical care system itself—an engine running out of control. This examination must focus on physicians. . . . In no other industry are senior decision-makers so unaccountable for the economic consequences of their actions." [35] Proposed changes include paying physicians a set amount depending upon the diagnosis rather than, as at present, paying a fee for each service provided. This change, it is argued, would "give physicians an incentive to hold down costs." [36]

In summary, Medicare has its serious faults, yet its accomplishments have been enormous. Virtually overnight, most elderly persons became eligible for hospital care, physicians' services, and other supportive help. Without basically altering the system of health services, Medicare provides the elderly with financing mechanisms to meet many of the costs of illness. Nevertheless, in at least two respects, all but the most affluent elderly remain vulnerable. In the event of catastrophic illness, or when long-term custodial care is required, the benefits of Medicare may be quickly exhausted. Then the only recourse may be to Medicaid, the federal-state program that varies greatly from state to state and is repugnant to many older people because of its welfare connotations. Thus, despite the advances that Medicare has brought, it can be considered only as a way station on the road to an adequate system of care for the elderly ill. And even the way station has become shakier of late with the mounting costs the patient is asked to assume.

MEDICAID

Medicaid is an assistance program operated by the states under federal and state guidelines. Its principal objective is to provide medical care for the poor. The program is applicable to certain categories of needy individuals—the aged, the blind, the disabled, and families with dependent children. In 1982, of Medicaid's 21.9 million recipients, 3.4 million or 15.4 percent were elderly. However, 36.3 percent of Medicaid funds were expended on those aged sixty-five and older. [37]

Medicaid Recipients, 1982 (in thousands)

Total recipients	21,936
Age 65 and over	3,368
Blindness	85
Permanent and Total Disability	2,836
Dependent Children under 21	9,656
Adults in Family with Dependent Children	5,402
Other Title XIX Payments	1,454

Medicaid Vendor Payments, 1982 (in millions)

Total payments	29,906
Age 65 and over	10,854
Blindness	174
Permanent and Total Disability	10,500
Dependent Children under 21	3,565
Adults in Family with Dependent Children	4,174
Other Title XIX Payments	638

Medicaid came into being in 1965, a "relatively unnoticed" companion to Medicare.[38] Emphasis upon hospital insurance and other health services for the elderly obscured the changes in the already existing federal-state program of medical assistance for the needy. The principle had been established three decades earlier when federal funds were made available to the states for the medical expenses of the needy unemployed. With the passage of the Social Security Act in 1935, provision was made for a social insurance system and also for a categorical public assistance system. The needy aged were one of the categories eligible for federal-state funds. Monthly assistance payments included limited medical care costs. Payments were made directly to recipients, a practice altered in the 1950s when the states were authorized to pay the vendor, that is, the doctor, nurse, or health institution. By 1960, four-fifths of the states provided limited medical services through the categorical assistance program.

Growing congressional concern for the aged ill was expressed through the passage of the Kerr-Mills Bill in 1960. A new categorical program—Medical Assistance for the Aged—provided somewhat higher matching funds for medical care. Moreover, a new concept was introduced: that of the medically needy. An aged person could receive assistance provided that his income, less his medical expenditures, placed him below the eligibility level. Federal reimbursement to the states varied from 50 to 80 percent, depending upon per capita income.

The new program was not well received. A few of the more wealthy states, notwithstanding their lower percentage of reimbursement, obtained most of the funds. For example, in the first two years, five states with 32 percent of the nation's elderly received 88 percent of the federal matching monies. At the end of three years only twenty-eight states had programs in operation.[39]

President Johnson's emphasis on health care for the aged in early 1965 resulted in legislation establishing two new titles in the Social Security Act: Title 18, Medicare, and Title 19, Medicaid. Included in the latter was a series of changes affecting medical assistance payments. Not only were the needy aged eligible for medical assistance but also those covered by the categorical programs of aid to the blind, aid to the disabled, and aid to families with dependent children. All were included in the new title, Medicaid.[40]

Types of Services

Federal regulations specify required services. Those of special importance to the elderly include:

Physician's services
Inpatient hospital services
Outpatient hospital services
Laboratory and X-ray services
Skilled nursing services
Home health services

Other services specified by federal law may be provided at the option of the individual states. Those applicable to the aged include:

Clinic services
Prescribed drugs
Dental services
Prosthetic devices
Eyeglasses
Private-duty nursing
Physical therapy and related services
Other diagnostic, screening, preventive, and rehabilitative services
Emergency hospital services
Podiatrist's services
Optometrist's services
Care in institutions for mental disease
Care in institutions for tuberculosis
Institutional service in intermediate care facilities

In addition, with the approval of the secretary of Health and Human Services, other services authorized by state law may be provided. The scope of coverage of the services—for example, the number of outpatient visits permitted within a given period of time or the number of inpatient hospital days allowed per year—is within the jurisdiction of the state. States may require nominal cost-sharing for optional services. For example, several states levy minor copayment charges on prescription drugs. The options, obviously, cause the costs of medical services in different states to vary substantially.

Eligibility

In thirty-five states, the criteria for Supplemental Security Income (Title XVI of the Social Security Act) are used to determine eligibility for Medicaid. Title XIX (Medicaid) authorizes, but does not require, a state to follow the

SSI definition. States may use a more restrictive standard, and fifteen states have chosen to do so.[41] However, the state must permit the individual to deduct medical expenses in determining income and to establish Medicaid eligibility by "spending down" to the eligibility standard in effect in 1972, when the act providing for SSI was passed.

States have the option of including in the Medicaid program those persons who are defined as "medically needy."[42] These individuals have sufficient income to pay daily expenses, but not enough to pay for medical care. Their income may be low, but not sufficiently low to qualify them for welfare cash assistance. An elderly individual receiving SSI would, in most states, quality as a medically needy person. In those states where the SSI recipient did not automatically qualify by incurring medical expenses, the person may "spend down" to the states determined level for eligibility as one of the medically needy. One great advantage of the program is the protection it provides against catastrophic medical expenses. The income level varies among the thirty states that have the program. At least five states (Connecticut, Louisiana, Michigan, Vermont, and Virginia) established different income levels within the state, depending upon the individual's location.

Payment for Services

The reimbursement rate is generally determined by the states. However, Medicare's reasonable-cost system must be followed for hospital care. Moreover, the secretary of Health and Human Services must approve the reimbursement arrangements for both skilled nursing and intermediate care facilities.

Reimbursement

Medicaid reimbursement to physicians is a tender issue. There is "no uniform national reimbursement philosophy."[43] Fiscal agents employed by the states administer fee schedules. The physician's charge may not exceed the established fee. Inadequate levels of reimbursement are cited as reasons for the refusal of some physicians to accept Medicaid patients. Indeed, roughly one-third of physicians are in this category. Efforts of the states to reduce costs by lowering fee schedules may be counterproductive. The patient unable to locate a physician may opt for the hospital outpatient department, usually a more expensive approach. The "medical mill"—providing an increased volume of often unneeded services—is one method used by unscrupulous physicians to circumvent the lower fee schedule.

Administration

Medicaid is an intergovernmental program involving federal, state, and local units. Each state is required by federal law and regulation to submit a plan of operations. If the plan is approved, federal funding amounting to between 50 and 83 percent of the cost of services is made available. The variation in the percentage is dependent upon the state's per capita income. Of total medical payments amounting to $32.2 billion in 1982, the federal share was $17.4 billion. State expenditures amounted to $14.8 billion. Medicaid funds provided 39 percent of all nursing-home-care expenditures.[44]

The states, in turn, depend upon local assistance offices, usually the county welfare or social services unit, to work with the individual recipients. The local unit determines the individual's eligibility in accordance with federal and state guidelines.

In most states the actual processing of vendor claims is handled by third-party fiscal agents under contract with the state. A few states administer their own programs, and a few have what are called health insuring agreements under which, for a per capita premium, the contractor pays claims. The end result is a host of separate programs that encompass, besides the states, the District of Columbia, Guam, Puerto Rico, and the Virgin Islands.

The enabling legislation gave the states enormous leeway in the kinds of services they would provide and in the methods they would use to distribute them. As a consequence, the federal government, through the Health Care Financing Administration, has had a relatively small amount of authority. One device recently developed to introduce a greater degree of uniformity in operating procedures is called the State Medicaid Management Information System (MMIS). HFCA will pay 90 percent of the system's development costs and 75 percent of the operating costs for each state. Whether this approach will reduce administrative conflict remains an open question. The federal stance has been to avoid conflict for fear of driving the states out of the program. A strict approach, it is argued, would deprive the recipients of needed services.[45] The elderly poor, as well as other recipients of Medicaid, would thus be without a major source of medical care.

Relationship with Medicare

Although Medicaid and Medicare are separate programs, they are related in ways that are important to the individual patient. For example, a low-income individual may be covered under both programs. Part A of Medicare takes care of inpatient hospital services. However, coverage under Part B, the supplementary medical insurance programs for physician services, involves a monthly premium. The Medicaid program under a "buy-in" agreement pays the premium, the deductible, and provides for any copayment items and services covered by Medicaid but not by Medicare. The states receive federal payments for the medically needy. Over 90 percent of the states and jurisdictions have "buy-in" agreements. This arrangement was used in 1978 to make payments on behalf of 83.8 percent of the 3.4 million elderly Medicaid recipients.[46]

Problems

Medicaid has had an unusual series of problems. Rapidly rising costs and abuses stemming from fraud of various kinds, such as the Medicaid mills, nursing home scandals, and a host of others, have resulted in corrective efforts at both the federal and state levels. In a number of instances the states have reduced the coverage of mandatory services. Certain of the optional services have been eliminated.

Although in numbers, as previously noted, the elderly constitute less than a quarter of Medicaid patients, they are responsible for approximately 40 percent of Medicaid's total expenditures. As costs have mounted, many proposals have been advanced to curb program growth. Among these are proposals to reduce eligibility and services, share costs, alter reimbursement policies, and many others.[47]

In summary, the dominant role given to the states by the basic Medicaid law has resulted in the offering of a different degree of service in each state. As costs escalate, the question being asked with increasing frequency is whether the federal presence should be altered. Some advocate giving the national government greatly increased control. Others argue that the nature of the services requires a closer relationship between recipients and local assistance staff than could easily be provided by a totally national operation.

In endeavoring to assess the strengths and weaknesses of Medicaid, a haunting question recurs repeatedly. Can a medical plan that attests to the nation's deep concern for its less fortunate members be devised and enacted? For all its good intentions, Medicaid is obviously not meeting the medical care requirements of many of the needy.

NURSING HOMES AND LONG-TERM CARE

In 1977 there were an estimated 1,126,000 elderly living in the nation's 18,900 nursing homes. The elderly made up 86 percent of the total nursing home population. Forty percent, were aged eighty-five and above, or two-fifths of that total age group. The ratio of women to men was approximately three to one, an evidence of the difference in life expectancy (table 2).

National, state, and local public monies accounted for 57.2 percent of nursing home expenditures, or $7.3 billion out of the total of $12.8 billion. The principal public source of financing was Medicaid, which accounted for 86 percent of the $7.3 billion. Medicare accounted for 5 percent of public funds. Other public programs and the Veterans Administration made up 9 percent.[48]

Extensive federal involvement in nursing homes did not develop suddenly. Nor was a plan for patient care the first consideration. In 1954, during the Eisenhower administration, the Hospital Survey and Construction Act of 1946, commonly known as Hill-Burton, was amended to provide $10 million

Table 2
Nursing Home Residents Aged 65 and over in 1977

	Number	Percent
Total 65 and above	1,126,000	100.0
65–74	211,400	18.8
75–84	464,700	41.3
85 and above	449,900	40.0
Sex		
Male	294,000	26.1
Female	832,000	73.9
Race and Ethnicity		
White (not Hispanic)	1,059,900	93.2
All others	66,100	

Source: National Center for Health Statistics, *Health, United States, 1982*, DHHS Pub. No. (PHS) 83–1232 (Public Health Service, Washington: U.S. Government Printing Office, Dec. 1982), p. 108.

for the construction of nursing homes by public and nonprofit agencies. The program was under the jurisdiction of the Public Health Service, which had the responsibility for Hill-Burton. Nursing homes were thus linked with hospitals. They "would never again be solely an extension of the welfare system; they now belonged to health policy as well."[49]

Proprietary nursing homes were not included in the 1954 legislation. However, through a newly formed lobbying organization, the American Nursing Home Association (now The American Health Care Association), authorization was obtained for federal help in financing capital costs.[50] In 1956, the Small Business Administration began to make loans for renovation and new construction. The loans, limited to one hundred thousand dollars, were often shared with local banks. A much larger program became operative in 1959 when the Federal Housing Administration obtained authorization to provide mortgage insurance to lenders of up to 90 percent of the cost of the project. These actions, combined with the advent of Medicare and Medicaid, provided a special stimulus to an expanding industry. Entrepreneurs discovered that large profits were possible from the operation of nursing homes, especially considering the liberal patient reimbursement policies.

In the late 1960s the stock of corporate chains of nursing homes sold at greatly inflated prices. The bubble burst in the early seventies because of various scandals and tightened regulations at both federal and state levels. Corporate chains remain prominent, although there has been no recent surge toward increased nursing home capacity.[51] As of early 1981, the two largest investor-owned firms were Beverly Enterprises with 38,488 beds in 327 facilities and ARA Health Services with 31,325 beds in 265 facilities.[52]

Help in the financing of nursing home construction is simply one area of federal involvement. A second area, obviously, is that of supplying public funds for patient care. In 1979, for example, roughly one-half of all nursing home costs were met by Medicaid. With federal approval, states develop "reasonable cost related" reimbursement rates.[53]

Requirements concerning operations constitute a third area of federal involvement. Nursing homes seeking reimbursement must meet the standards set forth in the Code of Federal Regulations. "Extremely detailed in some areas but extraordinarily vague in others," the standards are minimums that states may exceed.[54] Charges of inadequate standards by witnesses before the House Select Committee on Aging were summarized in the 1979 report of the Senate Special Committee on Aging: "Advocates for nursing home patients described continuing instances of indiscriminate drug therapy, inadequate food, severely limited nursing care and physician attention, little or no supportive social or mental health services, and inadequate rehabilitative therapy. Advocates said that nursing home patients were still being denied basic rights, including refusals to allow visitors, manipulation of patients' personal funds and indiscriminate and hasty transfers from one nursing home to another without sufficient notice or preparation."[55]

In addition to issues pertaining to quality of care, the projected substantial increase in the elderly population, particularly of those over age seventy-five, poses policy questions with respect to the availability of nursing home space. Estimates vary concerning the number of persons that will require institutionalization, but almost certainly it will be considerably greater than can now be accommodated. Alternatives such as adult day care, homemaker services, congregate housing, and others may partially stem the pressures for institutionalization. But what may be gained through increases in community-based services may be lost through changing family characteristics. The climbing rate of divorce and the increase in the employment of women diminish a family's ability to provide care for aging parents.[56] The end result may be a considerable expansion in various types of institutions such as skilled- and intermediate-care nursing homes as well as the largely custodial domiciliary-care institution. One recent study declared that "rising nursing home expenditures are likely to contribute to making long-term care the most problematic area of social policy over the next generation."[57]

Nursing home issues pertaining to space, adequacy of standards, and ever-rising costs are some of the facets in an increasing awareness of the need for other ways of achieving a comprehensive program of long-term care. The Federal Council on Aging, for example, has emphasized the necessity of providing programs to aid "the oldest of the old... usually but not always those over the age of seventy-five." Present policies, the council has declared, ignore those living at home, "whose best interests may be served by remaining at home."[58] A core of basic support services that would supplement the existing arrangements of relatives or others could enable many frail elderly to avoid institutionalization.

The Council on Aging has not been alone in the belief that a successful program of long-term care requires a multifaceted approach. The General Accounting Office has pointed out that federal programs such as Medicaid have greatly overemphasized nursing home care and have provided almost no help for community services. In 1978, for example, nursing home expenditures accounted for 41 percent of total Medicaid expenditures while less than 1 percent went for home health care services.[59]

Recognition of the imbalance in the current system of health services, has resulted in a variety of research and demonstration projects focusing on issues of long-term care.[60] Public awareness of the long-term care needs of the elderly is also increasing. It is doubtful, however, whether any large percentage of the population is aware of the startling increase in the number of long-term care cases that may be anticipated in future decades. From 1980 to 2020, the population of those over the age of eighty-five is expected to increase from 2.9 million to 7.9 million. A large percentage of this group as well as many of those in the sixty-five to seventy-five and seventy-five to eighty-five age groups will require nursing home or community-based health and social services. The development of an appropriate and affordable program of long-term care presents a challenge that will require sustained effort to meet.

In summary, the burgeoning nursing home industry has been supported in large part by public funds. The great majority of the patients in these institutions are elderly, and the very old are overrepresented. The growth in the number of nursing homes has been accompanied by much criticism because of overcosting and inadequate care. The federal government is attempting to address these issues. The future holds many problems since existing facilities may not be sufficient to accommodate the numbers of infirm aged in the coming years. Some feel that institutionalization is not always the best solution for the affected population and advocate a search for alternatives. As yet little of the public monies available have been allocated for such a search.

FEDERAL HEALTH RESEARCH AND SERVICES

Within the last decade, public awareness of the substantial demographic changes now under way has been increasing. One of the greatest of these changes is in the proportion of elderly to the total population. In 1900 only one in every twenty-five persons was over age sixty-five. In the early 1970s the ratio had escalated to one in ten. However, in the next fifty years, the number is projected to increase even more dramatically until by 2030 one person in five will be over sixty-five. Greater attention, certainly, must be focused upon research specifically directed toward the health problems of the elderly.

Research into the Aging Process

The origins of a specific governmental unit to concentrate on studies of aging date from 1940. With the aid of a grant from the Josiah Macy Foundation, federal health personnel working with staff from the Baltimore City Hospitals established a research unit that subsequently became the Gerontology Research Center in Baltimore. The agency is most widely known for the Baltimore Longitudinal Study of Aging, which began in 1958 as an annual two-and-one-half day examination of 650 volunteer male subjects. Some of the volunteers were in their twenties while others were in their nineties. Volunteers who died or left the program were replaced by other volunteers. Women were added in 1978.[61] Two years later, 180 women were enrolled.[62]

In 1948, research into the process of aging was made the responsibility of the National Heart Institute. When the National Institute of Child Health and Human Development was created in 1963, one of its missions was to conduct research on aging. A major step was taken by the Congress in 1974 with the passage of the Research on Aging Act.[63] The National Institute on Aging (NIA) was created "for the conduct and support of biomedical, social and behavioral research and training related to the aging process and the diseases and other special problems and needs of the aged."[64] In the next months the Geriatric Research Center and the Adult and Development Branch in the National Institute of Child Health and Human Development became the core units of NIA.

NIA carries on a variety of activities in the health field. For example, consensus development conferences make known new procedures and technology considered to be safe and helpful by exports on aging. To illustrate, a conference in 1980 attempted to point out the distinction between "curable physical and psychological diseases" producing impairment and brain disease that was irreversible. Another conference examined the management of terminal illness giving special attention to the hospice movement.

The expanded Social and Behavioral Research Program has recently been launched with emphasis upon aging as "part of the life continuum" rather than as an experience that begins at the age of sixty-five. Studies of a series of diseases of the elderly are the province of the Epidemiology, Demography and Biometry Program. The Basic Aging Program is concerned with the study of cells, and the Biophysiology and Pathobiology of Aging Program makes use of laboratory animals to accumulate knowledge about the aging process.[65]

In addition to studies by members of its own staff, NIA supports research into aging through grants to individuals in universities and hospitals. It also collaborates with other units of the National Instieus of Health and with roughly twenty other federal agencies involved in research into aging.[66] The National Cancer Institute, for example, is concerned with the aging cancer patient. The associated problems of cancer and aging require the mutual contributions of both institutes. Similarly, NIA has a variety of relationships with the Center for Studies of the Mental Health of the Aging, a unit of the National Institutes of Mental Health. Although NIA may now be said to occupy center stage in the field of aging research, it is by no means the only agency concerned. For example, the Department of Energy conducts research "directly concerned with the aging process" with certain contractor facilities, for example, with the Radiation Effects Research Foundation on atom bomb survivors and with the Los Alamos National Laboratory on plutonium workers.[67] Through eight Geriatric Research, Education and Clinical Centers (GRECC's) the Veterans Administration conducts research relevant to diseases of aging. In addition, the GRECC's promote clinical and psychosocial studies on aging at a number of VA medical centers.[68]

The budget of the National Institute on Aging, which has grown from $29,879,000 in 1977 to an estimated $95,670,000 in 1984, is one indication of the increased emphasis on research.[69] These figures must be compared with the total estimated outlay of $4.3 billion for federal health research in 1984. All research into aging amounted to slightly over 2 percent of the total.[70]

Notwithstanding the recent substantial increase in research studies related to aging, geriatric medical research is in an early stage of development. The former director of the National Institute on Aging, in testimony before the Select Committee on Aging, pointed out the need for research in instances where the elderly person is the victim of more than one disease.

It is really hard to believe, but it is true, that in the United States we do not have such studies. For instance, my own Institute at the moment does not have a research clinic program where we can study what it means to have an average of six drugs going into the body at the same time, the impact of one disease upon the other, the meaning of changes in the way in which symptoms present themselves as we grow older because of differences in our thermal regulation, our pain response.

We simply have to have that type of research, geriatric medicine. That is my name for it; but we do not yet in the United States have any significant major programs in those areas.

As I see it, we have about 20 years to catch up with it before we run into some very serious problems with the burgeoning population of older Americans, not to mention the fact that we have people today who deserve to have the kind of care that can only follow upon having the sort of knowledge that you get from direct scientific study.[71]

Health Services for Special Groups

Health benefits provided by the federal government to the elderly are extensive for some portions of the population and minimal, if not totally absent, for others. The existence of this condition is not because of indifference to the needs of many individuals and groups but rather because of the variety and complex nature of the problems. Some groups have been able to make their needs known. Others have been less fortunate. The programs, if any, that meet the needs of the latter have come in response to the requirements of a much larger population group. In these cases the elderly might constitute a small portion of the total served.

For example, Community Health Centers (CHC's) which numbered 588 in 1982, exist for the purpose of aiding approximately 4 million persons living in medically unserved or underserved areas. Of those receiving the services, 8.7 percent are aged sixty-five or above.

The Indian Health Service provides health services to the more than 800,000 Indians and Alaskan Natives who reside in roughly five hundred reservations scattered over twenty-eight states. The National Indian Council on Aging conducts annual conferences on the health of the elderly thus focusing attention on the 5.2 percent, or approximately 65,000 Indians and Alaska Natives, over the age of sixty-five.

Elderly migrant workers are aided by a 1978 amendment to the Public Health Service Act, which specifically authorized the 128 migrant health centers to provide services to former workers who because of age or disability could no longer be employed. Of the 394,000 migrants and seasonal farm workers served in 1982, about 5.6 percent were sixty-five years old or older. Merchant seamen, military personnel, and other "statistically defined population groups" eligible for treatment included numbers of elderly. Among the health professionals serving the special groups noted above were the 2,115 members of the National Health Service Corps. In 1982 they served 2.2 million persons. Approximately 9 percent of these were sixty-five years old or older.[72]

In summary, federally sponsored research in the field of aging has had a slow start, and although funds for this research are growing, they still constitute a small part of the research budget. While many aspects of aging are included in research options, geriatric medicine is in the forefront so that it can be tied in with other health care programs.

The federal government also intervenes by providing medical services to a number of special target groups. Only small proportions of such groups may be over the age of sixty-five but these programs do provide some options for older persons who might not be served under the more general health care programs.

3. Summary Analysis

Decades of effort failed to win sufficient support to mount a national health insurance program. Finally, a compromise was reached involving an incremental approach, and a pilot program for the elderly became the immediate goal. Elderly persons were selected as the first target group because it could be proved that they bore an uneven and far heavier share of medical expenses. In the early expansive years of the Johnson administration, priority was given to legislation for health care for older people. Passage of a somewhat awkward three-part bill was accomplished in 1965.

Medicare, intended entirely for older people, was divided into two parts. Part A, hospital insurance, involves compulsory coverage. A proportion of the monthly paycheck deduction for social security is earmarked explicitly for this purpose. About 96 percent of the monies paid out under Part A go for hospital insurance.[73] Although Part A also allows some reimbursement for skilled nursing and home health care, both of these are strictly tied to posthospitalization expenses. Approximately 2 percent of what is paid out under Medicare goes for each of these purposes. Medicare has been very severely criticized for its emphasis on hospital care, especially since a social security contributor has no choice but to buy into it. Critics argue that elderly persons are thereby pushed into hospitals when they have no real need to be there and that longer hospital stays are encouraged because home help for the convalescent is so difficult to obtain. Critics also maintain that paying so much money into hospital care is not only wasteful but inhumane. Much of the funds, they believe, could be better spent in finding alternatives that would serve the needs of the elderly in more satisfying ways. Although in very short supply, some alternatives are available for older persons who need care but do not need to be in a hospital. But Part A, from which the bulk of the money for Medicare comes, has included no coverage for anything other than hospital expenses and, until very recently, small amounts for posthospital care. It is now possible to turn to Medicare to pay costs for hospice treatment for dying patients. Wherever possible these patients, the great majority of whom are older persons, are kept in their homes and treatment is brought to them. While this development offers some balance in favor of home care, hospice patients are as yet relatively few in number. Also, hospice patients must be judged to be terminal, that is, beyond medical treatment except for the relief from physical pain. Home care for the medically treatable elderly ill remains virtually nonexistent.

Briefly summarized, the person covered by Medicare is entitled to a certain number of days in a hospital after an initial fee is paid out of his or her own pocket. The patient must also pay a partial fee after a specified number of days, and eventually the patient bears the full cost if the stay is a lengthy one. Medicare will also cover up to 100 days in a skilled nursing home if the treatment provided is related to the condition that required the patient to be hospitalized in the first place. A patient may also request a limited number of home health services from specific categories. But basically, Plan A provides for hospital expenses, and it is this hospital cost payment for which the social security payee contracts in the monthly paycheck deduction.

Part A is so concentrated on hospital care partly because of the felt need of legislators when Medicare was passed to pacify the American Medical Association. Part B of Medicare covers physicians' charges and outpatient costs. Over 80 percent of the monies paid out under Part B are used to reimburse patients for physicians' fees.[74] This part of Medicare is voluntary, however, and those who participate must pay a monthly premium in addition to the social security tax. The rule of thumb is that Medicare will pay for 80 percent of the "reasonable" charges made by physicians, while the patient pays the remainder. The retiree who belongs to Part B may also receive reimbursement for outpatient care, although in practice it is clear that physicians receive most of Part B funds.

The goal of the third part of the medical care legislation, Medicaid, is to help not only the elderly poor but also needy persons who are blind and disabled. This program is operated by the states under federal-state auspices. In most instances, Medicaid is tightly coupled with SSI. That is, if the person is eligible for SSI, he or she is also eligible for Medicaid. However, the individual states have a good deal of authority in administering Medicaid programs, and some states are more restrictive than others in their criteria as to who is "needy." The federal government does specify required services, but the states may add others. The states also make key decisions about service delivery, such as the number of inpatient visits that will be covered in a given time period.

Basically, Medicaid gives an eligible needy older person coverage equal to what would be given under Parts A and B of Medicare. As has been noted, eligibility may be judged somewhat differently from state to state. The federal government does require, however, that states permit deduction of medical expenses when determining income and that they also permit persons to gain eligibility by "spending down." Spending down means getting rid of any financial assets that might put the person seeking help over the specified income level. Critics of Medicaid label spending down "pauperization." It should be mentioned that although Medicare is linked to social security and Medicaid to SSI, persons not covered under those two programs may still be able to apply for either Medicare or Medicaid, depending on their circumstances. In fact, as was mentioned earlier, some older persons are covered by both.

Medicaid, in particular, is very closely linked to the nursing home industry, paying about two-fifths of nursing care expenditures. For the elderly, by far the largest population group residing in nursing homes, more than half of the costs are paid by Medicaid. The federal government has supported this industry in other ways as well. Large amounts of federal monies have been appropriated for the construction of nursing homes. As might be expected, Medicaid has been criticized, as was Medicare, for its emphasis on institutional care rather than on other options that might permit older persons to remain in their communities. Very little of the monies disbursed by Medicaid are for in-home services.

The federal government is involved in medical care for the elderly in other ways as well. A small but growing number of research dollars are devoted to geriatric medical research. And the government has a set of programs to assure that the unserved or underserved in the population receive necessary medical care. The barriers that otherwise might prevent access to care through the major programs for these special groups may be related to geographical isolation or to unique historical/cultural features.

In implementing Medicare and Medicaid, the federal government and the states have given a great deal of latitude to the private sector. Vendors such as hospitals, nursing homes, and physicians and intermediaries such as the Blue Cross Association have been largely responsible for cost standards. The same parties have had a determining voice in other aspects of service delivery, such as how long a patient needs to stay in a hospital or whether he or she needs to be in a hospital at all. Perhaps such a strategy was seen as necessary to get the medical programs approved in the first place. But this partnership between government and the private sector has not been a happy one for "the party of the first part." Costs have skyrocketed since the advent of the major medical programs, far outrunning all estimates. A part of the problem may be laid to inflation, but much has to be attributed to overcharging and even to overtly fraudulent practices. Since the early seventies the federal government, beset by scandals, has been working to tighten its regulations and to curtail costs. At the present time it is beginning to implement a plan that will match length of permissible hospital stay to particular illnesses and surgical procedures. Whether these efforts will effectively stem the terrible tide of rising costs has yet to be discovered.

In the meantime, older persons are bearing more and more of the burden of costs. For example the initial amount that Medicare patients must pay for hospital care and the supplemental payments after a specified number of days have increased sharply. Physicians have often refused to accept Medicare-stipulated fees, and, rather than paying the expected 20 percent of the costs for physicians' services, older patients are frequently paying as much as 50 percent. Medicare, once such a tremendous boon for older people, is becoming less and less helpful in defraying medical costs. There are many proposals to reduce the costs of Medicaid as well. These will also reduce the proportion of eligible older persons and the services that would be available to those still eligible. The great promise of the mid-sixties to free the elderly from their unusually heavy burden of medical costs has not been kept. The future of these major medical programs has been placed in some doubt and is yet to be determined.

VI / Two Auxiliary Programs

1. Introduction

While the attention of the nation has been riveted in recent years on social security and the major medical programs for the elderly, other smaller but still potentially vital services are getting short shrift. Of the two to be considered here, perhaps transportation should be given foremost attention. As was mentioned in chapter II in the discussion of the Aging Network, transportation has been a priority among the services afforded under the Older Americans Act. If other services are to be given to the elderly, ways and means must often be found to transport older persons to the place of delivery. This problem, especially as it pertains to older persons whose mobility is limited in some way, has proven to be an extremely complex one. Relatively little attention was given to transportation in chapter II, since the programs in this area address far more than a means of receiving needed services. There are in fact a large number of programs, each having different sponsorship and different conditions. The purpose of most is not to help the elderly in particular, although more specific attention has been given to older and handicapped persons since 1970. Transportation, because of its complexity and vital role in linking people to the world around them, deserves a section by itself. The efforts in behalf of the elderly have so far met with limited success, and there is evidence that those efforts may be declining.

Other programs that have met with only limited success, in spite of a demonstrated need for them, are those in the area of housing. Again, multiple approaches have been launched from different quarters with a notable lack of coordination and equity across sectors and target groups. Some of the programs have served primarily the elderly, and, again, concern for the housing needs of the elderly has increased over time. But the housing programs have addressed a number of target groups with only limited impact. Little has been accomplished in providing affordable and accessible housing suited to the special needs of the aging population.

Transportation and housing issues address basic needs for mobility and adequate shelter that those who are handicapped and/or economically disadvantaged find difficult to fulfill. The programs are not very substantial, but these crucial life areas do need to be included when policy for the aging is considered.

2. Transportation

Governmental programs to improve the mobility of the elderly have proliferated in recent years. The magnitude of the problem apparently was not fully recognized until the White House Conference on Aging in 1971, which ranked transportation third in importance. Only income and health were placed ahead of the "sleeper issue."[1]

At first glance, the problem of getting a person from here to there seems simple enough. Difficulties quickly arise, however, when the person has impairments of a physical, psychological, or economic nature. Problems are compounded by the location of the individual and by the transportation process itself. The combination of the individual's impairments together with the person's location and the kinds of available transportation result too often in a problem that evades solution. The end result is the absence of much-needed mobility.

Federal efforts to help the elderly have met with limited success. The primary objective of some programs has been to provide a social service; transportation has been incidental. This accounts in large measure for a considerable amount of legislation. Indeed, a congressional subcommittee is reported to have assumed that a staff research error was responsible for the announcement that transportation services for the elderly were funded by thirty federal programs. In fact, there had been no error. The subcommittee learned, somewhat to its dismay, that each program operated under totally different sets of guidelines. Restrictions governing participation that related to age, residence, income, physical condition, and other factors seemed reasonable when considered as a single program. "Taken together," the committee declared, "this maze of possible Federal financing has bewildered and hampered state and local officials across the country."[2]

Notwithstanding the more than thirty federal programs that may be used as potential sources for funding, there are only a few that deal with transportation per se. Most of the federal efforts to improve transportation are directed toward the entire population, of which the elderly may represent a small fraction. As an integral portion of the whole, the elderly benefit. But many of the eldely cannot benefit unless special efforts are made to make possible their participation in the transportation system.

PUBLIC TRANSPORTATION

The value of a public transportation system can scarcely be overestimated. With all of their advantages, however, most public transit systems present a variety of problems to the elderly, some of which are so serious as to render them impossible to use. In recent years the federal government has endeavored to identify these problems and, by means of research and demonstration projects and other devices, assume the leadership in improving the mobility of the elderly. But some aspects of the total problem virtually defy solution.

Lack of income is obviously a major factor in limiting mobility. The individual on a relatively fixed income may be hard pressed to meet the rising fares demanded by the transit agency, itself plagued by escalating fuel prices and increasing labor and equipment costs. Routing is also a major factor. The overriding purpose of a public transit system is to serve the work force. The central business district is the normal focus of transit traffic, although major factory or other work locations may also be important. Routes that are not important to the work force are usually nonexistent. This condition is understandable from an economic standpoint. As a consequence, however, use by the elderly is limited to routes that were established for purposes often having little relationship to the interests of this particular group of potential users. Related to the routing problem is the problem of scheduling. Long waits for vehicles of transportation are often necessary during the middle of the week and on Saturdays and Sundays as the transit agency endeavors to keep its operating expenditures to a minimum.

The use of public transit by the elderly is limited also by a host of barriers within the system. The frail elderly are especially vulnerable. The first barrier is that of getting to the bus stop or subway station. One or more blocks of walking may overtax the physical capacity of the aging person. Other barriers include inclement weather, extensive waiting and standing, the absence of shelter, fear of attack, and fear of darkness. Boarding the vehicle may involve steps that are almost impossible to negotiate, if it is a bus, or steps across a seemingly bottomless pit between the platform and the vehicle, if it is a subway car. Once the vehicle is boarded a new series of barriers emerges. The availability of seats, the often lurching vehicle, the difficulty of knowing one's location—these are a few of the problems confronting the elderly passenger. At the end of a bus or subway trip, the older person may be exposed to a repeat of the first series of problems.[3]

The barriers to mobility facing the elderly—and indeed, those of all ages—are especially acute for the group classified as the transportation handicapped. A national study released in 1978 indicated that 47 percent of the over 7 million urban transportation-handicapped population was over sixty-five years of age. The transportation handicapped were defined as those who, though not homebound, "experienced general problems" involving sight, hearing, the need for mechanical aids, and others, that impaired mobility.[4] According to the study, where there was a choice, the transportation handicapped used an automobile, although often as passengers rather than as drivers. Most used the bus; for some it was the only means of transportation. The percentage of subway usage by the transportation handicapped was less than half that by the nonhandicapped. Generally, they traveled during nonrush hours. Thirty-nine percent of the transportation handicapped needed personal assistance.

Programs of the Department of Transportation

Federal efforts to improve the mobility of the elderly fall largely within the jurisdiction of the Department of Transportation. The Urban Mass Transportation Agency is responsible for implementing the Urban Mass Transportation Act of 1964. The act's declarations of policy express the intent of Congress to recognize the special needs of the elderly. For example, an amendment in 1970 provided as follows: "It is hereby declared to be the national policy that the elderly and handicapped persons have the same right as other persons to utilize mass transportation facilities and services; that special efforts shall be made in the planning and design of mass transportation facilities and services so that availability to elderly and handicapped persons of mass transportation which they can effectively utilize will be assured."[5] Following are brief summaries of the major programs provided for by the act.

1. Section 3. Capital Grants. Grants are available to state and local public transit bodies for land, vehicles, and supporting facilities. Grants are to support projects largely in areas of fifty thousand or greater population (urban areas) and are to meet the needs of all, not just the elderly.

2. Section 5. Capital and Operating Formula Funds. Monies are apportioned to the states based on urbanized population and can be used for capital purposes or to defray operating deficits.

3. Section 5 (m). Reduced Fares. Transit bodies receiving Section 5 funds must offer reduced fares to the elderly and handicapped during nonpeak hours.

4. Section 6. Research and Demonstration Projects. Limited monies are available for the broadrange of special projects. Some of these are specifically related to the needs of the elderly.

5. Section 9. Technical Studies. Grants for technical studies could be utilized, for example, to relate the elderly individual to the public transit system.

6. Section 16 (b) (2). Nonprofit Corporations. Two percent of Section 3 monies may be granted to nonprofit groups for vehicles and equipment to meet the needs of the elderly and handicapped.

7. Rural Programs.

  a. Section 3. Areas with fewer than fifty thousand inhabitants may be included for MMTA capital grants.

  b. Demonstration projects in rural areas are authorized under the 1973 Federal Aid Highway Act.

c. Rural areas are included in Section 16 (b) (2) grants to nonprofit organizations.

REGULATIONS INTENDED TO AID THE ELDERLY AND HANDICAPPED

Mass transportation projects in most urban areas are the recipients of federal capital or operating assistance. In order to obtain the financial assistance, the transportation agency must comply with the laws of Congress and the regulations of the Department of Transportation, Section 504 of the Rehabilitation Act of 1973. The regulations interpreting this section have proved to be a major source of controversy. Section 504 provides that "no otherwise qualified handicapped individual in the United States . . . shall, solely by reason of his handicap, be excluded from participation in, be denied the benefits of, or be subjected to discrimination under any program or activity receiving Federal financial assistance."[6]

Three years after the act was passed, President Ford instructed the Department of Health, Education, and Welfare to provide guidance to the federal agencies.[7] In 1976 the Urban Mass Transit Administration issued regulations aimed at helping elderly and handicapped persons. The definition of the group for whom the regulations are intended is instructive.

Elderly and handicapped persons means those individuals who, by reason of illness, injury, age, congenital malfunction, or other permanent or temporary incapacity or disability, including those who are non-ambulatory wheelchair-bound and those with semi-ambulatory capabilities, are unable without special facilities or special planning or design to utilize mass transportation facilities and services as effectively as persons who are not so affected.[8]

Detailed regulations apply to newly constructed stations and terminals. There are, for example, regulations relating to boarding platforms, fare collections systems, and elevators. In newly procured buses, regulations specify maximum floor heights and require front door ramps or lifts and interior handrails and stanchions. An illustration of the degree of regulatory specificity follows: "The vehicle doorways shall have outside light (s) which provide at least 1 foot candle of illumination on the street surface for a distance of 3 feet from all points on the bottom step tread edge. Such lights shall be located below window level and shielded to protect the eyes of entering and exiting passengers."[9] The regulations endeavoring to provide full access to buses were reflected in a 1977 order by Secretary of Transportation Brock Adams that new buses should have a floor height no greater than twenty-two inches and that provisions be made for lowering the floor to eighteen inches at the loading point. Moreover, the bus was to be equipped with wheelchair lifts or ramps. The extensive costs involved in complying with the order resulted in requests for variances from a number of cities. In September 1980, the Metropolitan Transit Authority of New York voted not to comply with the access regulations relating to buses and subways.[10] Had this decision been implemented, the city might have lost $435 million in transportation aid. Recognition of the costs involved for all transit operators led the Congress to enact compromise legislation. Operators were permitted to by-pass the regulations, provided alternative service could be made available. However, a percentage of new buses were required to be equipped with lifts.[11] With the recent decrease in operating subsidies, scheduled for complete elimination by 1985, further flexibility will probably be introduced into the regulations requiring accessibility to public transit.[12]

Federal efforts to improve the mobility of the elderly and handicapped embrace the major forms of transportation. Following are recent illustrations of the types of activities of major units of the Department of Transportation as reported to the Senate Special Committee on Aging.

Federal Aviation Administration developing uniform procedures for transporting elderly and handicapped persons; funds for improving terminal facilities in accordance with American National Standards Specifications; information dissemination to advise airport personnel and handicapped persons about special services; training personnel for assisting elderly and handicapped in emergency situations.

Federal Highway Administration funds for facilities to accommodate elderly and handicapped on Federal aid highway systems; concern with the design and construction of pedestrian overpasses and underpasses; training courses relating to transportation for elderly and those involved with programs for the elderly.

National Highway Traffic Safety Administration developing performance and equipment guidelines for handicapped persons; encouraging states to develop programs for elderly with respect to driver instruction and pedestrian safety.

Urban Mass Transportation Administration funds for capital equipment to private nonprofit organizations; studies of wheelchair lifts for standard buses.

Research and Special Programs Administration insurance barriers faced by social service agencies in transporting elderly.[13]

TRANSPORTATION FUNDS FOR SERVICE DELIVERY

Although there are over thirty federal programs that may be used as potential sources for transportation funding, most are concerned with service delivery. The Comprehensive Older Americans Act Amendments of 1978 authorize grants to states for "transportation services to facilitate access to social services or nutrition services or both."[14] By regulation, area agencies may make agreements to share transportation costs with other agencies administering social service programs, for example, those under Titles XIX and XX of the Social Security Act.[15] Other programs that provide the elderly with transportation or transportation reimbursement include the various units making up the Department of Labor's Senior Community Service Employment program and ACTION's Retired Senior Volunteer Program, Foster Grandparents Program, and Senior Companion Program.

Transportation is vital to the success of many of the social services. It is not, however, the primary program objective. A major operating problem is that of providing a reasonable degree of coordination. The problem takes many forms. User eligibility restrictions, for example, stem from legislative action or administrative regulations. A social program to serve one group includes restrictions limiting the service to that group. Unless there is initial coordination between agencies in the preparation of administrative regulations, merging transportation needs to accommodate different groups becomes difficult. Age and income restrictions in determining eligibility for acceptance into a particular program may also be translated into restrictions applying to transportation.

In the past, those charged with developing social service programs have had few links with transportation experts. Indeed, the House Select Committee on Aging reported in 1976 that "transportation planning agencies concerned with the long range have generally shown little concern about the implementation of social programs and how their needs for transportation may be integrated into the regular transportation process."[16] This lack of coordination may result in the development of an expensive trial-and-error transportation system by the service delivery agency.

Coordination is also frequently difficult because of franchise arrangements. As a means of preserving an appropriate operating territory, the franchise may provide strict limits with respect to picking up passengers by buses, commuter railways, and taxicabs. Dial-a-ride systems, for example, have been struck down by the courts as franchise violations.[17]

Difficulties with coordination, in short, may arise from various sources. Seldom can they be overcome without a concerted attack from many levels.

RURAL TRANSPORTATION

Organized transportation services are almost totally absent in rural areas of the country. As a consequence, an estimated 3 million elderly and handicapped, in common with their younger and physically able fellow citizens, are limited almost entirely to one form of transportation—the private automobile. But for large numbers of the elderly and the handicapped—and for many others—the automobile is not a solution. As a consequence, many are "living lives of frustrated immobility."[18]

The Select Committee on Aging declared in 1976 that "there is no clear center of responsibility for rural transportation."[19] A number of the social agencies operate programs that cover rural areas to a limited degree. However, the transportation that may be provided incident to the specific service does not address the more general problem of the need for a transportation system.

Federal assistance for rural areas has been made available to a limited degree through Section 16 (b) (2) of the Urban Mass Transportation Act. In Missouri, for example, a nonprofit corporation, the Older Adults Transportation Service, Inc. (OATES), operated over 100 vans in 89 of Missouri's 115 counties. One-quarter of the vans are lift-equipped. The service is demand-responsive, that is, requested in advance. Membership in 1979, when there were thirty-two thousand enrolled, was limited to those over age fifty-five and to the handicapped. The fare varies among the counties, depending upon the amount of local support. The minimum was 4½ cents per mile. Revenues accounted for 20 percent of costs, the balance coming from donors and grants under the Urban Transportation Act, the Older Americans Act, and the Social Security Act.[20]

Another source of federal funding has been Section 147 of the Federal Aid Highway Act. Monies are confined to research and demonstration projects. Thus, the program does little to meet long-term transportation needs. Model projects, the Select Committee on Aging has pointed out, "have built in discontinuity. Often the local agencies cannot muster sufficient resources to continue even a successful demonstration once Federal Aid is terminated."[21]

In summary, the short-run prospect of increased federal attention and support aimed at improving the mobility of the elderly appears rather bleak. As federal operating subsidies are reduced, the already financially hard-pressed mass transit systems in many cities will be required to concentrate on economies rather than extensions of service or on costly alterations in vehicles and stations.

In the long run, however, government at all levels must strive to overcome the many kinds of transportation barriers that now impede a large percentage of the total population and are especially frustrating for large numbers of elderly and handicapped persons. For those in urban and suburban areas, public transportation systems provide a substantial segment of the population with "a lifeline to their community and a chance to remain involved in society's mainstream."[22] Lamentably, a considerable proportion of those living in rural areas are without any means of public transportation. Whatever the location, new approaches—especially new financial approaches—must be undertaken to provide "lifeline" mobility. Wherever they are located, older persons generally face significantly larger problems in getting to and making use of transportation systems.

3. Housing

Concern for the elderly played little part in the federal government's entry into the field of housing. Congress had conducted hearings on slums and blight as early as the 1890s. During World War I, several thousand units of housing, chiefly dormitories, were constructed to house workers in shipyards and munitions plants. However, substantial federal action did not come until the period of the Great Depression when the credit system failed and the entire economy was in deep trouble.

For many families, the danger of financial collapse was averted by the creation, in 1933, of the Home Owners Loan Corporation. It was given authority to purchase mortgages, thus eliminating the danger of foreclosure. At one point, over 15 percent of the country's mortgage debt was held by the corporation. With the improvement of the economy, the Treasury was fully repaid.

A system of mortgage insurance was established in 1934 with the creation of the Federal Housing Administration. As a consequence of this protection, lenders increased the length of time in which a mortgage could be repaid and lowered the down payment. The end result was that millions of families were able to purchase homes.[23]

However, the various financial arrangements that enabled Americans to purchase their own homes were seldom extended to those with low incomes. The elderly constituted a major segment of this broad classification. The best way to provide housing for the poor seemed to be public housing. The elderly were later singled out through other programs and given special aid. However, as a general proposition, federal aid to the elderly has been to renters rather than to home-owners.

Most elderly persons live in their own homes. According to the 1975 Annual Housing Survey, there were 14.4 million elderly households in the United States. Ten million were owner occupied, including 3.5 million single-person households. Renter-occupied households numbered 4.3 million; of these, 2.7 million were made up of single persons. Of the total number of elderly households, 3.3 million were classified as poor: 1.9 million home-owners and 1.4 million renters.[24] Of all elderly households, 88 percent were white, 10.4 percent black, and 4.3 percent Spanish-American.[25]

CLASSIFICATION OF PROGRAMS

In the decades since the Great Depression, many legislative actions have been taken with respect to housing. In order to keep track of the developing programs, both the government and industry referred to a specific section of the law. One observer has declared that the "legislative section numbers and housing-agency acronyms and jargon . . . are as much a part of the housing bureaucrat's language as the most common nouns and verbs in Webster's."[26]

Federal housing legislation in general, except for veterans' housing, is directed toward all persons in specific income categories. For example, an elderly individual may qualify for a particular program because of income status and not because of age. Thus, many elderly are included in the total number of persons affected by a specific program. The housing legislation that has been of greatest importance to the elderly is summarized below in table 3.

Table 3

Principal HUD Housing Programs for the Elderly

Section No.	Program	No. of Projects	No. of Elderly Units	Elderly Units as % of Total
Construction Programs				
Title II	Low-Income Public Housing	15,100	638,375	42.9
202	Direct Loans for Housing for Elderly and Handicapped-Active	1,458	95,340	89.6
231	Mortgage Insurance to Builders of Housing for the Elderly	504	66,228	100.0
221(d)3	Multifamily Rental Housing	3,591	23,892	75.1
221(d)4	Low-Income Rental	6,289	92,110	13.6
235	Home Onwnership-Inactive	255,435	not available	not available
235	Home Ownership	80,923	not available	not available
236	Rental and Co-op Assistance	4,055	55,278	12.7
232	Nursing Homes Mortgage Insurance	1,367	162,062	
Nonconstruction Programs				
8	Low-Income Rental Assistance			
	Existing	13,969	305,023	28.5
	New Construction	10,477	425,089	63.3
	Rehabilitation	1,925	52,512	40.3
312	Rehabilitation Loans	86,004	6,243	7.25

Sources: Adapted from "A Summary of HUD Housing Units for the Elderly," *Challenge* (HUD) 10, no. 8 (August 1979), inside cover (the table above omits several programs and columns of statistical data contained in *Challenge* and updates others according to data in *Developments in Aging: 1979,* part 2, pp. 213–17); *Developments in Aging: 1982,* vol. 1, p. 300. For Farmers Home Administration Programs, see ibid, vol. W, p. 3.

Initially, public housing was one of the packages of New Deal strategies to fight the depression. The emphasis was upon the creation of jobs. The goal of providing shelter for persons of low income was included in the statement of purpose of the Housing Act of 1937.[27] Nevertheless, the primary drive was to stimulate the economy. Social reform was secondary.

The thrust of the program shifted during World War II. There was no longer a need for housing construction simply to provide jobs. Instead, public housing, both permanent and temporary, was constructed for war workers and their families near major defense plants.

Following the war, new programs were launched. The Housing Act of 1949 declared that "the general welfare and security of the Nation and the health and living standards of its people required housing production and related community development . . . and the realization as soon as feasible of the goal of a decent home and suitable living environment for every American family."[28]

Federal grants were made available for slum clearance programs. A high rate of public housing construction was authorized, and families displaced by urban redevelopment were to be given preference.[29] The 1949 act authorized the construction of 810,000 units over a period of six years. Seventeen years later, in 1966, 431,000 units had been completed. (During that same period 300,000 families and single individuals had been displaced.) Extensive public opposition had blunted the original objectives.

Despite shifts in policy emphasis, the principal means of assisting low-income elderly has been to place them as tenants in federally subsidized public housing. The subsidy took the form of financial backing for local housing authorities chartered under state law. The tenant received no cash payment. Instead, the federal government stood behind the long-term bonds issued by the local authority to finance the construction and development costs. Moreover, by means of an "annual contributions contract," the federal government covered interest and amortization charges on the bonds of the authority. The bond thus became an attractive investment: the interest was exempt from federal taxation and the principal was guaranteed. The housing project was exempt from local real estate taxes, although an in lieu payment was required that amounted to 10 percent of shelter rents.

Rents varied, depending principally upon family income. A large family that required four bedrooms might be required to pay a small differential over the amount paid by the family requiring one bedroom. Tenant selection was a function of the local authority, operating, however, within guidelines concerning the maximum income and assets of an applicant. Preferences could be established according to residence in the area and the order of consideration of various categories of applicants. The following is illustrative:

Section 3. Preferences in Selection of Tenants

This authority will give preference in the selection of tenants to applicants who reside in Greene County for at least 18 months. Eligible tenants will be selected from among resident applicants for dwellings of given sizes and within such ranges of rent as may be established to ensure the financial solvency of the projects in the following order:

First— Transfer of overcrowded or overhoused tenants when appropriate unit size is available and at the convenience of the Local Authority.

Second—Elderly families, with displaced elderly families having preference over nondisplaced elderly families.

Third— Other displaced families, with families of veterans and servicemen having preference over other families in this category.

Fourth—Families of veterans and servicemen who have not been displaced.

Fifth— Other families: Within each of the above groups, due consideration will be given to the urgency of the family's need for housing. The above order will also be followed in selecting tenants from among eligible applicants who are not residents of Greene County.[30]

Not until the Housing Act of 1956 were the elderly specifically recognized. Indeed, prior to that time elderly single persons were not accepted for occupancy. The death of an elderly spouse meant that the remaining spouse had thirty days in which to find a new home. The 1956 act provided for single occupancy and authorized public housing for elderly families.[31]

Of the various categories of public housing in 1978, 46 percent of the nation's low-rent public housing units were occupied by families that "qualified as elderly on the basis of age, disability, or handicap."[32] Of the 1,100,614 units occupied, 47.1 percent of the families were black, 38.4 percent white, 12.2 percent Spanish American, 1.5 percent Indian, and .5 percent oriental.[33]

A signficant development beginning in the late sixties was the trend of local housing authorities toward converting dwelling units for use by the elderly. The elderly had an advantage in renting since the wear-and-tear costs they incurred were lower. There was a trend also toward increased occupancy by the elderly in high rises. Other ways of increasing the quantity and percentage of the elderly in public housing units included:

1. The leasing of newly constructed or rehabilitated housing from private owners. Classified as Section 23—Leased Public Housing, the program was also used in conjunction with the development of intermediate-care facilities. The sponsor would lease a portion of the facility, such as the food service area, to the housing authority.

2. The purchase of existing private housing.

3. The use of the "turnkey" device. The authority would purchase from a private contractor units designed specifically for the elderly. After receiving the authority's letter of intent, and after agreement had been reached on plans, the developer was responsible for obtaining the interim financing and for constructing the housing units. The contractor would then sell the projects to the authority.[34]

4. Congregate housing. The federal role in providing public housing for the elderly moved through several stages. In the early years, little attention was paid to any special needs of the elderly and the handicapped. The primary aim was to provide space. Then problems of location and design were recognized as important. The current emphasis is upon the need to aid the increasing number of functionally impaired elderly. Of the estimated 28 million elderly in 1990, roughly 11 million will be over the age of seventy-five. Among this group especially there will be many in need of assistance with housekeeping, meals, and personal services.

Congregate housing was authorized in 1970 in an amendment to the Housing Act of 1937. The provision was little used, however: as one observer said, the program "languished."[35] But the Congregate Housing Services Act of 1978 infused new life into the concept of extending special services to those elderly and handicapped who were unable to care for themselves.[36] The act was said to "finally implement housing law enacted in 1976 by providing a missing element—the availability of long term financing for comprehensive service packages."[37] The service contracts, however, could scarcely be classified as long term. Those arranged in fiscal 1980 were for five years.

The Congregate Housing Services Act authorized the Department of Housing and Urban Development (HUD) to contract for congregate services with public housing authorities and Section 202 (nonprofit) sponsors. As a means of coordinating housing and human services programs, local area agencies serving the aging were to be involved in funding proposals. The act authorized funds for a four-year period, enough for an estimated fifty to seventy-five demonstration projects.

The congregate housing services program has had the effect of requiring a considerable degree of collaboration between federal agencies. The Administration on Aging, for example, which has responsibility for nutrition and other service programs (see chapter II), has worked with HUD in developing procedures for the operation of the initial demonstration projects. HUD had declared that the "program will be a significant step in preventing the premature or unnecessary institutionalization of the frail or temporarily disabled resident of HUD public housing and section 202 projects."[38] However, recent emphasis upon reducing federal participation in social programs has made the word "languished" once again appropriate.

HOUSING ASSISTANCE PAYMENTS—SECTION 8

A new approach to assisting lower-income families was adopted in 1974 with the passage of the Housing and Community Development Act.[39] Families whose incomes are not in excess of 80 percent of the median income in the locality qualify for assistance payments in three categories of housing: newly constructed, rehabilitated, or existing. The payment is intended to close the gap between the approved rent for the unit and the amount required of the family—not less than 15 percent nor greater than 25 percent of the family's adjusted income.

With respect to the new construction and rehabilitation phases of the program, both for-profit and non-profit groups, and public housing agencies as well, are invited to submit development proposals. Once the proposal is approved HUD and the sponsoring groups enter into a Housing Assistance Payments Contract spelling out the rent structure, the maintenance services, and other factors. Upon completion of construction, the government makes a housing assistance payment for each unit occupied by an eligible family. Higher-than-established fair market rents can be charged when special amenities for the elderly are provided by the sponsor.[40]

The Section 8 Existing Housing Program has been declared by HUD to be the "Federal Government's major operating program for assisting lower income families in securing decent, safe, and sanitary housing."[41] The program enables a family, after receipt of a certificate of eligibility from the local public housing agency, to seek out its own housing. The agency is responsible for informing both the family and the sponsor of acceptable housing standards and must approve any agreement reached by the two parties. The public housing agency or other sponsor then enters into a contract embodying the terms of the agreement and providing for assistance payments by the agency. Except under special circumstances, the rent, including utilities, may not exceed the fair market rent levels established by HUD for the particular area. Assistance payments may be terminated by the agency if the sponsor fails to live up to the contract. Similarly, if the lease is broken by the tenant, the agency must continue assistance payments to the sponsor for a period of up to sixty days.

In order to assist in financing new construction or substantial rehabilitation projects, the government permits sponsors to make use of multifamily mortgage insurance programs such as Section 221 (d) (3) or Section 221 (d) (4), to be discussed later.

The contribution of the renter was changed by the Housing and Community Development Amendment of 1979 and again by the Omnibus Reconciliation Act of 1981.[42] Families having very low incomes (at or below 50 percent of the median) are required to contribute from 15 to 25 percent of their incomes.

The remainder is subsidized. Those with low incomes, as distinguished from very low incomes, are required to contribute from 20 to 30 percent of the family income. The eligibility limit was reduced from 80 to 50 percent of the median income in the locality.

The Section 8 program has been criticized in recent years because of the long period—twenty to forty years—that the federal government is obligated to provide assistance. Moreover, the amount of assistance needed over this time span cannot be calculated with precision. Additional subsidies may be required. These may take the form of a "financing adjustment factor" (FAF) or tax-exempt bond issues. In either case, these subsidies to the developer further increase the cost to the government.[43] The administration's budget proposal for 1983 reflected these criticisms of the program. The amount available for new subsidies was drastically reduced.

DIRECT LOANS TO SPONSORS—SECTION 202

Concern for the housing problems of the elderly was stressed in the Housing Act of 1959.[44] The Section 202 program established in the act enabled nonprofit sponsors of rental projects to obtain construction loans at low interest rates. The act was a recognition of the need for some kind of subsidy for the shelter costs of those whose incomes were marginally above those of residents in public housing. Moreover, the act recognized the place of the private, albeit nonprofit, corporation in a subsidy operation.

The interest subsidy included in the 202 program resulted in monthly rents substantially below those charged for housing financed through market rate mortgages. Income limits for admission, set up by HUD and based on family size and geographic area, were considerably higher than the limits set for admission to public housing.

The program ran into increasing opposition within the government since monies used for the purchase of a mortgage were counted as regular budget expenditures. The money loaned had to be appropriated by Congress; every project increased the deficit. As a consequence, in 1969 the program was suspended by executive order in favor of a new interest-subsidy program called the 236 Rental Housing Program. In early 1973, this program was frozen pending a review of the government's total participation in housing. Thus, for a time, there was no new subsidized housing specifically for the elderly.

With the passage of the Housing and Community Development Act of 1974, the Section 202 program was reinstated, but with revisions.[45] The Congress no longer makes an appropriation. Instead, the secretary of Housing and Urban Development is authorized to borrow specified amounts from the Treasury. These funds are then loaned to eligible sponsors such as nonprofit organizations and consumer cooperatives. Another mechanism is also

involved. The new act embraces the Section 8 Procedure of housing allowances to lower-income families. The government is authorized to contract
with the owner to pay the difference between the fair market rent and the
amount required of the tenant. The latter is to pay not less than 15 percent nor
more than 25 to 30 percent of adjusted income. Thus, the Section 202-Section
8 approach is a principal means of providing new housing especially for the
elderly.

MORTGAGE ARRANGEMENTS

Nursing Home Mortgage Insurance—Section 232

An amendment to the National Housing Act of 1959 authorized the government to promote the construction of nursing homes by providing mortgage
insurance for both proprietary and nonprofit corporations. The mortgage may
amount to 90 percent of the value of the project, including major equipment.
A minimum of twenty nursing beds is required. Nonprofit nursing homes may
obtain Hill-Burton grants as well as FHA mortgage insurance. State certification of the need for the nursing home is required.

Intermediate facilities may also be financed by mortgage insurance. These
are "supervised living environments" for the person who is not in need of a
nursing home but who nevertheless requires regular attention by trained
persons.

A supplemental amendment, Subsection (1), authorizes additional loans to
finance fire safety equipment. Through fiscal 1981, the Section 232 program
had insured mortgages in 1,326 facilities for the elderly containing 152,255
beds.[46]

*Below Market Interest Rate Mortgage Insurance—The Section 221 (d) (3)
and 221 (d) (4) Programs*

In 1961, private development of subsidized housing was initiated through
the adoption of the Below Market Interest Rate Program, designated as 221
(d) (3). Applicable to all rather than to the elderly alone, the act authorizes the
Federal National Mortgage Association to purchase mortgage loans made to
certain categories of private organizations, such as cooperatives. An interest
subsidy makes possible the reduction of monthly rent charges. The 221 (d) (4)
program, though similar, is applicable to public and profit-motivated sponsors. The two programs, since their inception, have been responsible for the
construction of over 937,000 units. About 10 percent of these were for the
elderly.[47]

Mortgage Insurance on Rental Housing—The Section 231 Program

The National Housing Act of 1959 established a plan for promoting unsubsidized rental housing for elderly people with incomes somewhat above the incomes of those eligible for either public housing or the 202 Direct Loan Program. The Federal Housing Administration is authorized to insure the lender against loss on a mortgage for construction or rehabilitation. If the project defaults, the secretary of Housing and Urban Development is responsible for operating or disposing of the property. For example, if the demand for housing for the elderly should no longer exist, the secretary is authorized to permit a prospective owner to convert the property to straight rental housing. In the early years of the program, the "default termination record" was not a good one. Of forty-three thousand units constructed between 1963 and 1970 under the Section 231 program and a companion 207 program authorized in 1956, over nine thousand, or about one-fifth, were taken over by the government.[48] Half of the total units were concentrated in four states—California, Arizona, Florida, and Texas.

One means of bolstering the program has been to utilize the rent supplement device authorized in 1968. Although technically the program is for unsubsidized multifamily rentals, nonprofit sponsors are eligible for rent supplements. The Housing and Community Development Act in 1974 retains the 231 program as "HUD's major program for developing unsubsidized rental housing for the elderly and at the same time make Section 8 payments available."[49] At the end of fiscal 1982, 66,228 units were included in a total of 304 insured projects.

Home Ownership Assistance—Section 235

Prior to 1968, subsidy programs were concerned almost entirely with rental units. In that year a homeownership program restricted to new or rehabilitated housing was initiated.[50] The purchase was financed by the homebuyer through government-insured market rate mortgages obtained from a private lender. The homebuyer received a government subsidy that reduced his payment to the amount he would have paid had the interest rate been 1 percent. The homebuyer was required to expend 20 percent of income in reducing the mortgage and in addition was made responsible for utilities, maintenance, and repairs. The down payment required was limited to 3 percent of the value of the house. Assistance payments were restricted to buyers whose incomes did not exceed 135 percent of the admission level for public housing.

The program was deactivated in the early seventies and the unspent funds were impounded. Pressures from housing groups combined with the sad state of the housing market brought a reversal in 1975. The revised program was aimed at a higher-income group than was the original. Families with incomes no greater than 80 percent of the median in their area were eligible to obtain an interest subsidy on a major portion, or all, of the mortgage, thus reducing their monthly payments.[51] The subsidy was paid by HUD directly to the lender. Appropriation for additional assistance commitments ceased in 1981.

DIRECT LOANS TO HOMEOWNERS

Home Rehabilitation Loans and Grants—Sections 312 and 115

Low-income homeowners in blighted areas, many of them elderly, experienced great difficulty in obtaining financing for home improvement. To overcome this problem, homeowners and, in some areas, tenants living in urban renewal areas were enabled, by Section 312 of the Housing Act of 1964, to obtain low-interest rehabilitation loans direct from HUD. A year later the Housing Act of 1949 was amended to authorize grants for rehabilitation purposes through Section 115. In 1980, of the total number of loans arranged, 16.6 percent had been granted to applicants sixty-two years of age or older. Actual processing of the loans is usually arranged by the unit of government that receives a community-development block grant. The elderly make use of the program largely to cover basic repairs.[52]

RURAL HOUSING

Of the 20 million families living outside metropolitan areas, about 2.5 million reside in dwellings lacking complete plumbing facilities, namely toilet, bathtub or shower, and hot and cold running water. In 1970, one-third of the 2.5 million were classified as elderly households. Most were black.[53]

Loans for rural housing were first authorized by the Housing Act of 1949. Section 502 of this act granted the Farmers Home Administration congressional approval to loan farm families money for the construction of houses on farms. The aim of the homeownership program was to aid families with incomes below the national median who were unable to obtain financing from other credit sources. The interest credit loans reduce the effective rate to 1 percent, or 20 percent of the adjusted family income, whichever is less. In recent years, new construction has been deemphasized in favor of the rehabilitation and repair of existing housing. This is believed to be less expensive on a per unit basis. Moreover, the shift favors the low-income family as opposed to the former practice of chiefly aiding those above poverty level. The normal interest rate is 13.35 percent. Low-income applicants, however, can obtain loans at a rate as low as 1 percent.[54]

Specific recognition of the elderly came in 1961 with legislation that authorized the Farmers Home Administration to select sponsors who would construct rental apartments or cooperatives for senior citizens in communities of not more than twenty-five hundred persons. Subsequent modifications increased the population limit to twenty thousand. Interest subsidies made possible lower rents, which were limited to 25 percent of income. In addition, the Housing and Community Development Act of 1974 authorized the payment of rent supplements for low-income families in rural rental housing. In

1979 the Farmers Home Administration, under the authority of the Section 515 rural housing program, together with the Administration on Aging launched demonstration congregate-housing efforts in each of the regions formerly under the jurisdiction of the Department of Health, Education, and Welfare. The loan funds for construction are provided by the Federal Housing Authority, while AoA supports the services.[55]

A Farm Labor Housing program has enabled farm laborers to obtain loans for construction or improvement of living quarters and related facilities such as water and waste disposal systems. The loan is limited to 90 percent of the project cost and is repayable in thirty-three years. The interest rate is 1 percent. Low-income owner-occupant residents may obtain home rehabilitation and repair loans of up to five thousand dollars, repayable in twenty years. Again, the interest rate is 1 percent. Loans of up to seven thousand dollars with repayment in twenty-five years may be obtained for the improvement of substandard dwellings. The interest rate varies from 1 to 3 percent, depending upon family income. These programs are open to all, including the elderly.[56]

Low interest loans of up to $5,000 are available (Section 504) for basic home repairs in rural communities of up to ten thousand inhabitants. In 1975 the commissioner of aging declared that this provision was "one of the very few financing opportunities for low income rural Americans."[57] Elderly applicants unable to repay the loan can apply for a grant. In fiscal 1981, 504 loans amounting to $24 million were scheduled to cover elderly applicants; $24 million was made available for grants.[58]

RESIDENTIAL RENOVATION AND REPAIR

The Older Americans Act Amendments of 1975 provided for a program of residential renovation and repair. Funds were authorized to bring homes occupied by elderly persons up to minimum standards and to adapt homes to meet the needs of disabled elderly people.

Winterization programs for the elderly may be funded through the Older Americans Act, through block grants of the Housing and Community Development Act of 1974, by community action agencies, or by the Farmers Home Administration of the Department of Agriculture. In some instances the Department of Labor's Green Thumb program has supplied the labor.[59] In 1976, the Department of Energy was also authorized to operate a program. Agency regulations limit the Department of Energy's assistance to eight hundred dollars per household.[60]

NEW APPROACHES

The various federal housing programs have been criticized as "inequitable" because they reach only a small percentage of the very poor, and as "inappropriate" because they have "little to offer" those classified as poor homeowners.[61] The authors of a study prepared for HUD in 1978 declared that "by categorically excluding homeowners, the current housing assistance programs exclude the majority of households headed by the elderly, the majority of households living in units that are physically deficient, and those who devote a disproportionate share of their income to housing. This situation means sharp inequities between elderly renters and elderly homeowners and results in substantial deterioration of the existing housing stock."[62]

To improve the program balance between homeowners and renters and at the same time help younger families in need of housing space, one proposal would urge the use of condominiums by the elderly. Since many elderly no longer need the space at one time essential to a growing family, the under-occupied shelter could be sold. The proceeds could be used to purchase a modest condominium. Any needed housing subsidy could be applied toward operating expenses such as utilities, taxes, and insurance.[63]

Condominiums are of two types—the newly constructed unit and the converted apartment. The unusually rapid expansion of both types in recent years has created new opportunities for the elderly and many unanticipated problems as well. Following the abusive practices of a "destructive minority within the development industry," Florida enacted what has been described as an "exemplary" condominium law.[64] National standards to protect the elderly have been proposed by the Senate Special Committee on Aging, but as of early 1983 these had not been enacted into law.

Another proposal would benefit the elderly homeowner with low income by employing a device called the Reverse Annuity Mortgage (RAM). The RAM is simply an agreement whereby a banking institution makes monthly loans secured by the value of the house. If the owner is unable to repay the loan, HUD assumes the monthly payment, providing it exceeds a given percentage of the owner's income and a percentage of the borrower's liquid assets. This proposal has the forbidding name "double reverse annuity mortgage."[65] In late 1978 the Federal Home Loan Bank Board authorized the nation's two thousand Federal Savings and Loan Associations to include the RAM among their mortgage instruments. While commending the RAM as a useful approach, the chairman of the Senate Committee on Banking, Housing and Urban Affairs has observed that it entails "more careful counseling and planning and occasionally much more involved calculations than any other form of mortgage if the best buy is to be obtained for the homeowner."[66]

A third proposal involves a modification of Section 8. Assistance payments for operating expenses only would be made available to homeowners. The program would require standards to assure that the house was properly maintained, a problem central to virtually all proposals for assisting homeowners in order to preserve or to increase the housing stock.[67]

A variation of this plan—the housing voucher system—would require that assistance payments be made directly to the renter. The case-equivalent voucher would enable the renter to exercise choice in the selection of housing, assuming that minimum quality standards were met. Obviously, more families could be assisted in this manner than through subsidizing new construction.

One alternative to the voucher system that stems from recent attention to the concept of the block grant would be to "fold" the separate housing programs into a housing assistance block grant. The most inclusive proposals would effect a major policy shift, transferring responsibility, in large measure, to state and local governments.[68] Federal guidelines, presumably, would target the income levels of the population to be assisted.

A presidential commission in 1982 recommended that new programs be developed to cope with the projected substantial increase in the over age eighty-five cohort. Instead of expensive new construction "serving a limited number of households at a very high cost to the government," programs would be developed that make better use of equity housing. The commission suggested "home sharing and accessory housing," meaning that the elderly homeowner would rent rooms after adding bath and kitchen facilities. The commission also suggested the development of special financing mechanisms such as the reverse annuity mortgage, previously noted, which would convert home equity into income. "Sale leasebacks" or "split equity" arrangements might be developed, by means of which an elderly person would sell his or her home to an investor with the stipulation that the right of occupancy would be retained for life or for a fixed term.[69]

In summary, federal programs of housing for the elderly have had limited impact. The number of persons affected has been relatively small. As the extensive legislation now on the statute books attests, public policy has lacked direction, being pulled first one way and then another by conflicting economic pressures.

The government's future role in assisting the elderly to meet the basic need for affordable and accessible housing is far from clear. The diverse requirements of the elderly merit reexamination with a view toward providing a range of programs especially for those with the greatest need.

4. Summary Analysis

Auxiliary ways to supplement the scarce resources, not only financial but physical and psychological, of elderly persons may be found in federal programs dealing with transportation and housing. Although transportation is more prominently featured, both of these areas receive attention in the Older American Act and its amendments. However, the programs are actually formulated and implemented under other auspices, a great many other auspices, in fact. As in other areas of public policy, therefore, complexity and confusion are endemic.

The major transportation concern of the Older Americans Act was to facilitate access to services. A much broader focus was to increase the mobility of elderly and handicapped persons. Programs to achieve these ends have been faced with barriers that stagger the imagination. For those elderly and handicapped whose mobility has been increased, the benefits in being able to get out in the world to meet people, to seek recreational activities, and to perform necessary shopping tasks are very large. However, implementation of planned programs, especially those that would serve rural areas, has proved difficult and very costly. The federal government is now reducing subsidies, and financially hard-pressed transportation systems are seeking economies rather than extension of services. It seems that the efforts that have been made in behalf of the elderly and handicapped persons are in progressive decline and that the grave problems these individuals have with mobility will persist.

Housing assistance can also make the world a more comfortable place, not only materially but psychologically. Federal housing programs have been quite numerous but have been oriented toward a variety of target groups and income levels. Limited benefit has resulted for the elderly. Although some housing programs, especially public housing, have concentrated on lower-income persons and are nearly 50 percent occupied by the elderly, such housing is not suitable for all older persons, and in any case it remains in short supply. Many older persons own their own homes and would prefer to remain in them if they could have necessary repairs made. Only a small trickle of federal monies is available for this purpose. Often elderly persons, especially those with chronic illnesses or handicaps, need specially designed facilities and services. Attention to these needs has been relatively recent, and so far programs are relatively small. The elderly can get assistance for other housing needs, but the programs are scattered and uncoordinated, so that needed help is often hard to obtain. Housing programs for the elderly are regularly being proposed, but although the growth of the older population, particularly the very old, with all its attendant problems is recognized, the development of housing programs does not hold great promise for the future. It is uncertain what will be the impact of a shift of responsibility from federal to state and local levels.

The needs for adequate mobility and shelter for the burgeoning older population, especially for those who are poor and/or handicapped, has in some way become articulated in federal policy. So far the thrust of policy in both these areas has been unfocused and uncoordinated. It is very difficult to know where to turn and in what direction programs will go in the future. In spite of a great many efforts, up to now the results have been disappointing.

VII / Government and the Older Worker

1. Introduction

Once upon a time, retirement was a rarity. But during this century, in fully industrialized countries, at least, a retirement phase of the life cycle has become more and more a normal expectation. As did other countries, in implementing social security legislation in the mid-thirties the United States chose the "magic age" of sixty-five as the appropriate time for retirement to begin.

As the century matured, however, and new amendments were applied to the legislation, the concept of sixty-five as the appropriate age become eroded. First female workers and then males were allowed to take "early retirement" at age sixty-two, albeit with reduced benefits, as discussed in chapter III. In that and the following chapter the numerous incidences of even earlier retirement under special arrangements were noted. Up to this time, then, the trend has been toward earlier and earlier retirement for more and more workers. What should be the appropriate age to retire became less and less clear.

The federal government is now attempting to reverse this trend, at least insofar as social security benefits are concerned. Gradually, very gradually, the retirement age for full benefits will be raised. The penalties for early retirement will be increased. Incentives in the form of higher benefits will be offered to those who remain in the labor force beyond the specified age, and those persons who want to take benefits but also work part time will also be allowed to retain more of what they earn.

These incentives aside, however, later retirement presents problems for older workers. Age discrimination and other social forces make it very difficult for many workers to find employment opportunities even up to the age of sixty-five, let alone beyond. This chapter is therefore devoted to an overview of federal programs aimed in one way or another at assisting the older worker, whether it be through legislation prohibiting age discrimination or through providing opportunities for job retraining or volunteer work. These programs will be reviewed in section 2 and their collective impact will be analyzed in section 3.

2. Programs Benefiting the Older Worker

The older person's employment problems have not been totally ignored by the federal government. But neither have policies been developed that could be described as consistent and clear-cut. Over the years the federal emphasis has shifted substantially.

The first expression of interest developed in the 1950s when the Bureau of Employment Security in the Department of Labor made efforts to define, through research studies, the special needs of older workers. Emphasis was placed on those seeking work and especially on the kinds of training that would most help them. In the intervening decades, attention has been focused upon the young and especially upon those who are disadvantaged.[1] By the beginning of the 1980s, federal involvement with older workers was limited to three areas of interest. One of these was legal in nature while the other two were specifically concerned with the employment of the elderly poor.

THE AGE DISCRIMINATION IN EMPLOYMENT ACT

A recent study of the Senate Special Committee on Aging declared that current employment opportunities for older workers were reduced by the "pernicious" practice of age discrimination.[2] Employers who refuse employment because of the advanced age of a worker or who for the same reason force early retirement or deny promotions and increases in salaries and wages may be in violation of the Age Discrimination in Employment Act.

Protection against age discrimination had not been included in the Civil Rights Act in 1964. Congress did, however, direct the secretary of labor to make a study of age discrimination. The report, submitted to Congress the following year, declared that there existed "a persistent and widespread use of age limits in hiring that in a great many cases can be attributed to arbitrary discrimination against older workers on the basis of age and regardless of ability."[3] The response of Congress was to enact the Age Discrimination in Employment Act of 1967 (ADEA).[4]

The promotion of employment based on ability rather than on age was declared to be the basic purpose of the act. One's age, thus, could not be used as a basis for discrimination. Initially, the act applied to persons between the ages of forty and sixty-five in businesses employing twenty-five or more workers. Over the next years, the act served as the basis for much litigation.

The first source of litigation was a provision that excused the employer when there was a "bona fide occupational qualification" (BFOQ) reasonably necessary to the normal operation of the particular business or when the differentiation was based on "reasonable factors other than age" (RFOA). The second exception recognized the possible existence of a "bona fide seniority system . . . which is not a subterfuge to evade" the act. This provision, in effect, made possible collective bargaining agreements that established the retirement age at some point below sixty-five. A third exemption protected the employer who "for good cause" might discharge a worker.[5] Insubordination, for example, might constitute "good cause."

The act was extended in 1974 to include federal, state, and local government employees. At that time, also, employers of twenty of more persons came under the act. It was not until 1978 that the age limit was raised to seventy.[6] This step was precedent-shattering for it signaled to both employers and employees that there was nothing sacred about the commonly accepted "normal" retirement age of sixty-five. Federal employees were not specified in the age limitation feature of the act. Thus, age discrimination protection was applicable to all federal employees regardless of age except for special groups such as prison guards and foreign service officers.

The 1978 amendments effectively abolished the second exception noted above relating to collective bargaining agreements establishing a lower retirement age. The "bona fide occupational qualification" exception remains a stumbling block: "the real issue seems to be the lack of functional criteria available to employers on which to base fair and sensible judgements regarding the ability of older workers to meet the demands of specific jobs."[7]

The 1978 act required the Department of Labor to conduct a study of the consequences of the new features of the act. Completed in 1981, the study reported that the postponement of mandatory retirement until age seventy "would not have an adverse impact on other segments of the population and would, in fact, stimulate jobs for more than 400,000 workers over 60."[8] This is a small percentage of the 28 million workers between forty and seventy years old who are employed in businesses and industries having twenty or more employees.[9] As older workers recognize age discrimination practices, litigation may increase. The end result could be a modest increase in the total economy as well as the reduction of personnel practices having a negative effect upon many elderly persons. As of mid-1983, efforts to eliminate all mandatory retirement by statute had not been successful.

EMPLOYMENT PROGRAMS

Federally sponsored work opportunities for older persons are limited. That they could be much less limited has been demonstrated repeatedly by a series of federally funded programs that have concentrated on the poor elderly. Ever so gradually over the years, these programs were enlarged. More recently the emphasis has been in the opposite direction—to reduce or to eliminate them entirely. From those few elderly having opportunities to participate has come substantial evidence of the value of the programs both to the individuals themselves and to society as a whole.[10]

Senior Community Service Employment Programs

Federally subsidized employment programs for older workers had their origin in 1965 when the "Mainstream Amendment" was added to the Economic Opportunity Act. Twenty percent of the funds appropriated for Operation Mainstream were to support economically disadvantaged persons aged fifty-five and older. The first grant was awarded in 1966 to Green Thumb, Inc., a branch of the National Farmer's Union. Operations were begun in four states: a total of 280 persons were employed.

Operation Mainstream was transferred to the Department of Labor in 1967. With the Green Thumb experience as a model, the department arranged with three national organizations of the aging for somewhat similar programs. The National Council of Senior Citizens established the Senior Aides Program, the National Council on the Aging developed the Senior Community Service Project, and the National Teachers Association/American Association of Retired Persons inaugurated the Senior Community Aides Program. By 1972 the funding level amounted to $13 million, and five thousand older persons were employed. A fifth national contractor, the U.S. Forest Service, was added the same year, and the program became known as the National Older Workers Program—Operation Mainstream.

In the next years the employment programs were the subject of extensive legislative-executive controversy. Although the programs were maintained, the overall title was eliminated as they were absorbed under Title IX of the Older Americans Act.[11] In the 1978 revision of the act, the programs were authorized under Title V. Their collective title is the Senior Community Services Employment Program (SCSEP).

The administration of the program is the responsibility of the Department of Labor, which is authorized to arrange with public or private nonprofit agencies to servce as project sponsors. Project sponsors are expected to maintain "working linkages" with Department of Labor manpower agencies and with state and area agencies on aging. Except in emergencies, federal funding is limited to 90 percent. Matching funds are nearly all in-kind. The Forest Service, the only federal agency that acts as a sponsor, makes a 20 percent in-kind contribution covering "training, counseling, supervision, supplies and materials."[12]

Although the national sponsoring organizations operate in accordance with federal regulations, they are nevertheless free to determine their own organizational structure. Green Thumb, Inc., for example, has operated for the most part in rural areas. Green Thumb assumes direct responsibility: their own employees are in charge of all activities. NRTA-AARP and the Forest Service follow the same pattern. The National Council on the Aging and the National Council of Senior Citizens operate through subcontractors. Actual operations are conducted by public or private nonprofit sponsors at the state or local level. At the local level, the national contractors have "host" agencies that utilize the services of the older workers—the enrollees.[13]

The program is aimed at "economically disadvantaged" persons who are fifty-five years old and older and who are eager to work and to earn income. Federal regulations speak of "the restorative experience of community service work."[14] Priority in hiring is given to those aged sixty and above. Annual family income may not exceed 125 percent of the poverty level. The work period is limited to twenty hours per week. Workers receive the minimum wage. Sponsors are informed that the program is not intended to displace an already employed worker. An objective of the program is to move enrollees into unsubsidized employment as quickly as possible. The employment needs of minorities are to be considered and the hiring of minorities should be in proportion to their numbers within the state's population.

One major recent development has been the inclusion of the states as sponsors. Three states and four territories were awarded grants in the 1976–1977 program year. In the following years additional states were added. The growth of state interest is indicated by the fact that of 4,750 new jobs for the 1980–1981 programs and 1,950 new positions for 1981–1982, 55 percent were to be filled by state sponsors. Total positions authorized for 1981–1982 amounted to 54,200. This number included three new national sponsors added in 1978: the National Urban League, the National Center on Black Aged, and the Associación Nacional Pro Personas Mayores (National Association for Spanish Speaking Elderly.)[15] The appropriation for all programs in recent years has grown markedly to a high of $277.1 million in fiscal 1982.

Information about the characteristics of those enrolled in the program and about the kinds of services they are providing may be obtained from the following data issued in 1983 for the year ending June 30, 1982.[16]

Senior Community Service Employment Program Performance Report

Enrollment (July 1, 1981 to June 30, 1982)	54,200
Authorized Funding	$277,100,000
Characteristics	
Male	33%
Female	67
Education	
Grades 1 through 8	35
Grades 9 through 11	21
Grade 12	29

1–3 years college	11
4 years college and above	4
Family income at or below poverty level	85
Veteran	9
Ethnic group	
White	67
Black	23
Hispanic	7
American Indian/Alaskan	1
Asian/Pacific Islands	2
Age	
55–59	20
60–64	28
65–69	27
70–74	17
75 and over	10
Services to the general community	54
Education	12
Health/hospitals	4
Recreation/parks/forests	9
Social service	11
Public parks and transportation	5
Other	13
Services to the elderly	46
Health and home care	5
Housing and home rehabilitation	3
Recreation/senior citizens	9
Nutrition programs	12
Transportation	3
Outreach/referral	7
Other	7

A national survey of those over age sixty-five by the Louis Harris Association in 1976 found that there were 4 million persons who, though unemployed or retired, wanted to work.[17] Some, undoubtedly, would back off if confronted with the opportunity. However, the experience of the national organizations of the aging in the operation of the Senior Community Service Programs demonstrated that large numbers of older persons desire employment.

Recent administrative efforts to reduce social service expenditures resulted in the proposed extinction of Senior Community Service Programs. Funds were provided through June 1984 only after Congress overrode a presidential veto. The 1984 budget proposed that funds be transferred from the Department of Labor to the Administration on Aging. The Leadership Council of

Aging Organizations in March 1983 declared that "it is clear that the national contractors who have successfully operated and advocated for the program would no longer administer Title V."[18]

The future of the program is uncertain. Among principal supporters are leading organizations of the aging, some of which are the recipients of government contracts. Thus, advocacy is tinged with self-interest. One of the principal criticisms of the program relates to the small number of persons affected. Although part-time job opportunities for the elderly have increased from five thousand to fifty-five thousand in the last decade, only a tiny fraction of the potential beneficiaries have been affected. Pennsylvania's secretary of aging, Gorham Black, has observed that "much more serious actions must be taken if we are to provide all older persons with the opportunity to work."[19]

OTHER FEDERAL EMPLOYMENT SERVICES FOR OLDER WORKERS

CETA and the Older Worker

A relatively small percentage of older persons were employed in the early years of the Comprehensive Employment and Training Act of 1973 (CETA).[20] Basically, CETA was a revenue-sharing program concerned with enabling sponsors, such as state and local governments, to provide training and employment opportunites for persons of all ages. Administered by the Department of Labor, the program operated through grants to state and local agencies. Workers received the national minimum wage. The sponsor was not required to supply matching funds. When the act was first passed, the secretary of labor was authorized to establish training and employment programs for the unemployed of all ages, including "special target groups." Middle-aged and older men and women were recognized as one special target group. Further attention was drawn to the needs of older workers by amendments to the act in 1978. Sponsors receiving CETA funds were required to take into account the needs of older workers. Any special services were to be coordinated with those provided under other programs, especially those of the Area Agencies on Aging.[21] The pressure of Congress for more attention to the older worker was understandable, since fewer than 3 percent of CETA enrollees were over fifty-five years of age and only 1 percent were over age sixty-five.[22]

Among federally sponsored programs that employed older CETA workers was the weatherization program for low-income persons, particularly the elderly and the handicapped. In 1979 about two thousand workers were said to be engaged in weatherization services. Several federal agencies were involved. Included were the Department of Energy, the Community Services Administration and Community Action Agencies, the Department of Housing and Urban Development, and the Administration on Aging.

CETA expired in 1982 and was replaced by the Job Training Partnership Act (JTPA), scheduled to begin October 1, 1983. The act, to be administered at the state level, is intended to benefit principally those in the younger age brackets. However, 3 percent of the funds are to be available for the training of older workers.[23]

U.S. Employment Service

Older workers are classified by the U.S. Employment Service as a priority group. The federally financed and state-operated agency defines the older worker, however, as one aged forty-five and older. Emphasis upon placement productivity in the over twenty-four hundred offices throughout the nation has allowed relatively little time for focusing on the problems of the older applicant. Often the employment service position of "older worker specialist" has been eliminated or simply made a part of one person's "special service" activities for minorities, veterans, older workers, and others.

VOLUNTEER EMPLOYMENT PROGRAMS

Volunteer service programs funded by the federal government have been in operation for almost two decades.[24] Three of these, classified as the Older American Volunteers Program (OAVP), are under the jurisidiction of ACTION, an independent umbrella agency created by the Executive Reorganization Plan No. 1 in July 1971. ACTION operates domestically through ten regional offices and forty-nine state offices to provide technical assistance to sponsoring organizations and training of project staff.

Through interagency agreements, the Older American Volunteer Programs have been tied to a number of federal departments delivering social services. For example, by means of an agreement with the National Fire Prevention and Control Administration of the Department of Commerce, volunteers take part in an educational program to reduce fire loss. Similarly, through agreement with the Department of Transportation, the Administration on Aging, and ACTION, volunteers aid isolated elderly in utilizing transportation services.[25] A number of state and local governments, by agreement with ACTION, identify themselves with one or more of the programs and provide financial support over and above matching funds required of local project sponsors.[26] A description of the three major volunteer programs follows.

Retired Senior Volunteer Program (RSVP)

Authorized by the Older American Act Amendment of 1969, the Retired Senior Volunteer Program was transferred from the Administration on Aging to ACTION upon the creation of the latter. The purpose of the program is "to develop a recognized role in the community and a meaningful life in retirement for older adults through significant volunteer service."[27] A program information statement issued in January 1972, underscores one sentence declaring that "the focal point of RSVP activity is the needs and interests of Senior Volunteers."[28] The Senior Volunteer is a person sixty years of age and older. There are no requirements relating to income, education, or experience. Volunteers receive out-of-pocket expenses only, such as transportation money. In many cases they work only a few hours each week. Public liability, automobile liability, and accident insurance are provided by the grantee.

Financial assistance for the programs is in the form of grants to local public or nonprofit private organizations. The organization making application for funds is required to specify goals, indicate geographical boundaries, create an advisory committee, and develop plans for obtaining nonfederal financial support.

RSVP programs cover a wide range of activities. An early report declares that "examples are schools, courts, libraries, museums, hospitals, nursing homes, day care centers, institutions and programs for shut-ins."[29] Regardless of the particular assignment, the volunteer is not to displace an employed person.

Energy conservation is among the more recent program areas to receive special attention. In 1979, volunteers "promoted consumer education in energy issues, disseminated information on simple home weatherization, provided basic energy audit assistance to individuals seeking help with energy conservation, and participated in referral systems for people seeking information on special energy saving problems."[30] Other newer programs include (1) various aspects of the treatment and rehabilitation of those suffering from alcohol and drug abuse, (2) helping juvenile offenders, and (3) working with mentally and emotionally handicapped persons. A program initiated in Denver in 1975 and known as the RSVP/FIC Project (Retired Senior Volunteer Program/Fixed Income Counseling) provides assistance on consumer-related issues.[31]

In the early years of the program, RSVP was criticized for its emphasis on satisfying the volunteer rather than on providing an experience that, in addition, would be of help to those in greatest need. Other criticisms were directed at the numbers of persons involved and at the limited minority and ethnic representation among the volunteers rather than at the program quality. An agency spokesman in 1979 declared that "aggressive steps" were being taken to meet these criticisms.[32] An Agency profile that same year indicated that women constituted 78.3 percent of the total number of volunteers; 14.5 percent of the volunteers were over eighty years of age; 82.9 percent were white, 12.3 percent black, and 3.2 percent of Hispanic origin.[33] In 1982, the budget amounted to $26.3 million. It provided for over 722 projects involving over three hundred thousand senior volunteers.

Foster Grandparent Program (FGP)

The Foster Grandparent Program was first developed in 1965 as a cooperative effort between the Office of Economic Opportunity and the Administration of Aging. Twenty-one pilot projects were begun with the objective of utilizing the services of older persons in helping institutionalized children and young teenagers. In 1969, amendments to the Older Americans Act transferred full responsibility to the Department of Health, Education, and Welfare. The Administration on Aging funded and administered the program until it was transferred to ACTION in 1971. Current authorization of the program stems from the Domestic Volunteer Service Act of 1973.[34]

The program is project-oriented in nature. Grants are made to public agencies and to private nonprofit sponsoring organizations. The institution in which the foster grandparent serves, called a volunteer station, is not eligible for sponsorship. Normally the grant will cover up to 90 percent of the operational costs, although this proportion may be increased in the event of an emergency or other special need. In 1982 eighteen thousand foster grandparents were serving over fifty-four thousand children in 237 federally funded projects encompassing the entire country, Puerto Rico, and the Virgin Islands. The operating budget was $46.1 million.

Foster grandparents are men and women over age sixty with low income, who are recruited to provide supportive services to children—chiefly in institutions—having special needs. The income eligibility level is set at 125 percent of the national poverty line. However, this level is increased by the amount of the state supplement in those states that add to the Supplemental Security Income payment.

While the program is designed by ACTION as volunteer, it does offer a number of rewards, some of which are over and beyond those normally associated with strictly volunteer activity. For example, the foster grandparent receives a small stipend for his or her work (two dollars per hour in 1982) which is limited to four hours per day, five days a week. The volunteer may also receive one meal, transportation costs, accident insurance, an annual physical examination, and counseling from the professional staff on the benefits available through various government programs. Though the volunteer, receives a small stipend, he or she is not classified as a part of the work force. Project staff employees are not federal employees. They are responsible to the project sponsor. The foster grandparent's stipend does not reduce the volunteer's eligibility for assistance under any governmental program.

A cost benefit study conducted by Booz, Allen Administration Service,

Inc. in 1971 and 1972, indicated that foster grandparents received substantial noneconomic benefits. Of roughly nine hundred individuals interviewed, most reported improvement in various life attributes.[35]

Attribute	Improved
Health	52%
Independence	87
Feeling of Usefulness to Others	94
Lessening of Isolation	88
Satisfaction with Life	95
Self-Respect	81
Happiness	92
Feeling Loved	86
Less Financial Worry	92

In the same study, members of the professional staff of the institutions indicated their impressions of the impact of the foster grandparents upon the children themselves.[36]

Attribute Improved	% of Children
Physical Health	53
General Disposition	60
Relations with Authority Figures	36
Sense of Security	75
Self-Image	33
Communications Skills	53
Other Skill Development	51
Maturity Level	31
Decreased Antisocial Behavior	26
Performance in School	16

Proponents of the Foster Grandparent Program argue that the very nature of the operation assures a positive effect upon the community in which the program is located. The dual clientele is a feature that sets the program apart. The older person's meaningful activity enhances his or her income and morale. If what the volunteer does contains a strong element of love, patience, and compassion for the child, the chances of a positive response from the child are increased. The achievement of the child further enhances the sense of accomplishment of the grandparent. Similarly, the child benefits immeasurably. A poignant staff report, though somewhat outdated, seems pertinent: "Kids are walking. Kids are talking. Kids who use to have to be tranquilized aren't being tranquilized anymore. Kids who couldn't go to school, go to school now. It just makes all the difference in the world. For the first time in a child's life, he's got someone who is all his." [37]

The success of the Foster Grandparent Program has resulted in financial support from other than federal sources. In 1982, ACTION reported that over forty states had appropriated funds to expand the program. For example, in that year 360 low-income elderly residents in Michigan were working in seven nonfederally funded projects. [38]

Most foster grandparents are women. In 1979, the ratio was 83.3 percent female to 16.7 percent male. Ethnic background percentages were white, 63 percent, black, 27.8 percent, Hispanic, 6.1 percent, and American Indian and Alaskan, 2.1 percent. [39]

The Senior Companion Program

A third major volunteer program was authorized by the Older American Comprehensive Service Amendments of 1973. Initially limited to demonstration projects, the objective of the Senior Companion Program is to enable low-income persons over age sixty to provide supportive services to individuals, other than children, with "exceptional needs." [40] Thus, the program has a dual purpose: to aid both the senior companion and the person served.

ACTION grants may be made to public agencies and to nonprofit private organizations. The grants cover up to 90 percent of the development and operational costs. A larger percentage may sometimes be approved, such as in poverty or disaster areas or in instances where the nature of the program has been determined to be "of exceptional value." [41] New programs require consultation with the State Agency on Aging or, when appropriate, the Community Action Agency.

Volunteers serve at Volunteer Stations. These are of three principal types:

1. Residential Care Volunteer Station—A minimum of thirty persons with special needs is required for this classification. There must be at least ten senior companions for the facility.

2. Nonresidential Care Volunteer Station—A minimum of fifteen persons with special needs is required. At least five senior companions must be placed in the facility.

3. Private Home Placement Volunteer Station—One senior companion may be assigned to a private home if the person in the home has special needs. [42]

The services of the senior companion are intended to aid the person or people in the volunteer station. These services may be simple neighborly acts such as visiting, shopping, getting in touch with agencies that can assist with problems, and, in general, endeavoring to be of help to the homebound person. The individual being helped may or may not be elderly. However, 80 percent of those served must be over age sixty.

The income of a senior companion may not be above the poverty level. In particular geographic areas this figure may be increased to reflect a higher cost of living. Conditions for employment stipulate a period of service of twenty hours per week. The stipend in 1980 was two dollars per hour, which was not to reduce the eligibility for assistance from other governmental programs. Sponsors are required by regulation to arrange for transportation, meals, and accident and liability insurance for the senior companion.[43]

The program is relatively small. In 1982, there were eighty projects and 5,280 senior companions. The operating budget was $12.2 million.

OTHER VOLUNTEER EMPLOYMENT PROGRAMS

Service Corps of Retired Executives (SCORE)

Established in 1964 by the Small Business Administration, SCORE is a service organization whose membership consists of business and professional persons. In 1982, there were 398 chapters throughout the country with a membership of over 11,500 volunteer retired business persons. Volunteer business persons who have not retired may join the Active Corps of Executive (ACE).

The SCORE volunteer endeavors to help solve the management problems of small businesses. The work is performed within the home community of the volunteer or within a fifty-mile radius. There is no salary or payment for the volunteer's time. However, there is government reimbursement for out-of-pocket and travel expenses.

The activities of the volunteers cover a wide range. Since the establishment of the program, over 1 million businesses have been counseled by SCORE members.[44]

Volunteers in Service to America (VISTA)

The primary objective of VISTA, a unit of ACTION, is to help the poor, including the elderly poor, "achieve a measure of self-sufficiency through participation in the democratic process and the use of available resources."[45] To achieve this goal, in 1979 over four thousand volunteers worked with 695 sponsors to help approximately 1,250,000 poor persons participate in a variety of community projects. Roughly one-quarter of the volunteers were involved in activities relating to senior citizens, such as working in community centers, assisting with food and health cooperatives, or acting in an advocacy capacity to improve local institutions such as nursing homes. Thirteen percent of all of VISTA's volunteers were over age sixty.[46]

Locally recruited volunteers made up 70 percent of the work force. Of these, roughly 40 percent were persons with low-incomes. The term of service was normally one year. The volunteer received subsistence expenses.

3. Summary Analysis

Recently a composite body at both the executive and congressional levels of the federal government worked together to attempt to solve the funding problems that have been plaguing social security. Although there was reluctance to tamper in any way with legislation that had achieved such a high level of national support, it was agreed that some steps had to be taken to address the budgetary crisis. Among other alterations, the resultant legislation decreed that the fully pensionable retirement age would increase over a number of years and also instituted larger pension penalties for early retirement.

While "saving social security" is a national priority espoused not only by legislators but also by the general public, that part of the resolution of the dilemma that involves pressuring workers to remain in the labor force in later life seems contrary to the concerns of the federal government as described in this chapter. For example, the Age Discrimination in Employment Act (ADEA) of 1967 demonstrated explicit awareness of the problems of older workers in retaining jobs or entering new employment at ages far younger than those presently specified under social security. In that context, older workers are defined as those aged forty years or older. Even with this relatively low age limit on what constitutes an "older worker," the conditions of the act are difficult to regulate or, from the point of view of the employer, even to comprehend because of the exceptions made for "good cause", i.e., reasons why an older worker could legitimately be dismissed or not hired. It seems evident that even when a relatively young person can be defined as an older worker, problems arise around a distinction between age per se and functional incapacities that might limit job performance. The implication is that the two are somehow interrelated and that the performance abilities of the older worker are thus inherently subject to doubt in comparison with those of the younger worker. The thread of concern for "older" workers far younger than age sixty-five or even age sixty-two can be discerned in other federal programs. The United States Employment Service lists older workers as one of its priority target groups, but in this case the older worker is defined as aged forty-five and older. The Comprehensive Employment and Training Act of 1973 also included consideration for older workers, but only as a special target group within a much larger population singled out for concern. CETA defined "older" workers as those aged at least fifty-five. Workers or persons desiring work in the age range of sixty and older have received very few services and very little attention under these programs. Implicitly, it then seems evident that the federal government is well aware that age discrimination in employment begins far earlier than the current social-security-specified retirement age. It also seems clear from the descriptions in this chapter that these programs waste little time on persons at or near age sixty-five, or even age sixty-two. Given this apparent fatalism about the worker beyond age sixty and his or her employment possibilities, it does seem contradictory to pressure workers to go on working to even older ages than they can manage at the present time.

Employment opportunities in later life are, of course, unevenly distributed, and the worker with the lowest level of skills and whose skills are most likely to be perceived as obsolete is at a distinct disadvantage in the job market, especially as he or she grows older. It is these aging persons, too, who are the most likely to need all the economic resources they can muster. The federal government has instituted a number of programs for older persons seeking employment that generally target poorer economic groups and either specify or state a preference for workers sixty years of age or older. Whether identified as employment programs, as are Senior Community Service Programs, or volunteer employment programs, as are the Retired Senior Volunteer Program, the Foster Grandparent Program, and the Senior Companion Program, these activities seem to satisfy needs of both the older person and the recipient of his or her services. If is unfortunate that they seem to be so vulnerable to cutbacks and even extinction.[47]

VIII / The Aging Veteran

1. Introduction

The prototype of Federal intervention efforts to ensure the welfare of any population group is that instituted for veterans. Presumably, the nation, although in general opposed from the outset to government involvement in such matters, was nevertheless especially indebted to those who offered the supreme sacrifice for national survival. The ensuing pages will show that more programs and associated services have been offered and still are being offered to this group than have been offered to any other social group in the United States. The programs and services are not always well coordinated, since there is a notable degree of confusion as to which veterans are best served by particular programs and under what circumstances. Nevertheless, the veteran and his survivors receive an unusual amount of largesse from the federal pocketbook. When the proportion of veterans in the population was comparatively small and/or relatively youthful, a grateful society had no qualms about large expenditures per individual for this group.

At the present time, the proportion of veterans in the population is visibly expanding and at the same time "graying." Decade by decade, the numerical bulge produced as a consequence of World War II is ascending, as if on an escalator, into the higher age ranges. With the aging of the veteran population, an increasing concern with long-term care has evolved because of the large proportion of chronic disabilities, whether service or nonservice connected, within this group. The enormously powerful lobbies for veterans, which have been until the recent past also reflective of an unusually cohesive legislative block in U.S. politics, have more or less underwritten a carte blanche for all benefits advocated for veterans over age sixty-five. But since the Korean and particularly the Vietnam "wars," some cracks have appeared in the cohesive structure. These in turn are related to the massive budgetary allocations to the expanding and aging veteran population and to the questions being raised by politicians and the public at large as to the feasibility of maintaining the present level of benefits and, if so, for whom these benefits should be allocated.

It is worthwhile to consider the historical roots of the programs for the veteran as well as the programs themselves because of the unusual features of the policy aimed at this particular group. Such a comprehensive approach with such cohesive channels of responsiveness to perceived needs is highly universal in our society. In the next section, we will describe the history and present status of programs for veterans, with particular attention to the aging veteran. In a third section, the programs for veterans will be analyzed in the light of other policy efforts directed at the aging.

2. The Aging Veteran

The aging veteran population will increase substantially in the next decade. In September 1982, there were 3.5 million aged veterans. Roughly one out of eight was over sixty-five. By the early 1990s, the number will have more than doubled as World War II veterans move to the age sixty-five and older category. In the year 2000, there will be more than 9 million veterans over age sixty-five.

Estimated Age of Veterans, September 30, 1982 (in thousands)[1]

Age	Number
All ages	28,522
Under 20 years	9
20 to 24 years	735
25 to 29 years	1,718
30 to 34 years	2,890
35 to 39 years	3,364
40 to 44 years	2,485
45 to 49 years	2,538
50 to 54 years	3,326
55 to 59 years	4,133
60 to 64 years	3,838
65 to 69 years	1,917
70 to 74 years	836
75 to 79 years	301
80 to 84 years	149
85 years and over	303

Veterans' benefits are wide ranging, covering programs in health care, compensation and pensions, education, housing, and life insurance. Each year, new laws and regulations add to an already extensive set of rules developed over virtually the entire history of the nation. The geometric increase in the over-sixty-five age group in the next decades will require special attention to the needs of this segment of the total veteran population.

In terms of precedent, the governmental benefits programs supervised by the Veterans Administration (VA) are virtually unequalled. One hundred forty years before the signing of the Declaration of Independence, a Plymouth Colony law declared that anyone returning "mamed & hurt" from military service "in his Majesties name . . . shall be maytayned competently by the colony during his life."[2]

With the adoption of the Constitution, the federal government assumed primary responsibility for the pension benefits of veterans of the Revolution. The construction of special facilities for aged and disabled veterans began with the establishment of the U.S. Naval Home in 1833 and the U.S. Soldier's Home in 1851. Widows' pensions date from 1836. However, during the first half of the nineteenth century, veterans constituted a small fraction of the population. At the outbreak of the Civil War, there were approximately 80,000. Within four years there were approximately 2 million, nearly all from the Union Army.[3]

There were similar large increases in the number of veterans following each of the major wars of the twentieth century. World War I added 4.7 million; World War II, 16 million; the Korean conflict, 6 million; and the undeclared war in Vietnam, 9 million. In September 1982, there were 28,522,000 veterans. This number constituted less than one-third of the potential recipients of VA benefits. Taking into account dependent children, spouses, widows or widowers, and dependent parents of deceased veterans, the potential beneficiaries numbered 83.8 million, or over 36 percent of the nation's total population.[4]

THE VETERANS' LOBBY (THE IRON TRIANGLE)

Any discussion of governmental policy as it pertains to elderly veterans must first address, however briefly, the extraordinary political strength that veterans as a body have commanded over the years. Although driven out of Washington by the U.S. Army during the famous Bonus March in the summer of 1932, the veterans now exert a remarkable degree of political strength.[5] A former administrator of the VA, Max Cleland, has declared that "veterans' groups start out in a special category. I think the average member of Congress puts the veteran on a pedestal."[6]

Small wonder, then, that the wishes of the roughly 30 million veterans are more likely to be heard in the halls of Congress than those of any other group of similar size. Veterans' legislation has long been developed in what has been described as a "closed system." Congressional committees concerned with veterans' legislation team with veterans' lobby groups and the VA to operate in concert. Their control of programs has been virtually absolute, so much so that the three groups have become known as "The Iron Triangle."[7]

Legislative proposals must first be approved by the Veterans' Affairs committees of the House and Senate. Both have been described as "unabashed advocates of existing programs rather than . . . overseers."[8] In recent years, the Senate committee has been more receptive to new proposals. In the House, proposals have oftentimes been introduced under suspension of the rules permitting no amendments.

For seventeen consecutive years congressional appropriations for veterans' programs exceeded the White House budget proposal.[9] The generous approach of the Congress was due in part to the personal convictions of the members. A second important element was the veterans' organizations, whose lobbyists developed a special expertise in making Congress aware of the wishes of the membership.

The largest veterans' organization is the American Legion, with a membership of 2.7 million. The Legion also has a women's auxiliary of 1 million members. The Veterans of Foreign Wars is second in size, with a membership of 1.8 million and an auxiliary of 620,000. The Disabled American Veterans, with 666,000 members, is said to be the "fastest growing and most progressive of the Big Three."[10] Other organizations include the American Veterans of World War II, Korea and Vietnam, the Paralyzed Veterans of America, the Blinded Veterans Association, and the Vietnam Veterans of America.

The third leg of the Iron Triangle is the Veterans Administration, second only to the Department of Defense in number of permanent employees. The major veterans' lobbying groups are provided office space in the fifty-eight regional centers of the VA. Through offices, hospitals, and a variety of field arrangements in roughly 150 cities and towns, the VA network covers the entire country.

Although not classified as part of the Iron Triangle, the state and county offices concerned with veterans' affairs constitute another important link to the aging veteran. For example, veterans' affairs offices in many counties assist veterans in obtaining federal and state benefits. In rural areas, far from federal veterans' offices or facilities, the county veterans' officer is the principal link in dealing with the financial and health needs of the veteran.

FINANCIAL BENEFITS

In 1982, there were 1,584,188 persons sixty-five years old and older receiving cash benefits from the Veterans Administration. This number included 843,161 veterans, 649,478 widows, 75,817 mothers of veterans, and 15,732 fathers of veterans.[11] Roughly one-quarter of the veterans were receiving service-connected benefits.

Compensation   Veterans may receive compensation for disabling injuries or diseases incurred in line of duty during wartime service unless willful misconduct is involved. VA rating boards, using a predetermined "Schedule for Rating Disabilities," establish a degree of disability ranging from 10 to 100 percent. Additional payments are made for "certain specific severe disabilities."[12] Monthly allowances vary in accordance with regulations relating to the percentage of disability and the number of dependents. Dependency benefits are paid for service-connected disabilities rated 30 percent or above. In theory, the monthly benefits are based upon the impairment of earning capacity had the veteran been injured in a civil occupation.

Compensation for Service Connected Disability[13]

Degree of Disability	Monthly Compensation
10%	$ 62
20%	114
30%	173
40%	249
50%	352
60%	443
70%	559
80%	648
90%	729
100%	1,213

In the event of a veteran's service-connected death, benefits known as dependency and indemnity compensation may be paid to a widow, widower, child, or parent. The monthly rate of payment is tied to the pay grade of the veteran. However, the payment to parents is based on a means test.

Pensions   Pensions may be paid to veterans with limited incomes for nonservice-connected disability. The objective "of pension legislation has been to keep veterans and their survivors from want and degradation."[14] In order to simplify the system of payment that had been developed through the passage of numerous legislative acts, the Congress enacted the Veterans and Survivors Pension Improvement Act of 1978, to become effective January 1, 1979.[15] Under the previous legislation a number of categories of income were not counted. The 1979 act dropped most of these. The act contained a grandfather clause, however, so that no veteran would receive less than he had been paid under the earlier regulations.

The new formula established a minimum annual income. For example, on June 1, 1982, a veteran without dependent spouse or child was entitled to an income of $5,328. The amount of the pension was determined by subtracting any countable income, such as social security, from the $5,328.

Maximum Non-Service-Connected Pension, June 1, 1982[16]

Individual Veteran	$5,328
Veteran with One Dependent	6,980
Each Additional Dependent Child	903
Veteran Needing Regular Care	8,524
World War I—Additional Payment	1,202

A major objective of the act is to ensure above-poverty-level support. Moreover, automatic inclusion of cost-of-living increases in social security is written into the legislation. A cost-of-living increase in social security no longer results in a decrease in the pension. On the contrary, the support level is raised to provide an increase in both the social security benefit and the pension benefit. For example, assume that the veteran receives $3,000 in social security benefits and $1,460 in VA pension benefits. An 8 percent cost-of-living increase amounts to $240.00 additional social security benefits. The 8 percent increase applied to the pension amounts to $116.80. The two increases total $356.60 as an additional annual benefit. This amount is added to the previous support level for a new total level of $4,816.80.

The eligibility requirements are concerned with the amount of wartime service (ninety days in service, at least one day in wartime), discharge other than dishonorable, disability, and low income. For pension law purposes, veterans sixty-five years old and older and not working are classified as permanently and totally disabled.

The veterans' pension program, social security, and supplementary security income together have resulted in raising virtually all aged veterans above the poverty level. This is a major accomplishment.

Compensation and pension benefits continue long after a war has ended. For example, in 1981, forty-seven widows and 111 children of Civil War veterans were receiving payments, 116 years after hostilities had ceased.[17] Payments to widows of Revolutionary War veterans ended in 1906, 123 years after the war.[18]

MEDICAL CARE

The Veterans Administration operates an extensive medical-care delivery system employing over 195,000 persons in 1982. The system was established following World War I to care for those with service-connected disabilities. At that time, hospital facilities throughout the nation were considered inadequate to provide for the increased load of wartime casualties. The system was expanded after World War II, and the eligibility rules were altered. An entitled veteran, that is, one with an honorable discharge who has "been on active duty (for nontraining purposes) for at least one day," is eligible for hospital and other care.[19] The veteran must certify inability to pay.

A significant step occurred in 1971 when Congress eliminated the certification-of-need requirement for veterans over age sixty-five. The full impact of this change upon the medical care programs provided by the Veterans Administration may be some years in crystallizing. According to estimates contained in a report of the National Academy of Sciences, the next two decades will see a major shift in the number of veterans over age sixty-five. By the year 2000, according to the study, 25 percent of all surviving veterans will be aged sixty-five and older, assuming the absence of war or other catastrophe.[20] By 1990 over half of all males in the United States over age sixty-five will be entitled to veterans' health care benefits.[21]

Three broad categories of veterans use the health services of the VA: (1) those with service-connected disabilities who receive compensation; (2) those with nonservice-connected disabilities who are receiving pensions; (3) other eligible veterans. As noted previously, those over age sixty-five do not have to certify need.[22]

The various health services may be divided into three broad components of care: hospital, long-term, and outpatient. The Veterans Administration classifies eight "level of patient care" as follows:

0	no disability
1	minimal disability
2	mild disability
3	moderate disability
4	moderately severe disability
5	severe, chronic, stable disability
6	severe, chronic, unstable disability
7	acute disability or diagnosis
8	severe acute disability[23]

Hospital Care

The study of the National Academy of Sciences indicated that the compensation and pension groups accounted for only 11 percent of the veteran population. However, they made up 57 percent of the hospital inpatient census.[24] The Veterans Administration report of January 10, 1983, to the Senate Special Committee on Aging indicated that "almost half of the approximately 50,000 veterans in extended care programs" were aged sixty-five and older.[25]

General Medical and Surgical Hospitals

In 1982, there were 172 VA medical centers and a number of satellite clinics. The medical centers "operated" over eighty thousand hospital beds in medical, surgical, and psychiatric sections. The bed occupancy rate was 81 percent.[26] The largest units were the 144 General Medical and Surgical Hospitals. Taken together, these units provided an extensive range of services relating to levels 6, 7, and 8, noted above.

Extended Hospital Care

Patients who have survived an acute illness may require some months of hospital care that includes close physician supervision, skilled nursing, and numerous professional services. These patients were formerly classified as intermediate care patients, but the VA now uses the expression Extended Hospital Care to distinguish these patients from Medicaid's intermediate care patients, who require no professional care. The number of beds in the Extended Hospital Care category has increased substantially in the last decade because of referral of patients to the VA when private insurance and other arrangements are exhausted.[27]

Psychiatric Hospitals

In recent years there has been an emphasis decreasing the number of centers classified as psychiatric hospitals. From 1967 to 1977, the number of these institutions declined from forty-one to twenty-eight. The number of beds also decreased, from approximately 53,000 to 28,000. At the same time, the number of persons receiving mental health treatment increased. The variance was caused by several developments, including a change in the philosophy and character of rehabilitative measures as well as the conversion of some centers to General Medical and Surgical Institutions.[28]

LONG-TERM CARE

The long-term or extended care component of the services provided to veterans embraces a variety of separate programs. Included are VA nursing home care, community nursing home care, hospital-based home care, VA domiciliary care, personal care homes, and the state home program.

Nursing homes were established with a view to freeing up "frozen" hospital beds for patients who were acutely ill. A 1961 survey reported that 42 percent of psychiatric hospital patients had been hospitalized for over ten years. The VA was authorized three years later to operate nursing homes and to contract with private nursing homes.[29]

VA Nursing Home Care

In 1982, nursing-home-care units were in operation at ninety-seven VA medical centers. Chronically ill veterans requiring skilled nursing accounted for an average daily census of 8,442.[30] The resources of the medical center are available to the patient in the nursing unit. Although priority is given to veterans with service-connected disabilities, the majority of patients are "elderly, single, poor men whose discharge from the nursing home care unit is most frequently due to death."[31] An extensive study of the VA nursing home system in 1977 by the independent National Academy of Sciences resulted in various criticisms. Nevertheless, the report declared, "It should be noted, with regard to the physical nursing care provided, that all the units were found to be generally satisfactory."[32]

Community Nursing Home Care

The VA in 1982 has placed veterans in over thirty-one hundred nursing homes through-out the country. In general, these are proprietary homes that operate on a per diem contract basis. Over thirteen hundred provide skilled nursing care and the balance provide intermediate care or combined skilled and intermediate care. There is no time limit for the veteran with a service-connected condition. The average daily census of veterans in 1982 was 9,533. Over 31,000 were served by the program; about 50 percent were over sixty-five years of age.

Domiciliary Care

The origin of domiciliary care dates from 1866 when Congress provided for eleven National Homes for Disabled Volunteer Soldiers. The domiciliary—a converted barracks—was declared to be "an institution which provides a home—bed, board and incidental medical care."[33] Service in the military and inability to earn a living were the basic criteria for admission.

The goal of the domiciliary care program is to aid those who are disabled "by age, disease, or injury" but who do not require hospitalization or skilled nursing services.[34] In general, the domiciliaries are similar to homes for the aged, but, in addition, they are now used to assist younger men with psychiatric difficulties. In 1982, VA domiciliaries had an average dialy census of 7,087. A two-hundred bed replacement facility recently completed at the medical center in Wood, Wisconsin, is the first domiciliary to contain units for female veterans.

State Home Program

A number of the states operate hospitals, nursing homes, and domiciliary facilities for veterans. For example, in 1888, eleven states had homes for veterans. Legislation enacted in 1964 established grant programs to assist the states. One per-diem grant enables the state to provide hospital, nursing home, and domiciliary care. A second type of grant provides 65 percent federal funding for construction. In 1982, thirty-two states and the District of Columbia operated forty-five homes and seventeen thousand beds to provide hospital, nursing home, and domiciliary care.[35]

Outpatient and Noninstitutional Extended Care Programs

The VA operates over two hundred outpatient clinics. However, most of these are based at VA hospitals. Distance thus creates a problem for many ambulatory patients. Several programs have been introduced to assist veterans whose health problems do not require institutional care.

Hospital-Based Home Care

The goal of hospital-based home care programs is to facilitate the return of the veteran to his own home as well as to reduce the necessity for readmissions. A hospital-based treatment team provides medical and other services and trains family members to assist the patient. This recently developed extended care program was made available on a limited basis by thirty VA medical centers in 1982. Approximately 20 percent of the sixty-five hundred patients had terminal cancer.

Residential Care

Noninstitutional extended care or residential care programs provide a homelike setting for the patient. The veteran is responsible for paying placement charges. Inspections are made by staff from a VA hospital, with the social worker concentrating on relations between the veteran and the family and between the veteran and the community. In 1978, a General Accounting Office study recommended expansion of the program as one alternative to hospitalization.[36]

A POLICY DILEMMA

The expansion of the aging veteran population over the next decades raises issues concerning appropriate steps to be taken in the future. The recent study of the National Academy of Sciences, while complimenting many facets of the VA medical system, nevertheless called attention to a number of areas of concern. Among these were the following:

1. In view of the age distribution, the need for acute and geriatric care for aging veterans will increase substantially.
2. The capacity to provide outpatient service is "relatively sparse."
3. The hospital system has a far greater bed capacity than is necessary to care for veterans with service-connected disabilities.
4. Veterans with service-connected disabilities constitute only 30 percent of the long-term-care patient load.
5. Substantial funds are being expended on a construction program notwithstanding the surplus of VA hospital beds and, in most areas of the country, the sufficient capacity of community hospitals.
6. Excessive hospital admissions and longer than necessary stays result in excessive hospital use.

Although the study called attention to the service-connected versus the nonservice-connected disability, the committee concluded with the assumption that current eligibility requirements would not be altered. However, the committee recommended that "VA policies and programs should be designed to permit the VA system ultimately to be phased into the general delivery of health services in communities across the country."[37] A five-year "integrated demonstration" program was recommended. If successful, the program should then be extended to "become part of the community system of medical care accessible to nonveterans, as well as veterans."[38]

Although the Senate Veterans' Affairs Committee held hearings on the report, the proposal got nowhere. The staff director of the study is reported to have said, "I think it's highly unlikely the Veterans Administration will ask the Academy to do anything else."[39]

OTHER PROGRAMS TO ASSIST THE AGING VETERAN

Medical Research

Efforts to define and meet the special needs of older patients have resulted in the establishment of Geriatric Research, Educational, and Clinical Centers.[40] In 1982 the GRECC program consisted of eight centers that emphasized the development of a highly qualified staff in the field of geriatrics. Special units containing from ten to thirty beds have been established for intensive diagnosis of aging patients. The staff at each unit normally concentrates research upon one or a few diseases of the aged.

Mental Health and Behavioral Science Service

Emphasis upon improving conditions for older psychiatric patients by what is referred to as the MH and BS Service has resulted in a variety of approaches. Special training programs and instructional manuals for staff personnel have been developed to aid aging victims of alcohol and drugs. A recent initiative has been the establishment at the Palo Alto VA Medical Center of an Elder Veterans Service Center, where new concepts in the treatment of psychiatric patients are being developed.

Special Services

Social work, rehabilitative, dietetic, and nursing services of the VA provide various forms of assistance to veterans and their families. The objective of these individual services of social workers, home-health aides, and an extensive body of volunteers is to enable the aging veteran to recognize and utilize his own strengths and thus to achieve maximum independence and self-respect.

To assist in the care of veterans, a voluntary service program has been developed. Elderly volunteers are reported by the VA to be the "mainstay" of the service. However, in recent years increasing numbers of young people have become involved.

Education

Educational benefits for service-disabled veterans are available to all veterans aged sixty-five and older. In addition, the widow of a veteran whose death was service-connected, or the wife of a permanently and totally disabled veteran is also eligible for educational benefits. In 1982, about 220 persons over age sixty-five were recipients of educational benefits; 80 of these were women, chiefly widows of veterans who had died of service-connected causes or wives of veterans who were totally disabled from service-connected causes.

Housing

Although housing assistance would normally be applicable to younger veterans, the elderly veteran is not precluded from loan guaranty and mortgage insurance benefits because of age. Farms, mobile homes, and condominiums are included in the types of housing for which government loans may be obtained.

Information and Referral

The VA conducts an extensive information and referral service to acquaint veterans with the benefit structure. For example, with the approval of Agencies on Aging, senior citizen centers are visited by veterans' benefits specialists who inform the elderly of the various benefit programs. This service has proved of special value to aged widows of veterans.

3. Summary Analysis

The programs for veterans are most interesting when compared to federal policies in general. Intervention of behalf of veterans was a historical precedent. Over the years the nation has continued to have special concern for veterans' welfare. Extensive financial, health, and auxiliary service programs have been developed to aid not only veterans who suffered disabilities in military service but also those with nonservice-connected disabilities. Collectively these programs may be called comprehensive because they include virtually every service that has been made more selectively available to other more recently targeted groups. Programs for veterans are also remarkable because the legislation of them has been concentrated in two committees, one in the Senate and one in the House, rather than spread over a number of legislative bodies.

While the numerous programs that have been established in response to the identified needs of veterans, are not well coordinated, the thrust of legislation has been cohesively organized *and* cohesively supported up until quite recently. The mood of Congress, supported by the executive branch, has for many years been articulated roughly as "we cannot do enough for our veterans." The general public has also been supportive of this evaluation of veterans as a special population worthy of extra consideration.

Two unpopular military interventions overseas, the Korean "police action" and the undeclared war in Vietnam, have undermined the consensual backing for virtually unlimited support for veterans. Veterans themselves have become involved in debates over which veterans deserve how much consideration and under what circumstances. During this same period, the proportion of aging veterans and their beneficiaries has increased markedly. A larger and larger crop of veterans is identifiable in the general population. More and more of these are entitled to health care as currently articulated and will also be needing long-term care in the not-too-distant future. The expense of this care will necessitate the reevaluation of benefit levels for a particular preferred group whose population has exploded not only in terms of numbers but also in terms of relative expensiveness of care.

As the number of veterans over age sixty-five increases from roughly 3 million in 1980 to over 9 million in the year 2000, there is bound to be national reaction to the sharply increased costs of pensions and health care, particularly for recipients with nonservice-connected disabilities. The veterans themselves, as mentioned, have already begun to react. For example, in 1978, one body of Vietnam veterans criticized a proposed expansion of non-service-connected pension benefits as a disservice to the disabled veteran.[41]

As the need for acute and geriatric care of veterans over age sixty-five increases, so too will questions about the need for facilities and services for those of advanced years. Should the system be dismantled, as some have suggested, or be preserved, as veterans' organizations insist, or serve as a basic element of and a partial model for a national health service?[42] Serious debate about these proposals can be expected over the near future.

IX / Public Policy and the Aging Summarized

A primary objective of this book has been to provide an overview of public policy for the aged in the United States with a particular emphasis on programs initiated at the federal level. More than any other population group, the elderly have become dependent on publicly funded resources in many areas of their lives. Efforts on behalf of the elderly have been increasing markedly over the last decades, and the "slice" of the budget allocated for programs for the elderly is now very large. Yet the many programs have been developed in a piecemeal fashion and do not represent anything that could be termed a cohesive national policy for older persons. Accordingly, there is vast array of resources and services available to older persons, or at least to some segment of the elderly population, but the linkages among them are obscure and sometimes nonexistent.

We have tried to introduce some elements of order in the previous chapters by making logical groupings of programs wherever possible. This effort constitutes a part of another objective of this book, which is further carried out in the summary analysis of each chapter. In this section, the programs covered were examined in relation to one another and to the population group served. Even at this partial level of analysis, it was apparent that there was a high level of inconsistency and lack of coordination among and between programs. This outcome is to be expected, given the incremental approach to policymaking in the United States. As has been noted, this approach is not applied only to legislation in the area of aging, but rather is a typical "model" for policymaking in general.

In this concluding chapter, the task to be accomplished is threefold. First, a highly condensed description of all the previous chapters will be given. It is hoped that this overview will enable a grasp of the major programs, of what they offer, and of the groups they are available to. Second an analysis of all the programs taken together will be presented. The analysis will be directed toward reviewing the auspices under which the programs are implemented and carried out. Descriptions will be offered of their relations with one another, insofar as these exist, of their degree of fit and consistency, and of the extent of coverage offered to aged population groups. The final section will be devoted to a discussion of the implications of public policy toward the aging as it relates to the present situation and the potential for the future.

1. Descriptive Overview

THE POLITICS OF AGING

The problems of the aging, or indeed of any population group, were not high on the agenda of the framers of the Constitution. More than a century and a half elapsed before the establishment of the social security system. Another three decades went by before the Older Americans Act was passed. During this lengthy period, governmental procedures at both the federal and state levels became rather firmly fixed. The function to be performed, whether for the defense of the nation or for the promotion of agriculture, took precedence over the clientele to be served, with one exception, the American veteran. As a consequence, the congressional committee structure became geared to the functional pattern. It is obvious that this pattern was not easily changed. In effect, it helps to explain why even today programs for the aged are spread out across so many different "functional" committees.

The tables on pages 11 and 12 of chapter I demonstrate at a glance the distribution of legislative issues concerning the aging among the congressional committees. The two specifically designated committees on aging, the Senate Special Committee on Aging and the House Select Committee on Aging, have the right to investigate issues of interest to the aging but have no authority to propose legislation. This statement is not meant to imply that the two committees are powerless. On the contrary, the committees are free to range widely without risking the charge of infringing upon another committee's domain, giving them not only the ability to maintain a watchful eye on all prospective legislation affecting the elderly but also the freedon to investigate the actual operation of ongoing programs.

The large number of congressional committees concerned with one or more issues concerning the elderly has serious disadvantages when it comes to formulating a cohesive policy for the aging. But while the disadvantages are real, they are not necessarily crippling. There is a major advantage that must be recognized; namely, the development of an awareness of matters of interest to the aging among large numbers of legislators exposed to such issues because of their memberships on one or more of the functional committees. Thus, many if not most legislators are likely to become aware of issues concerning the elderly.

Legislative and public awareness of these issues has greatly expanded in recent years because of the growth of special interest groups. By far the largest of these, the American Association of Retired Persons, was originally an offshoot of the National Retired Teachers Association. In 1982, however,

NRTA became a division of AARP. The total membership of roughly 15 million persons far exceeds that of any other organization of elderly persons. Other major interest groups include the labor-union-oriented National Council of Senior Citizens, the aging-specialists-oriented National Council on the Aging, the Gray Panthers (a body "concerned with actions for change rather than service"), and the National Association of Retired Federal Employees.

Interest groups do not necessarily work in concert, since they represent different segments of the aging population and highlight different issues. Recently, however, the above-mentioned and many other groups involved with issues concerning the aging have joined together to create a Leadership Council on Aging. This move toward greater unity has evolved partly in response to the threat to social security, an issue affecting the entire aging population. If this unity can be reenforced and consolidated, the joint influence of interest groups representing the aging, coupled with the increase in the number of elderly in proportion to the total population, will almost surely expand the political potency of the aging.

The phrase "Aging Network" would seem to designate an all-embracing organizational structure concerned with the total governmental effort to aid the elderly. Nothing could be farther from the truth. The Aging Network, in fact, constitutes but one segment of the considerable governmental bureaucracy concerned with problems of the aging. The expression "Aging Network" technically refers to the array of public and semipublic agencies responsible for giving life to the Older Americans Act—the "sole federal social service statute designed exclusively for seniors."[1]

Enacted in 1965, the Older Americans Act has undergone a series of revisions, the ninth in 1981. The Congress has been supportive of the objectives of the act but at the same time reluctant to provide operating authority for an extended period. The 1981 amendments, for example, carry the act only through 1984. However, in two decades, a rather elaborate organizational structure, headed by the Administration on Aging and its regional offices under the direction of the Office of Human Services in the Department of Health and Human Services, has developed. There is also a small review and appraisal group called the Federal Council on the Aging, In addition, within the fifty-seven states and other jurisdictions there were, in 1982, 676 Area Agencies on Aging supervising various contractual agencies responsible for direct services to the elderly. For example, almost seven thousand multipurpose senior centers were in existence.

The declaration of objectives contained in the Older Americans Act covers a number of major social services. Many of these are the responsibility of federal departments and agencies having specifically legislated authority over national programs affecting the entire population. However, by means of formal and informal agreements at both the federal and state levels, the network is able to bring attention to the special needs of the elderly.

Financing the network programs is largely, but by no means totally, a federal responsibility. From an initial budget allocation of $6 million in 1965, annual federal appropriations grew to almost $7 billion in the early eighties. Recent budget reductions of programs for the elderly have been somewhat less harsh than those of agencies concerned with the entire population.

There is almost no limit to the number of specialized services that could be provided, especially to the over ages seventy-five and eighty-five cohorts. Through the federal-state supervision of the Area Agencies on Aging, the promotion of research and demonstration projects, and the establishment of multidisciplinary and long-term-care gerontology centers, the network can, over time, contribute much to the solution of problems of the aging. However, to finance programs a larger-than-current degree of support is required from the entire citizenry. At the present time, only a small proportion of the elderly are being reached.

GENERAL FINANCIAL AND RETIREMENT PROGRAMS

Social Security

When President Reagan declared in March 1983 that "a dark cloud has been lifted," perhaps he should have added the word "momentarily." A frightened people were grateful that the Congress and the president could agree upon a series of changes to assure the solvency of the system. The Social Security Amendments of 1983 made history. But, almost certainly, public satisfaction will be short lived. The solution is not yet in sight.

From its inception, social security was intended to occupy a position over and beyond that of any existing program. It was not to be public welfare, nor was it to have strictly the features of a private pension system. Rather, its authors hoped that social security would supply to retirees a "minimum level of well being." The system was to be equitable, recognizing the workers's contribution and thus her or his right to benefits. It was also to be adequate, recognizing the weighting concept favoring the low-wage earner.

The system got off to a modest start with a payroll tax of 1 percent—to be matched by the employer—on the first $3,000 of income. Over the years, following the addition of features such as disability and hospital insurance, the tax gradually increased until in 1984 the rate was 7 percent on both employee and employer, covering an income of up to $37,500.

As first implemented, the system was to cover only about 20 percent of retired workers. Almost immediately, the legislation was revised to include dependents and survivors. Over the years coverage was extended to encompass ever-greater proportions of the retiring population. Today social security is truly the cornerstone of financial support of older persons, since almost all of the members of the aging population are entitled to benefits of some kind. Although the amounts of benefits vary greatly and the problem of adequacy has not been solved, the system has very nearly achieved the universal coverage originally envisioned by Roosevelt.

For much of the period following the passage of the Social Security Act in 1935, the program was accepted without question. Indeed, as noted previously (p. 57), one of those involved in the development of the system declared that the words "social security" had become "a common and comforting expression in the American language."

In time, the various liberalizations of the system, together with inflation-adjusted benefits, resulted in expenditures greater than the economy could or would support. Indeed, after 1974 the balance in the Old Age and Survivors Insurance (OASI) Trust Fund declined year after year. Borrowing was necessary in October 1983 to meet benefits due in November.

Proposals to assure the solvency of the system were wide ranging. The bipartisan National Commission on Social Security Reform was appointed by the president to recommend a solution. Unfortunately, the membership could not agree. A major crisis was averted only by an extraordinary Accord reached by the president, the Congress, and the commission. The Social Security Amendments of 1983 resulted from that Accord.

The nation has successfully weathered the considerable trauma associated with the passage of the amendments. No one can predict with certainty whether the lull will continue or new crises will arise. The crisis of the early eighties reached a crescendo over funding issues. Future major issues may also relate to financing, but they may center on factors not now deemed crucial. For example, the ratio of those paying into the system is declining relative to the number of those receiving benefits. What will be the result of this shift? Certainly, workers in their thirties or forties will not receive benefits in relation to contributions that begin to compare with those received by current retirees in their seventies or eighties. In one year the latter may receive benefits that exceed their total contributions. In short, equity as much as funding might be the basic cause of a future crisis. Economic conditions will play a large role in determining public acceptance or rejection of the system as it now stands. Almost certainly, congressional fine-tuning will be required to eliminate inequities before they become crises.

Supplemental Security Income

Basically, the Supplementary Security Income Program, although administered by the Social Security Administration, must be considered as separate and apart from social security. Intended to replace Old Age Assistance, a grant-in-aid program administered through the states, SSI was to provide federal monies for the low-income elderly and for blind and disabled persons. Begun in 1974, the program was funded from federal general tax revenues. The states, if they chose, could add to the monthly cash payments.

Unlike social security, the program has no relationship to an individual's work record. It is not a retirement program. The original objective was to provide a basic, minimum for the elderly poor. Eligibility depends upon a person's income and resources. What may seem a simple matter—the determination of income and resources—in practice has proved to be far from simple. There is an unearned income disregard and an earned income disregard; there are regulations governing the value to be attributed to individual assets such as automobiles, household goods, personal effects, and life insurance. In one state the SSI recipient is eligible for Medicaid; in another, no such eligibility exists. The SSI recipient is eligible for food stamps. Yet over 1 million eligible people do not participate, probably because they associate the program with welfare.

Reports of recent national commissions have recognized that, notwithstanding many features of SSI that are subject to criticism, the program has provided a substantial safety net for many elderly poor. The objective of providing financial support sufficient to upgrade individuals at least to the poverty level nevertheless awaits fulfillment.

The Food Stamp Program

Few governmental measures to aid the poor have gone through the ups and downs of the Food Stamp Program. For over four decades the use of food stamps has survived either as a limited experimental venture or, since 1973, as a national program mandated by Congress and operated by the Department of Agriculture in conjunction with the states.

In the first years following the establishment of the nationwide program, a family wishing to participate was required to purchase food stamps—the monthly purchase requirement—in accordance with eligibility limits relating to the household income and the number of persons in the family. The family then received an allotment. The total number of coupons in the allotment was greater than the amount of the purchase. The difference—the bonus— increased the family food buying capability. However, the requirement of a cash outlay created problems, and in 1977 the monthly purchase requirement was eliminated. Coupons are now allotted on the basis of cash income after deductions. In-kind income, such as a rent subsidy, is not counted, which raises questions of individual equity.

The Congress has resisted a number of proposals that would substantially reduce food stamp expenditures. Of the reductions that have been effected, most have spared the elderly, who constitute a small (10 percent) but increasing ratio of the total participants.

The Regulation of Private Pension Plans

The regulatory function of government is well illustrated by legislation to protect workers from income loss upon retirement. Too often employees in business and industry have relied on the promise of a retirement pension, only to discover that the promise was totally lacking in substance. For one reason or another, the employee did not qualify, or, owing to mismanagement and sometimes outright fraud, there were inadequate funds available.

With the passage of the Employees Retirement Income Security Act (ERISA) of 1974, a whole series of protective devices were introduced. Rules were established relating to the employee's eligibility for membership in the pension plan and to the process of accruing credits for years of employment. The principle of nonforfeitable rights, or vesting, was established. Guidelines were set forth to prevent the misuse of assets by the fiduciaries, that is, the officers and trustees of the plan. Information relating to the operation of the system was to be made available to the employees and to the government. To assist in preventing plan terminations, a new government agency was created, the Pension Benefit Guaranty Corporation.

The series of protections afforded by ERISA has done much to improve the prospects for reasonable worker retirement benefits. However, a host of issues remains unsettled. The lack of any provision in most plans for inflation adjustments, the small percentage of women who have been able to qualify because of vesting or portability problems, a growing argument over worker versus management control of pension fund investments, the concept introduced by the President's Commission on Pension Policy of a minimum universal pension system, the relationships with social security—these are among the problems awaiting resolution.

Federal Civilian Employees Retirement

A number of federal agencies, such as the Foreign Service and the Central Intelligence Agency, have their own retirement systems. Most federal employees, however, are members of the United States Civil Service Retirement and Disability System. CSR, as this system is called, provides benefits to approximately 1.9 million persons. In 1981, the annual cost was about $18 billion.

CSR was established in 1920, well over a decade before social security came into being. For years after social security was established, the contribution paid by the government employee into the Civil Service Retirement and Disability fund continued to be much greater than the small tax paid by employees and employers into the Old Age and Survivors Insurance Trust

Fund. Owing to the difference in the contribution rate that existed over several decades, the CSR retiree had many advantages and, as a consequence, wanted no part of social security unless, in some fashion, its benefits could be an "add on."

In recent years, the costs of CSR have become a matter of concern. In 1980, for example, general fund appropriations accounted for nearly half of CSR income. One result was a hard look at retiree benefits. Why, for example, should the public employee be eligible for full retirement income at age fifty-five? Not only is this provision extremely costly, but it results in the loss of many able employees at the peak of their productivity. Not all retirement provisions for the person in CSR, however, favor the employee. Often they put the employee at a great disadvantage. An example is the absence of pension portability for those leaving the government before meeting the five-year employment requirement.

The Social Security Amendments of 1983 constitute a first step in what must become a major revision of the retirement system for federal employees. Those hired on or after January 1984, are required to be covered under social security. Eliminating windfall benefits received by those whose working lifetime was not entirely covered by social security constitutes an initial step only. Of equal if not greater importance will be the series of steps required to provide current and prospective retirees with the benefits they have a right to expect, based on the laws and regulations in effect at the time of their hiring. There must be developed a structure to provide the newly hired civil servant with a social-security-plus framework of benefits comparable to the better plans long in effect in business and industry. It will take much time and effort to carry federal employee retirement reform through to completion.

State and Local Retirement Systems

Over the last decades, the Federal Employees Retirement Income Security Act has introduced a considerable degree of order into the pension systems of business and industry. However, ERISA has nothing to say about the activities of public systems. Efforts to establish the Public Employees Retirement Income Security Act (PERISA) have been unsuccessful. Literally thousands of public systems provide some measure of security for the employees of state and local governments. However, several hundred thousand public employees, chiefly those at the municipal level, are members of systems that are financially unsound. The newspaper that portrayed the plight of social security during the early eighties—"Will It Be There When You Need It?"—is currently applicable to a large number of local systems.

One comforting factor for many public employees is their membership in social security. In some states all are covered; in a few states no public employees are covered. One-third of the employees in the country as a whole lack membership. The 1983 Social-Security Amendments permit groups who had terminated their coverage to rejoin the system.

A joint survey in 1979 by the Advisory Commission on Governmental Relations and the National Conference of State Legislatures asserted their conviction that "great strides" were being made in improving public pension systems. Progress might be further enhanced by the passage of regulatory legislation such as PERISA, a proposal endorsed in 1981 by the President's Commission on Pension Policy.

Railroad Retirement

Railroad employees have the unique distinction of being members of a retirement system administered by the federal government. The railroad industry had the political strength during the Great Depression period of the thirties to obtain legislation setting up a retirement structure that became operable prior to social security. The three-member Railroad Retirement Board, representing labor, management, and the public, was established to administer the system. Benefits were to be paid from Railroad Retirement Account in the U.S. Treasury.

Contributions to, and benefits from, the new system were considerably larger than those in social security. As a consequence, railroad employees initially wanted no part of the latter. But as the industry declined over the next decade, financial problems increased. As social security benefits expanded in scope and amount, railroad workers wanted not only those benefits but benefits comparable to these found in industries whose workers were covered by both social security and private pension plans. In 1974, legislation was passed creating a two-tiered system that provides, in effect, for social security coverage (Tier 1) and for a private pension (Tier 2). In its attempts to account for various categories of employee awards the benefit structure has become "a claim examiner's nightmare."

The solvency of the system, seemingly assured in 1974, was continually threatened by unanticipated further decline in railroad employment—from 600,000 in 1974 to 388,000 in 1983. Moreover, income from the pension fund was used to cover jobless benefits. In August 1983, Congress was forced to act: taxes on both employers and employees were increased, and for the first time a tax was levied on Tier 2 benefits. Minor changes in benefits were made to reduce costs. Once again, with substantial contributions from the federal treasury, solvency seemed assured, at least for a few years. Assuming that the extraordinary complexity of the system can be substantially lessened, the railroad retirement structure might serve as a useful model in constructing an integrated retirement system for the civil service, military retirement, and other federal pension programs.

Military Programs

The military retirement system needs reexamination. For a minority of members of the armed services, the retirement system is virtually idyllic, providing a generous retirement benefit at an early age. For too many, however, the system approaches total catastrophe, providing social security coverage but nothing more as a reward for less than twenty years of service in the armed forces.

Normally, the word *retirement* connotes the end of one's working life. However, in the armed services retirement may mean reaching the end of a twenty-year period of service before the age of forty or slightly above. Although only a small percentage of the officers and enlisted men remain in the armed services for twenty years, the 1984 military retirement budget amounted to almost $17 billion. In 1978, only 12.2 percent of the retirees were over age sixty-five.

In contrast to the rewards accorded the service member who retires at an early age is the seeming total lack of consideration for the member who leaves before completing 20 years of service. For that person, there is no vesting whatever.

The military retirement system merits reexamination not only from the standpoint of the individual members of the armed forces but also because of its impact upon the national economy. The individual makes no contribution toward the military annuity, nor are tax monies set aside. The lack of any funding to meet future liabilities can have only one result—continually increasing military retirement expenditures.

The Black Lung Program

A very high proportion of black lung compensation payments goes to older persons because the pathology arising from environments involving hazardous materials develops only after many years of exposure. Congressional supporters of the act favored monthly benefits for those suffering severe lung impairment as a consequence of prolonged exposure to coal dust. The program was not to be related to state workmen's compensation, nor was it to be related to social security. Rather, black lung benefits were a special compensation to be met out of federal funds and to be given only to those who had contracted the specific devastating disease while working in an essential industry.

At first, use of the X-ray was the sole means of determining the extent of the disease. Authority over the act was placed in the hands of the Social Security Administration, which came under severe criticism for its high percentage of claim denials. The act was liberalized in 1972, and other evidence was accepted in determining the extent of respiratory impairment. Authority over the program was divided between the Social Security Administration and the Department of Labor. Continued unhappiness over program administration, however, led to a second revision of the act in 1977 and further liberalization of the eligibility requirements.

At first, the payment of benefits was assumed totally by the federal government. Not until 1974 were operators required to pay claims, and then only if the responsible operator could be determined. The 1977 revision placed a tax upon mined coal that was to support the Black Lung Disability Trust Fund. Unfortunately, the amount of tax levied was insufficient to pay approved claims, and in 1981 the tax rate was doubled and eligibility standards were tightened.

The assumptions in the early years of the program that the disease could be eliminated in a short time or that state workmen's compensation laws would take over new cases proved to be erroneous. The 1977 revision, unlike the 1972 amendments, provided no termination date.

The Black Lung Program experience has been unique. Whether it will remain so is questionable. What should the federal government do for workers who, years after exposure, develop "brown lung" (byssinosis, from cotton dust), "white bug" (talicosis, from dust in talc mines and mills), silicosis, or asbestiosis? What about victims of disease-bearing consumer products or of chemical wastes? To ask the questions is simple; to develop reasonable and generally acceptable answers may take decades.

Legal Services

The elderly poor are often in need of legal assistance. One of the most common areas of misunderstanding grows out of the administration of public benefits. The individual may feel aggrieved, for example, over an interpretation of the regulations pertaining to Supplementary Security Income or to any one of the several governmental programs that provide financial assistance. The need for legal services may also pertain to totally different matters, such as problems relating to commitment to an institution or to the selection of a guardian.

The agency that was created by the Legal Services Corporation Act of 1974—the Legal Services Corporation—has promoted the establishment of hundreds of neighborhood offices where individuals, many of whom are elderly, may obtain legal help. As a consequense of joint efforts at cooperation, the corporation in 1982 was the major "delivery mechanism" for legal services funded by the Older Americans Act.

Criticism of the corporation because of the types of actions it sometimes undertook, plus efforts by the president to remove the agency from the federal budget, created in the early eighties a crisis of substantial proportions. Congress refused to abolish the agency, although the appropriation was reduced. The Leadership Council of Aging Organizations has declared that elimination of the corporation would put "the most fundamental of safety nets, equal justice under law," out of the reach of the elderly poor.

Tax Benefits

The tax benefits to the elderly take several forms. For example, an elderly couple need not file a return if their gross income is under $7,400. Their personal exemptions total $4,000. If they are over fifty-five years of age, they may have a one-time exclusion of $125,000 of the gain on the sale of their home. Tax credits may be obtained by a couple filing a joint return, providing adjusted gross income is below $17,500 or if taxable pension and annuity income do not exceed $35,500.

The elderly benefit also from tax expenditures, that is, special exclusions that result in revenue losses to the government. For example, the absence of any tax on social security income—except for those persons in the higher tax brackets—accounts for a substantial saving to the individual, and similarly, a substantial revenue loss to the government. Other kinds of income that is not taxable are energy assistance, food stamps, veterans benefits, black lung benefits, and basic railroad retirement benefits.

Energy Conservation

Federal efforts to help solve the financial needs of the elderly poor have taken many forms. One of these has been the cash payment to help meet home heating costs. Begun in 1976, the program later was enlarged to include the distribution of goods such as heaters and blankets to those who qualified. In recent years, the states have been given greater authority. For example, with the passage of the Home Energy Assistance Act of 1980, the Department of Health and Human Services established guidelines for income eligibility. The states, however, were authorized to set limits below the federally established maximum. The administration of the program has been criticized for the absence of long-range planning, but the program has been recognized as a "significant source of support" for the low-income elderly.

Federally financed weatherization services have also benefited considerable numbers of the poor elderly. Begun on an experimental basis in 1973, the program has undergone various shifts in administration. The Congress rejected the president's proposals in 1982, 1983, and again in 1984 to eliminate the program, although appropriations were slightly reduced.

MAJOR MEDICAL PROGRAMS

Medicare

For the elderly, 1965 was a landmark year. Not only was the Older Americans Act passed that year but also the extremely important health insurance legislation establishing Medicare and Medicaid.

Medicare has two parts. Part A, linked to social security, provides for compulsory hospital insurance through an additional tax on wages. Part B incorporates a system of monthly premiums, deducted from the individual's social security benefits, to pay for a portion of doctors' services. Part B is voluntary, and many eligible elderly do not elect to pay the monthly premium. General supervision of this widely accepted program is a function of the Health Care Financing Administration (HCFA) in the Department of Health and Human Services. HCFA deals with intermediaries such as the Blue Cross Association, which in turn work with hospitals and other service providers. The processing of physicians' claims under Part B is also a function of the intermediary rather than the HCFA. Direct federal control is highly limited in the context of Medicare.

Steadily increasing hospital and physicians' charges, together with more sophisticated and more expensive patient treatment, have resulted in rapidly expanding costs for Medicare. A part of the burden has been shifted to elderly patients by increasing the contributions they must make toward their own care. Efforts have also been made to restrain the charges of providers. The most recent effort to stem increasing costs resulted in the adoption, in 1983, of the so-called "prospective" payment plan, by means of which patient needs are to be classified according to DRG's, or diagnostic related groups. There are 467 such groups, and each has a different payment rate. The plan is just now going into effect and its impact is as yet unknown.

Past efforts to control costs have not been particularly effective. Professional Standards Review Organizations, for example, have seemingly had no effect on stemming the tide of rising costs. These will be replaced by Peer Review Organizations, a more streamlined structure, in 1984.

Medicaid

In contrast to Medicare, Medicaid is a medical assistance program for the needy operated under federal and state guidelines and funded in large measure by the federal government. In 1983, 15.4 percent (3.4 million) of the recipients were elderly, although 36 percent of the funds were expended on elderly patients. In two-thirds of the states, eligibility to participate hinges upon meeting the criteria for participation in Supplementary Security Income.

Among the difficult problems relating to Medicaid is that of physician reimbursement. One-third of physicians refuse to participate on the grounds that the fee schedule is inadequate. One of the most interesting features of the Medicaid program is the linkage to Medicare. Four-fifths of the aged Medicaid recipients are under "buy in" arrangements that enable them to be covered by both programs.

Medicaid monies provide the principal source of public funds for nursing homes. Over four-fifths of the total nursing home population is elderly. Forty percent of these are aged eighty-five and older. Of the total number of elderly patients, women outnumber men three to one.

The federal government's involvement with nursing homes is of a threefold nature: assisting in financing construction, providing public funds for patient care, and establishing operating standards. Nursing home issues include particularly the problem of increasing costs. One partial solution receiving increased attention concerns the provision of home health-care services.

TWO AUXILIARY PROGRAMS

Transportation

For well over a decade, transportation has been recognized as one of the elderly's most important problems. Indeed, this "sleeper issue" came out of the woodwork, so to speak, at the White House Conference of 1971. Transportation was rated the third most important issue, exceeded only by issues of income and health.

The problem of providing transportation for the elderly may seem simple. In fact, it is extraordinarily complex. Physical impairments and the individual's location may make the use of public transportation difficult and often impossible. Those in rural areas often have no means of travel whatever unless they are in the fortunate position of being able to rely upon a friend or upon a public agency that is operating under special subsidy arrangements.

The federal government has attacked the elderly transportation problem from two principal directions. First, laws and regulations administered by the Department of Transportation relate to criteria in the field of mass transportation, such as floor height in buses, where federal funding is involved. Highway construction, traffic safety, airplanes and aviation facilities, accessibility to trains and train stations — all of these and more have elements of governmental regulation intended to aid those who are elderly and/or handicapped.

Transportation is also important in providing social services. The elderly receive transportation or transportation reimbursement through a number of totally separate social services. The problems of coordinating transportation funding and of providing services that answer the elderly's need for "lifeline mobility" often become uncommonly complicated.

Housing

A number of federal housing programs have singled out the elderly for special aid. However, in the mid thirties, when the government entered the housing field, participation of the elderly came not through homeownership but rather through tenancy in subsidized public housing. Indeed, the elderly were not specifically recognized until the Housing Act of 1956, which authorized public housing especially for the elderly.

Low-income families, including the elderly, received help in obtaining rental aid in newly constructed, rehabilitated, or existing housing through the passage of the Housing and Community Development Act of 1974. By 1978, elderly families inhabited 46 percent of the nation's low-rent public housing units.

Recent legislation provides for the government subsidy of very-low-income families, who are required to pay rental amounting to between 15 and 25 percent of their incomes. However, the amount available for subsidies to new developers has been substantially reduced. This will, of course, restrict further expansion. Over the years several government assistance programs have been provided for developers, such as direct low-interest loans, below-market interest rate mortgage insurance, and other devices. Elderly families occupy a relatively small percentage of homes developed by these means.

Homeownership assistance programs have also operated to a greater or lesser degree since 1968. They have taken the forms of government assisted mortgages or low-interest loans to the owner rather than the developer. A limited number of low-interest loans for rural housing was made available through the Farmers Home Administration. The emphasis in recent years has been upon rehabilitation and repair as distinguished from new construction.

In 1982, a presidential commission suggested that new-programs were essential to cope with the increasing numbers of elderly in the higher age cohorts. The emphasis upon expensive new construction had to be replaced. Special financing mechanisms, for example, could convert home equity into income.

Notwithstanding the variety of housing legislation in recent decades, the impact on the elderly, especially the elderly poor, has been limited. This issue is one that merits further attention and a shift of emphasis from the interest of the developer to the needs of the elderly.

GOVERNMENT AND THE OLDER WORKER

Federal legislation to assist older workers has been threefold—the prevention of discrimination in employment, the encouragement of volunteer employment programs, and the subsidizing of a limited number of older workers under project contractors, who in turn are supervised by the Department of Labor.

The Age Discrimination in Employment Act of 1967 applied to persons between forty and sixty-five years of age in businesses employing twenty-five or more workers. Subsequently, the age level was raised to seventy, the minimum number of employed reduced to twenty, and the coverage extended to federal, state, and local government employees.

The Older American Volunteer Programs are tied to federal social service agencies. First authorized in 1968, the Retired Senior Volunteer Program is under the Direction of ACTION. Volunteers work in a wide range of settings, such as schools, hospitals, and nursing homes. They may receive out-of-pocket expenses only. The volunteer is not to replace an employed person. The Foster Grandparent Program, first developed in 1965, and the Senior Companion Program, begun in 1973, pay small stipends to low-income persons for up to twenty hours of work per week.

Work opportunities for older persons are authorized under Title V of the Older Americans Act and in 1983 were supervised by the Department of Labor. Project sponsors such as the U.S. Forest Service, the American Association of Retired Persons, the National Council on the Aging, the National Council of Senior Citizens, individual states, and others arrange for the employment of roughly thirty thousand workers through "host" agencies at the local level. Again, the work week is twenty hours at the minimum wage. The number employed is obviously a small fraction of the potential. Efforts to eliminate the programs entirely were rejected by the Congress, which provided funds through June 1984.

THE AGING VETERAN

The preceding chapters have been concerned with governmental policy toward a specific population group—the aging. An increasing fraction of this population group relates to those aging persons who are also veterans. For many decades, the combination of veteran status and age was a matter of little moment. However, now and in the immediate future the veterans' benefits structure that has been gradually built up assumes increasing importance. In the year 2000, for example, the 9 million veterans then over age sixty-five will undoubtedly place a severe strain upon the nation's ability to provide already promised health services.

Veterans' organizations constitute a potent political force. The Iron Triangle, as the combination of the Veterans Affairs committees of The House and Senate and the Veterans Administration is called, has in the past developed the reputation of being a "closed system." Legislation favorable to the interests of veterans was enacted with little difficulty.

Wide-ranging benefits include (1) compensation—liberal monthly payments for those disabled in the line of duty, (2) pension—a monthly payment to the disabled or low-income veteran, and (3) medical care for those having service-connected disabilities and for those certifying inability to pay. For those over age sixty-five, the certification of inability to pay was eliminated in 1971. The full impact of this action has not yet been fully realized. By 1990, roughly half of the entire male population over age sixty-five will be eligible for veterans' health care benefits.

The Veterans Administration, through its over 170 medical centers, provides extensive hospital, long-term, and outpatient care. This care is already being provided to many who do not have service-connected disabilities. The

1971 act classifying the nonworking veteran over age sixty-five as permanently and totally disabled opens up the possibility that a large percentage of the elderly male population will be cared for through the veterans' health care system. In view of the rapid escalation of health care costs throughout the nation, the question arises whether the care now given the veteran with nonservice-connected disabilities should be curtailed or whether the system should be expanded, perhaps as a major beginning step toward a national health service.

SUMMATION

Programs for the elderly, which initially focused on income, now encompass a whole gamut of life supports. Income in old age remains a central concern, and social security has emerged as a truly universal giant, with a number of smaller programs existing on its periphery or side by side with it. Concern of legislative bodies with health care for the older population started with relatively modest plans but in the sixties culminated in the full-blown programs of Medicare and Medicaid. Programs to meet the needs of the elderly have also been developed in other areas, although the impact of these is less significant. Efforts have been made to improve housing and transportation. The older worker has received attention from several perspectives. And, finally, the Aging Network offers a number of personal services authorized under the Older Americans Act and its amendments.

It would seem that little has been left out that could contribute to the quality of life for the older person. Yet the programs, given the mode of development, do not cohere into a national public policy. There are some linkages among programs, but these tend to be relatively few and rather weak. Also, there is a number of areas where programs are virtually duplicated but are applied to different population segments or are targeted for relatively narrowly defined segments. As a consequence, there are overlaps as well as gaps in the programs under consideration. It is also clear that the sharing-out of benefits from various programs is anything but even-handed. This is partly because of the many agencies that have a hand in the implementation of the various programs as well as because of the influence of special-interest organizations representing a better educated and better organized segment of the population. It is this "tangled web" that is the subject of the next section of this chapter.

2. Summary Analysis

There can be no doubt that massive efforts have been made in support of the elderly. The large portion of the budget that goes to aging programs, or programs from which the aging benefit, attests to this fact. So does the multiplicity of life-support areas, seemingly addressing every need, that are encompassed by these programs. Yet the frequent complaints, that have been recorded throughout this book of fragmentation, lack of coordination, and confusion are well grounded. This state of affairs obviously cannot be laid to ill will. In large part, the failure to develop a cohesive national policy for the aging can be attributed to the structure and process of policymaking in the United States. Later in this section, it will be shown that there are some emerging points of coherence in policy for the aging, but these have been a long time coming. The barriers to comprehensiveness and universality are very real and cannot be overlooked by those who are interested in the policymaking scene. Let us recapitulate briefly.

Federal policy for older Americans has been developed piecemeal and incrementally over many years. This approach to policymaking is applicable to all efforts in the United States, and development in the field of aging is simply one example of the process as a whole. In comparison with other Western industrialized nations, the United States began tardily and reluctantly to address the needs of special population groups. Prior to the 1930s federal policy was limited to functional sectors such as agriculture and defense. The division of responsibilities among congressional legislative committees still reflects this traditional approach. Other historical forces that have led to complexity in the field of aging, as well as elsewhere, include the relatively late appearance of federal pension and unemployment legislation. The economic picture had been so bleak for so many years prior to that time that many private and public pension plans were already in effect. In the public sphere, the federal level was involved in a very limited way in forming policy for special groups such as veterans and certain categories of federal employees. But there were many scattered public plans at the state and local community levels. Many of these predecessors of social security and related legislation continue to exist, making any semblance of uniformity very difficult to achieve.

In this book an effort has been made to restrict the examination of policy to federal programs for the aging. As the reader will have discovered, this effort has not been entirely successful, since many programs involve a great deal of spillover into other spheres of authority. The individual states and local communities often have a great deal of say in how programs are implemented even when these programs are federally initiated. This division of responsibility extends far beyond programs that provide income to older persons. It is pervasive, again because of traditional rules of power dispersion stemming from the Constitution.

Taking the federal level of policymaking in itself, the legislative process around programs for the elderly is already highly fragmented. The two Houses of Congress and, of course, the executive branch are all involved in legislation to benefit the elderly. Roughly a dozen functional committees in the Senate and another dozen in the House of Representatives have legislative responsibilities for particular programs. In each of these bodies, one of the committees is an oversight committee for all elderly programs. Oversight committees have no right to introduce legislation. Their responsibilities are primarily informational, although members can and do keep an eye on legislation for older persons and help the process along. In general, however, separate pieces of legislation for specific areas are assigned to different committees for action. To say the least, this mode of policy development interferes with program coordination. It helps to explain why the many programs tend to be instituted on an ad hoc basis, without reference to existing programs.

Policymaking at the federal level is, in any case, a process of conflict and compromise. Even within the committees responsible for a particular sphere of policymaking, several rather different perspectives are likely to be represented among the members. Thus any particular piece of legislation undergoes severe scrutiny, revision, and amendment before passage, if indeed it is passed at all. A similar process occurs as equivalent committees in the two houses attempt to reconcile differences on any given bill. And, after all this, there are still the president's wishes to be considered, lest a veto or other obstruction to passage be applied. Thus while the provisions for some programs for the elderly appear to be quite sweeping, when one examines the fine print it becomes clear that only a trickle of services will result. The Older Americans Act is a classic example of this phenomenon.

The legislative process, complex as it is in itself, does not exist in a vacuum. Many powerful interest groups representing the aging attempt to bring their weight to bear upon legislators. Although there seems to be some movement among a number of these groups, each representing a somewhat different constituency, to present a more united front, up until the present time they have often been in competition with one another. The individual legislator, while he or she may be grateful for the information supplied by interest groups, is often placed in an awkward situation in terms of decision-making. Nevertheless, the major interest groups do exert an undeniable influence, and their demands for their aging constituencies must be taken into account. Also to be considered are aging voters. The growing proportion of the population that is labeled as elderly represents a potentially powerful force at the ballot box. While, as shown in chapter II, older people are a heterogeneous group and do not as yet vote in anything resembling a bloc pattern, the possibility of bloc voting is always there. Older people are consistent and reliable voters, and this well-established fact, in addition to their growing numbers, cannot be ignored. Rare is the politician in recent years who fails to attempt to establish his or her advocacy for older people. But just what to advocate remains a delicate and intricate puzzle.

The problems of the politicians and the legislators do not stop there. Although these are elected to attempt to solve problems at the national level, it is in fact the voters "back home" who are responsible for getting them in—or out—of office. Thus senators and representatives cannot neglect the views of their state and local constituencies in making legislative choices. The legislator hears those voices, in addition to all the others, in considering legislation. Sometimes trades-offs can satisfy otherwise conflicting demands. For example, more conservative legislators from the farm belt may join more liberal legislators in voting for the Food Stamp Program. Forming this coalition provides benefits for agriculture as well as for older persons. However, in many cases, such happy solutions are not possible, and the legislator is forced to act cautiously while sorting out what are bound to be somewhat conflicting messages from many influential sources.

Through the electoral process, then, what happens at the federal level is directly related to the concerns expressed at state and local levels. Formal legislation, too, delegates much responsibility for program implementation to public bodies at the state and local levels. In some cases, most notably in the health area, responsibility is also shared with the private sector. As a result, what appears to be an evenhanded program when initiated federally may actually operate quite differently in different parts of the country. This diversity is directly attributable to the separation of powers between different levels of government and, in this long-hallowed context, is probably unavoidable.

When the Administration on Aging was instituted, many thought it would bring order into the relative chaos of policy for the aging by performing an overall coordinating and administrative role. In fact, the AoA has never been awarded anything resembling such a high level of authority. Even in relation to the Aging Network, for which it does take administrative responsibility, its powers are strictly limited. The Older Americans Act cites a number of services that are actually under the auspices of other organizations. Although recently charged with the responsibility of coordinating the various bodies involved in bits and pieces of policy for the aging, the AoA has been given no real authority to accomplish this. Generally, the AoA is reduced to negotiating with the various relevant federal bureaucracies to provide services it is not entitled to supply.

The AoA does have overall authority to administer, via The Aging Network, service programs related to the Older Americans Act. Implementation of the Older Americans Act and its amendments is accomplished by delegating responsibility to successively lower levels of public bodies and eventually even private bodies. Modeled on policy implementation in other spheres, administrative layers reach down to the community level. Since at each level some leeway is afforded because of different conditions that may exist within the elderly population, some diversity in implementation inevitably occurs. The trickle-down approach to policy implementation, then, also means that the program at the top level will be more unified than the one that is actually put into practice at the various local levels. The AoA is directly responsible only for administering the ten regional agencies. Each regional agency, in turn, is responsible for a cluster of state Offices of Aging. The state offices administer within-state or community-level regional offices called Area Agencies on Aging. Administrative responsibility is therefore delegated by successive steps to ever-narrower spheres of authority. And all of this takes place at the purely administrative level: the actual delivery of service is accomplished for the most part through contracts with service providers, including private organizations, at the local level. Although coordinating functions are prescribed at both the state and local levels, the situation is very similar to the one at the top. State offices have no authority to coordinate all aging programs in a given state, and the Area Agencies on Aging have no authority to coordinate the available service providers at the local level. Again, negotiation is used as much as possible to stimulate coordination and cooperation.

This device of delegating administrative authority to ever-lower levels may, as some argue, make the Aging Network and its attendant services more visible and responsive to the needs of the older population simply because it does enable participation at the community level. The point to be made here, however, is that this approach encourages greater fragmentation because it adds local input to what has already been established at the federal level. Not only will the availability of services vary from locality to locality, but the quality of the services can also be expected to vary. Accordingly, the dispersion of powers across a number of levels creates another dimension to the general disarray in policy for the aging. The Aging Network is to some extent an extreme example, although by no means a unique one, of the consequences of this approach. What can be obtained under the Older Americans Act constitutes a relatively small part of the total service programs intended to benefit the elderly. Many other programs, however, are affected by the dispersion approach. Individual states in particular are often highly influential in determining who is eligible for given programs as well as the nature and extent of benefits to be provided.

For all these reasons, it has been argued throughout this book that there is no such thing as a national policy for the aged in the United States. Although most of the legislation for the aging does indeed originate at the federal level, the responsibilities for implementing programs for older persons have been parceled out in such a way that coordination or even orderly progression has been impossible. Many legislators with diverse perspectives hold some responsibility for pieces of legislation, but no body has the power to pull the pieces together. In fact, so many different forces play a role in developing programs for older persons that the whole process is fraught with compromise, trade-offs, and contingencies. The situation at the federal level represents a part, perhaps the most important part, of the picture. It has been impossible, however, to limit discussion of public policy for the aged to the federal level. Almost inevitably, when implementation processes come into consideration the role of the individual states, and to a lesser extent of local communities, has to be considered. It can be said in rather simplistic summary fashion that fragmentation of policy for older Americans occurs at two levels: in policymaking at the federal level and in policy implementation by public governing bodies at subfederal levels.

The question can then be raised as to whether there is any semblance of order among the various programs instituted for the older population. More precisely put, are there any viable linkages that relate programs to one another and create standards that apply across programs rather than being applied individually from program to program. The answer is that there are some linkages and that the central core, to the extent that there is one, rests with social security legislation. The only program relying solely on federal government criteria, social security has emerged not only as a nearly universal source of income for retired workers and their survivors and dependents but also as an extremely useful "yardstick" to determine eligibility for other programs and/or as a backup measure of income security for other pension plans.

Given the problems in policymaking, social security is almost incredibly effective in providing economic support. One way or another almost every older citizen of the United States is now within the reach of the social security network. Because it is entirely federally and therefore centrally administered, social security is also remarkably cost efficient compared to other programs. Less than 2 percent of the monies flowing through the system are used for administrative costs, while the remainder goes to the recipients.

For all its advantages, however, there are still some older persons who are not eligible for social security or who receive inadequate benefits. Despite the adequacy principle in the formula for calculating benefits, the goal of providing a minimum floor of well-being is not always met. For that reason, without the Supplementary Security Income Program and the Food Stamp Program, many persons would still be very poor in old age. Federal control over these programs is weakened. There is a linkage between social security and SSI, since the Social Security Administration is the general reference point for deciding when and if an older person is eligible for SSI. In fact, individual states have a great deal of discretion in determining eligibility and benefit levels. Accordingly, the universal aspect attached to social security criteria is greatly diluted, to the detriment of large numbers of elderly persons, especially in certain states. The link between SSI and food stamps, however, is very direct: if one is eligible for the former, one is eligible for the latter.

In spite of divergencies at the state level, it should be emphasized that the Social Security Administration exerts a powerful influence on the states, and therefore the linkage between social security and SSI is quite real. SSI, in turn, is tightly tied to the Food Stamp Program. The federal government in recent years has also taken a much more active role in relation to both private pension plans and those instituted at the state and local levels. The linkages with social security are sometimes direct, but more often, they are indirect. Across the board, however, the standards of social security as related to contributions and expected postretirement rewards have been evoked to spell out what private and nonfederal plans must undertake to ensure respectability and reliability. Many complaints about weaknesses in the federal role regarding pension plans remain, and it would be greatly overstating the case to claim that anything approaching order and consistency exists. At the same time, there can be no doubt that a much greater measure of security has been achieved for those who are involved in private and nonfederal public pension plans. This statement is probably especially true in relation to the highly vulnerable state and local plans, in which the large majority of those covered are now also directly part of the social security system. Linkages between social security and multiple other plans for federal employees are now in the progress of being strengthened as well.

The central point, however, is not the degree to which social security governs the way in which the various programs that provide financial benefits in old age are carried out. What makes social security definable as a central core is that it is constantly and increasingly being used as a reference point around which current and future decisions about pension plans are evaluated.

Social security also provides a vital link between the two areas that concern older people most, according to the White House conferences: income and health. Eligibility for Medicare rests solely on social security criteria. In fact, compulsory hospital insurance payments (Plan A) are part of the pay check deduction for social security. This linkage is very clear. Every social security recipient has hospital insurance, at least. The second part of Medicare (Plan B), which covers a portion of physicians' fees, is voluntary. Since participation requires the payment of an additional monthly premium, many older social security recipients have chosen not to participate. Still, it is social-security eligibility that governs access to this type of coverage as well as to hospital care.

In its turn, Medicaid provides the same services to needy older persons. The linkage to SSI, a sister to social security, is not as direct for several reasons. Primary among these is the decisionmaking authority allocated to the states. In most cases an older person who receives Supplementary Security Income is also entitled to Medicaid. However, the individual states have discretionary powers over eligibility to Medicaid, just as they do over SSI eligibility and payments. In a minority of states, as a result, whether or not an older person is entitled to Medicaid is a separate issue rather than an automatic consequence of whether he or she is an SSI recipient.

Beyond the linkages with social security, the remaining programs do not stand in any readily discernible relationship to one another. Many politicians and other spokespersons for the elderly had hoped and indeed anticipated that programs for the aged would be coordinated under the Older Americans Act. The goals of the act, as reported in chapter II, certainly suggested such a potential. The goals, however, were very far out of line with reality, and over time the potential has remained just that. The Older Americans Act emphasizes transportation as necessary for service delivery and also speaks to housing needs among older Americans. The Aging Network was not and is not authorized to provide these services, however, and must negotiate with the responsible bureaucracies in behalf of elderly clients. The Older Americans Act and its amendments have authorized the provision of a number of services to the elderly. These include multipurpose centers, nutrition programs, a number of personal services, and paid volunteer programs for low-income older persons. Under the Aging Network, then, another smaller and weaker cluster of programs for the aging can be identified.

What order exists under public policy for the aged can be found in relation to social security and, to a lesser extent, the Aging Network. Some of the linkages around social security are very clear and direct; other are more nebulous. Policy for the aging has a nexus that stretches at least across the two vitally important areas of income and health. Social security also increasingly forms a reference point, and sometimes even an anchoring base, for non-federal pension plans. At the federal level, recent legislation to "save social security" also includes a step toward closer linkage between social security and the various plans for federal retirees. These developments are promising, for they auger more consistency and evenhandedness as well as possible savings in administrative costs. Nevertheless, there is a very long way to go before a state of affairs resembling coherence is achieved. And the barriers to be surmounted are formidable and quite probably impossible to breach beyond a certain point.

A second organizing focus around policymaking for the aging can be found in the Aging Network, authorized by the Older Americans Act and its amendments. This legislation appears to be a logical coordinating base for programs for the aging, given its exclusive concern with the elderly, but the necessary authority is simply not given. Much has been accomplished in "putting the network in place" and also in serving older Americans in important ways.

Whether the up-until-now relatively small impact of the Aging Network upon the elderly as a total population will continue to expand is questionnable in the current funding climate. A number of legislators have advocated strengthening its integrative functions, but a move in this direction also seems unlikely in the near future.

It is possible, then, to suggest that there are some discernible organizing points in policy for the aging. That they have been emerging or increasing fairly recently suggests some potential for future coherence. On the whole, however, the dispersion of powers within the federal operations and between the federal and other levels of authority leads to a pessimistic forecast for a national policy for the elderly in the foreseeable future. The traditions of power dispersion are very strongly embedded in American democracy. Still, when one looks back to the early decades of this century, one cannot avoid recognizing that the approach of the United States toward caring for its people has changed dramatically.

In spite of the presence of organizing clusters, the consequences of general fragmentation are manifest in the gaps and overlaps in meeting the needs of older persons. The most significant gap is the failure to eliminate poverty among older Americans. The multiple programs, addressing virtually every area of life, and the by-now huge budget expenditures have not produced a reasonably secure existence for a large number of the elderly in this country. Using the principle of adequacy in social security combined with back-up programs in SSI and food stamps has not solved the problem. The heaviest burden falls on minorities and women, especially very old women. Those persons who, for one reason or another, had the least ability to build up an adequate social security base either on their own or as dependents are not raised above the poverty level through the adequacy principle. SSI may help if it is available and/or acceptable to them. These same people are also usually those who had no access to private pension plans or other means of supplementing income in old age. A history of poverty is a path to a disadvantaged old age. There is some recognition of this fact, obviously, in federal policy, and some strides have been made, but poverty in old age continues, and it continues to affect some groups more than others. With the increasing graying of America and the higher proportions of women in the very-old-age brackets, and with the current high levels of unemployment that affect minorities far more than whites, the issue will sharpen, not lessen, over time.

The many smaller programs intended to defray taxes or provide relief from the burden of, for example, home heating and insulation costs reach only a limited number of elderly persons and in addition have very limited benefits. Such programs, while certainly well intentioned and welcome to the recipients, attack the problem obliquely and ineffectively. Housing programs could be enormously important to the well-being of elderly persons, particularly those who are handicapped in some way. However, the numerous programs are scattered and disorganized, and as yet are little focused on the needs of the very old. Efforts at making the transportation "lifeline" more accessible to the elderly, especially those who are poor, handicapped, or in need of services of some kind, have met with some success, but the problem has proved monumental. In the current economic climate, efforts in the area of transportation are declining if not being dropped altogether in some vital areas. The promise of the Older Americans Act and its amendments, too, has been far out of proportion to their actual impact. And the future does not look any rosier. Here again, many services that may be essential to the well-being of the very old, the chronically ill, and the homebound and isolated can only be needed more rather than less extensively as the age profile extends into the upper reaches of the life cycle.

Finally, there is a gap in health care coverage for the current crop of older people in this country. Medicare is becoming more expensive, that is, the proportion of income older persons must pay to receive services is rising. Since all persons must pay the same amount regardless of income, the burden falls most heavily on the poorer segments of the aging population. It is possible to fall back on Medicaid, but this involves divesting oneself of virtually all assets, and even this option is not available to some older people. Some elderly persons may simply have to do without care; others not previously impoverished may become so in the process of receiving care for extended or costly illnesses. Again, there seems to be little attention to the future.

While these gaps exist in economic, health, and a variety of other vital services to the older population, there are also significant overlaps. For example, too many programs give pensions to selected segments of the population. Administrative costs, combined with special benefit advantages, make these overlaps not only costly and unwieldly but also inequitable. Better-off older persons in this nation are also able to amass benefits from various sources and can take greater advantage of tax provisions and other loopholes to maintain a very comfortable lifestyle. Much of this comfort is achieved at the expense of the taxpayer in general and of funds for the less-well-off elderly in particular. The economic advantage naturally leads to other advantages, such as ability to procure adequate health care, housing, transportation, and other services.

It is not the American way to deprive persons of advantages they may have amassed over a lifetime, and we would not anticipate equality of income in old age any more than at any other phase of the life cycle. We do think that government should be somewhat more evenhanded in the distribution of public benefits so that at least the minimum needs of the elderly are met in all the important areas of their lives. Taxing social security benefits for the elderly in higher income brackets is a step in the direction of reducing excess public expenditures for those who are already comfortably off. But little has been heard to the effect that some of the savings could be used to redress the plight of the elderly poor. There was surprisingly little outcry about the decision to tax social security benefits above a certain income level, possibly because this measure was successfully presented as necessary to preserve social security. In the current political climate, it is unlikely that significant steps will be taken to improve life circumstances in old age. Rather, we seem to be drifting in the opposite direction. Yet given the characteristics of the aging population, this is a problem that looms very large in the future.

3. Conclusion and Implications

In the preceding chapters, an effort has been made to set forth the dimensions of the major federal programs affecting the elderly. Each program was established in response to a specific need. In some instances, the essential element related to income, in others it related to the provision of a service. The programs developed over several decades. Although the desirability of establishing an overall national policy was recognized, the achievement of that goal remains on the distant horizon, even though some beginnings of cohesion have emerged over time.

A brief recapitulation of the numbers of elderly suffices to demonstrate the existence of a major national policy problem. There were in 1980 25.5 million persons over age sixty-five, and the numbers of aged, especially those seventy-five and eighty-five and over, will increase dramatically in the next two decades. Thus, those least able to care for themselves will in the year 2000 constitute 17.3 million or 50 percent of the projected 35 million persons over age sixty-five.

The full ramifications of what has been labeled a "demographic tidal wave," and the solutions to the multitude of resulting problems have thus far escaped public grasp.[2] The government can scarcely be accused of shirking the task, as attested to by the annual expenditure of billions of dollars on programs of vital significance to the aging. However, as the number of elderly and their proportion in the general population escalates, present weaknesses become more apparent.

The absence of a national policy has been caused by no single factor. It has been emphasized in this book that the structure and process of policymaking in the United States make comprehensiveness and universality extremely difficult to achieve. Another factor has to do with the input from the elderly themselves. The elderly may be the most concerned about policy for the aging, but as a group they have lacked the cohesiveness and drive normally associated with successful political action. Of the nation's 25.5 million persons over age sixty-five, nearly half belong to at least one organization of the aging. Yet membership in an organization has in no sense been the catalyst needed to achieve either a single-purpose objective or a series of unified programs.[3] But the relative political effectiveness of the aging as a group could change rather quickly in coming decades as new and more sophisticated cohorts of the elderly grapple with the increasing complexities of issues involving the aging.

Thus the absence of any all-embracing national policy cannot be charged solely to the weaknesses of the political system at the formal level. Admittedly, the considerations of issues involving the aging in the Congress, the highest legislative authority, is made difficult by the nature of the committee structure. The division of authority among a host of committees multiplies the task of obtaining consensus, although it does have the great virtue of enabling a considerable proportion of federal legislators to become informed about the issues of concern to the elderly. The problems at the "top" are compounded throughout the several levels of the political system.

With all the difficulties in the system itself and although the population most affected is inconsistent and ineffectively organized, many gains have been made for older people, and support has indeed increased mightily over time. With minor modifications, the objectives of the Older Americans Act of 1965 have been retained. This act is the "sole federal social service statute designed exclusively for seniors."[4] The 1981 amendments constituted the ninth revision of the act. In less than two decades a rather elaborate Aging Network has been developed, with the funding level increasing many times.

The programs included in the Aging Network are, in reality, no more than a minor part of the total government effort directed toward the elderly. Indeed, the largest single program, social security, was initially not directed at the retired person; instead it was a system to produce benefits when all workers attained a fixed age. Today the costs of social security and the various federal retirement systems amount to over 100 times those of the Aging Network programs. The costs of social security have risen astronomically over time, and the same may be said of the major medical programs. A commitment to elderly concerns has thus been demonstrated, but it may be wavering.

The elderly, more than any other segment of the population, are vitally concerned with the special policy issues relating to those over sixty-five years of age. But other segments of the population are affected and may be especially burdened under rising costs. For example, those who are working are paying a considerable social security tax, which is transferred quickly for the benefit of retirees. Other population cohorts lack the elderly person's intimacy with a given policy for the aging. As the budget bite gets larger, what the aged may consider a matter of life and death may not be viewed as very worthy of support by younger cohorts.

From this point of view, perspective on the part of the elderly persons may be lacking. Without perspective, there may be an undue emotional linkage with a particular issue concerning aging. When this occurs, there is a risk of endangering intergenerational relationships. While obviously many elderly persons are not getting sufficient assistance, there are others who feel entitled to benefits that may seem excessive to other population segments. A part of this problem may be caused by a lack of understanding of the benefit structure, but it could endanger the generally sympathetic public climate in which programs to benefit the aging have emerged and grown. It is important that elderly persons consider the needs of the total society rather than make demands based exclusively on their own interests. To do otherwise is to invite the downgrading of all programs for the aging by younger workers who might become disenchanted with evidences of greed on the part of large numbers of elderly. To prevent this catastrophe, it would be a vital step to launch a major educational effort centered on the responsibility of the elderly and indeed all population groups to strive toward a more evenhanded distribution of the nation's public resources.

The nation is beginning to devise future plans for redistributing resources and reducing costs in the face of the changing age structure. The Select Committee of the House of Representatives has asserted that the most appropriate steps toward an acceptable and affordable policy for the aging must be directed toward the "elders" those over age seventy-five. They are the most vulnerable and "are significantly worse off than senior adults (65–74)."[5] The latter should receive services, however, providing they have needs that can be documented. The committee declared that with greater emphasis upon preventive measures, all elders could, within a decade, be provided with a "full floor of care" at no greater cost than is now expended on a much smaller number.[6] Doubtless many other proposals will be presented and discussed over the next years, and doubtless they will not address some of the major problems identified in this book. Addressing the issue of affordability via targeting especially vulnerable segments of the elderly population and working outward from there, for example, is not a new idea, and it is one that has encountered much resistance in the past and presents tremendous problems in implementation.

From what has been reported, the faults of the nation's programs for the aging may appear to be without limit. The strong language of Congressman Pepper merits repeating: "fragmented, inefficient, unmanageable, and incomprehensible."[7] In addition, certain of the programs have features that appear to be shockingly unfair. Other programs are simply symbolic tokens of what might be. Even with all the budgetary outlay, the Select Committee on Aging has declared that "the rhetoric far outdistances the reality."[8]

Nevertheless, considerable accomplishments must be recognized. For example, the incomes of literally millions of seniors have been substantially raised by means of social security, Supplementary Security Income, veterans' and miners' benefits, and special retirement programs for federal employees and military and railroad personnel. As a consequence, poverty has been markedly reduced. Similarly, through Medicare, Medicaid, and veterans' medical benefits many older people receive an amount and quality of medical care scarcely imagined two decades ago. Other older Americans are protected by federal laws and regulations concerned with, for example, retirement systems of business and industry and, age discrimination in employment.

In spite of these notable achievements, the costliness, the unwieldiness, the all-too-apparent inequities have caused widespread disenchantment with policy for the aging. The next years are not promising for those who contemplate a never-ending expansion of financial benefits and social services for the elderly. The current trend toward austerity points in precisely the opposite direction. The implications surrounding the nature of policymaking in the United States are clear in times of entrenchment. Little in the way of sweeping change or broad-gauged planning is occurring, but rather a chipping away at the edges that promises little in terms of increased policy coherence. The chipping away will be more restrained in an election year, and the president's budget calls for a rather modest cut in domestic programs. A comparatively larger cut has been proposed for programs for the needy than for those affecting a broad segment of the population where more powerful political opposition can be mobilized.[9] This year social security will be left largely untouched, and a proposed cut in Medicare has been withdrawn, although beneficiaries will still have to pay more if the budget passes as written.[10] While it is forecast that there will be "some tough bullets to bite" in 1985[11] and that Medicare is a prime target, we can anticipate that a "decremental" approach will continue to be the order of the day unless the political and economic climate changes markedly. The economy appears to be improving, but intimations for the future are conflicting, and the picture is, to say the least, murky.

Yet the projected changes in the older population, especially in segments that are likely to become more rather than less needy because of functional reductions. Attention from all levels of government working in coordination would seem to be required. This kind of coordinated effort would be very difficult to achieve in the American system, no matter how pressing the problem.

Events will ultimately force a resolution. At the present time, there seems to be a movement away from a nationwide approach, leaving some important questions about consequences. What, for example, will the touted New Federalism mean for the programs described in the preceding chapters? Will they continue to be federally administered or, perhaps through block grants, be made almost totally subject to widely varying state and local controls? Almost certainly, in the political climate of the mid-1980s few programs will be expanded unless there is a groundswell of recognition that the needs of many older Americans are compelling. In the short run, the likelihood of such a groundswell seems very small. In the near future, a number of existing programs, especially those of a token nature, may well disappear. Other programs will probably undergo cutbacks or modifications of one kind or another. The basic programs will be reassessed and revised, but they must survive. In the long run, the nation will almost surely recoil against those suggesting a less caring approach to the problems of the elderly.

Appendix

Notes

Index

APPENDIX / A Profile of the Aged and the Aging

The Number of Elderly

The twentieth century has seen a dramatic increase in both the number and percentage of the elderly. The Census Bureau has determined that the population of the United States in 1980 was 226,504,825.[1] Of this number, 25,544,137, or 11.3 percent, were aged sixty-five and over. One person in nine is now an "elder" (see table A); a considerable contrast to the 1-in-25 ratio of 1900 (see table B).[2]

Specialists in demography point out the dangers in assuming that all those aged sixty-five and over belong to one homogeneous group. Just as there are major differences between twenty-year-old persons and those thirty or forty years of age, so there are differences between sixty-five-year-old persons and those seventy-five, eighty-five, and above. Indeed, in these latter categories, there are "many sharp differences with respect to such characteristics as living arrangements, marital status, work status, income, education, health, kinship support, and use of leisure time."[3] Of the approximately five thousand persons who celebrate their sixty-fifth birthdays on any given day, most have experienced a life history substantially different from those in the last decades of the nineteenth century.

Table A

Those aged 65 and Over, Number and Percentage

Age	Total	Percentage
65 and Over	25,544,133	100.0
65–69	8,780,844	34.4
70–74	6,796,742	26.6
75–79	4,792,597	18.8
80–84	2,934,229	11.5
85 and Over	2,239,721	8.8

Source: U.S. Department of Commerce, Bureau of the Census, *1980 Census of Population, Age, Sex, Race, and Spanish Origin of the Population by Regions, Divisions, and States:* 1980, PC 80–S1–1, May 1981, p. 3.

239

Table B
Aging Population as Percentage of Total Population, by Decades

Year	Total Population (in thousands)	Aging Population (in thousands)	Percentage of Total
1900	76,094	3,099	4.1
1910	92,407	3,986	4.3
1920	106,461	4,929	4.7
1930	123,077	6,705	5.5
1940	132,122	9,031	6.9
1950	151,684	12,362	8.2
1960	180,671	16,675	9.3
1970	204,879	20,085	9.8
1980	226,504	25,544	11.3

Source: U.S. Department of Commerce, Bureau of the Census, *Historical Statistics of the United States, Colonial Times to 1970,* September 1975, part 1, p. 10. For 1980, see table A.

One of the more startling features of the population over age sixty-five concerns both the number of persons in the over seventy-five and over eighty-five cohorts, that is, those born within a stated period, and the large percentage increase in those groups (see table C).

Individuals are living longer. This increase in length of life is due to a number of factors, including progress in medicine and in science. However, the principal factor accounting for the increase in the number of elderly stems from the high fertility rates in the last decades of the nineteenth century and the early decades of the twentieth century. A less important factor during this period was immigration. A recent study of projected growth during the period 1976–2000 estimated that the 65–74 age group would increase 23 percent, those aged 75–84 by 57 percent, and the 85 and over age group by 91 percent.[4] These large Projected increases obviously must be taken into account in the formulation of policy for the aging.

Sex Ratio and Marital Status

The sex ratio of the aging population is no less startling than the overall increase in numbers. At birth, the number of males and females is substantally equal. In past years, the ratio remained equal. In 1900, for example, the ratio between men and women of all ages was virtually the same. There were 101.9 white males per 100 females and 102.9 black males per 100 black females.[5]

In recent decades, a major shift has taken place. The life expectancy of females is now much greater than that of males. By 1980, the sex ratios in the general population had changed markedly, and this change is reflected most dramatically in the older population (see table D). Due to the longer life expectancy of women, women were highly overrepresented compared to men

Table C
The Growth of the Older Population Actual and Projected: 1900–2050 (in thousands)

Year	Total Population, All Ages	55–64 No.	55–64 %	65–74 No.	65–74 %	75–84 No.	75–84 %	85 & Over No.	85 & Over %	65 & Over No.	65 & Over %
1900	76,303	4,009	5.3	2,189	2.9	772	1.0	123	0.2	3,084	4.0
1910	91,972	5,054	5.5	2,793	3.0	989	1.1	167	0.2	3,950	4.3
1920	105,711	6,532	6.2	3,464	3.3	1,259	1.2	210	0.2	4,933	4.7
1930	122,775	8,397	6.8	4,721	3.8	1,641	1.3	272	0.2	6,634	5.4
1940	131,669	10,572	8.0	6,375	4.8	2,278	1.7	365	0.3	9,019	6.8
1950	150,697	13,295	8.8	8,415	5.6	3,278	2.2	577	0.4	12,270	8.1
1960	179,323	15,572	8.7	10,997	6.1	4,633	2.6	929	0.5	16,560	9.2
1970	203,302	18,608	9.2	12,447	6.1	6,124	3.0	1,409	0.7	19,980	9.8
1980	226,505	21,700	9.6	15,578	6.9	7,727	3.4	2,240	9.9a	25,544	11.3
1990	249,731	21,090	8.4	18,054	7.2	10,284	4.1	3,461	1.4	31,799	12.7
2000	267,990	23,779	8.9	17,693	6.6	12,207	4.6	5,136	1.9	35,036	13.1
2010	283,141	34,828	12.3	20,279	7.2	12,172	4.3	6,818	2.4	39,269	13.9
2020	296,339	40,243	13.6	29,769	10.0	14,280	4.8	7,337	2.5	51,386	17.3
2030	304,330	33,965	11.2	34,416	11.3	21,128	6.9	8,801	2.9	64,345	21.1
2040	307,952	34,664	11.3	29,168	9.5	24,529	8.0	12,946	4.2	66,643	21.6
2050	308,856	37,276	12.1	30,022	9.7	20,976	6.8	16,063	5.2	67,061	21.7

Source: U.S. Department of Commerce, Bureau of the Census, Decennial Census of Population, 1900–1980 and Projections of the Population of the United States: 1982 to 2050, Current Population Reports, Series P-25, No. 922, October 1982. Projections are middle series.

a. The authors believe this is a misprint. The proportion should read 0.9.

Table D
The Aging by Sex

Age	Male	Female	Ratio Women per 100 Men
Total	10,302,601	15,241,532	148
65–69	3,902,083	4,878,761	125
70–74	2,853,116	3,943,626	138
75–79	1,847,115	2,945,482	159
80–84	1,018,859	1,915,370	188
85 +	681,428	1,558,293	229

Source: U.S. Department of Commerce, Bureau of the Census, *1980 Census of Population, Age, Sex, Race, and Spanish Origin of the Population by Regions, Divisions, and States:* 1980, PC 80–S1–1, May 1981, p. 3.

in the upper age brackets. Furthermore, this overrepresentation became even more striking as the highest age brackets were reached.

The ratios bear upon the marital status of the aging population. As a consequence of the greater female life expectancy, together with the tradition that in most marriages the groom is somewhat older than the bride, the number of elderly widows greatly exceeds the number of elderly widowers. Theoretically, both may remarry. In fact, however, in 1979, 70 percent of women aged seventy-five and over were widows,[6] while a similar proportion, 69 percent, of men aged seventy-five and over were married.[7]

Distribution by Race

According to provisional data of the 1980 Census, 83.2 percent of the total population declared themselves to be of the white race. Blacks made up 11.7 percent, Asian and Pacific Islanders, 1.5 percent, American Indians, Eskimos, and Aleuts, .6 percent, and others, 3 percent.

White elderly constituted 12.2 percent of the white race. Black elderly made up 7.9 percent of the total black population. Only 4.9 percent of those of Spanish origin were over age sixty-five. Within racial groups, it is clear that life expectancy is higher for whites (see table E).

Geographic Distribution

The proportion of elderly in the population varies widely from state to state, as the 1980 census of the population shows.[8] The variety ranges from Florida with its high percentage (17.3) to Alaska with its low percentage (2.9). Five of the seven states classified by the Census Bureau as West North Central have an aging population of at least 13 percent of the total: Iowa (13.3),

Table E

The Aging by Race

	65–69	70–74	75–79	80–84	85+
White	7,811,071	6,094,178	4,309,286	2,684,793	2,044,705
Black	776,597	563,377	387,231	199,760	158,861
Spanish origin[a]	236,698	193,416	136,376	66,465	48,830
Asian and Pacific Islanders	79,723	58,042	39,154	21,061	13,854
American Indian, Eskimo, and Aleut	28,256	19,886	13,472	7,052	5,852
Other	85,197	61,269	43,184	21,563	16,449

Source: U.S. Department of Commerce, Bureau of the Census, *1980 Census of Population, Age, Sex, Race, and Spanish Origin of the Population by Regions, Divisions, and States: 1980, PC 80–S1–1,* May 1981, p. 3.

a. According to the Census Bureau, "Persons of Spanish Origin may be of any race."

Kansas (13.0), Missouri (13.2), Nebraska (13.1), and South Dakota (13.2). This proportion is equaled (or surpassed) by three widely scattered states, Arkansas (13.7), Florida (17.3), and Rhode Island (13.4). A few other states are approaching the 13 percent level, having a proportion of at least 12.5 percent; these are Maine (12.5), Massachusetts (12.7), and Pennsylvania (12.9). Only three states in addition to Alaska (2.9) have an aging population of fewer than 8 percent of the total: Hawaii (7.9), Utah (7.5), and Wisconsin (7.9). The remaining states cluster near the national proportion of older people, 11.3 percent. Whether their older populations were relatively large, relatively small, or around the average, all states except one showed an increase in the proportion of elderly between 1970 and 1980. Only Wyoming showed a slight decrease.

Although there is no clear pattern of distribution among states, it is apparent that there are wide discrepancies between states in proportions of elderly. Across the board, increases in proportions of elderly are to be anticipated. Where and to what extent this will occur, however, depends somewhat on other factors. The changes that occur in various segments of a state's population affect its proportion of elderly. For example, the out-migration of those in their twenties and thirties who may be looking elsewhere for improved economic opportunities increases the proportion of those over age sixty-five. A lower-than-average fertility rate has the same result. On the other hand, the high fertility rate of the fifties and the low fertility rate of the seventies will, other factors remaining normal, result in a still higher proportion of elderly in the period around 2020. This has been referred to as the graying of the baby boom generation.[9]

In summary, the proportion of the aged in the United States has grown steadily over this century and promises to continue to grow over the near future. Presently, those aged sixty-five and older constitute 11.3 percent of the total population, or one in every nine Americans. The numbers and proportion of those in very late life stages—over ages seventy-five and eighty-five—are growing more rapidly than the older population as a whole. Given the differential life expectancies of males and females, as the population grows older there are far more women than men in any age bracket. Women are highly overrepresented among the old and especially among the very old. They are far less likely to be married than men, and many seem to be living disadvantaged and socially isolated lives in old age. For minority groups a somewhat opposite problem occurs: compared to *all* whites, they have significantly shorter life expectancies, a phenomenon that is attributable to poorer economic circumstances and poorer health care in the younger years. Differential distributions of the proportion of the elderly by state means that some states will be spending more of their resources on services to older persons than other states. All of these statistics are therefore of concern to those interested in public policy and the aged.

Notes

1. U.S. Department of Commerce, Bureau of the Census, *1980 Census of Population,* PC 80-S1-1, May 1981, p. 1.

2. Herman B. Brotman, *Every Ninth American* (1982 edition), An Analysis for the Chairman of the Select Committee on Aging, House of Representatives, 97th Congress, 2d Session, July 1982, p. 1.

3. Jacob S. Siegel, "Prospective Trends in the Size and Structure of the Elderly Population, Impact of Mortality Trends, and Some Implications," in *Consequences of Changing U.S. Population: Demographics of Aging,* Joint Hearing before the Select Committee on Population, U.S. House of Representatives and the Select Committee on Aging, 95th Congress, 2d Session, May 24, 1978, Vol. 1., 77.

4. Ibid., p. 78.

5. Jacob S. Siegel and William E. O'Leary, "Some Demographic Aspects of Aging in the United States," *Current Population Reports,* Series P-23, No. 43, February 1973, U.S. Bureau of the Census, p. 7.

6. Brotman, *Every Ninth American,* p. XXXIV.

7. Richard C. Crandall, *Gerontology: A Behavioral Science Approach* (Reading, Mass.: Addison-Wesley Publishing Company, 1980), p. 17.

8. U.S. Department of Commerce, Bureau of the Census, *1980 Census of Population,* PC 80-S1-1, May 1981, pp. 4-5.

9. Shirley H. Rhine, *America's Aging Population: Issues Facing Business and Society* (New York: The Conference Board, Inc., 1980), p. 8.

Notes

Chapter I. The Politics of Aging

1. Charles Lindbloom, *The Policy-Making Process,* 2d edition (Englewood Cliffs, N.J.: Prentice-Hall, 1980), pp. 1–15.

2. Robert B. Hudson and Robert H. Binstock, "Political Systems and Aging," in R. H. Binstock and E. S. Shanas, eds., *Handbook of Aging and the Social Sciences* (New York: Van Nostrand Reinhold, 1976), pp. 360–400.

3. See, for example, Andrew Achenbaum, *Shades of Gray: Old Age, American Values, and Federal Policies Since 1920* (Boston: Little, Brown, 1983); Ralph Dolgoff and Donald Feldstein, *Understanding Social Welfare* (New York: Harper & Row, 1980); and Ruth Crary Bank, "A Changing Worklife and Retirement Pattern: An Historical Perspective," in M. H. Morrison, ed., *Economics of Aging: The Future of Retirement* (New York: Van Nostrand Reinhold, 1982).

4. Max Weber, *The Protestant Ethic and the Spirit of Capitalism* (New York: Scribner's, 1958), pp. 1–20.

5. H. D. Lowther, *Problems of Aging* (California: Dickenson, 1975), pp. 15–20.

6. J. A. Garrity, *The American Nation: A History of the United States* (New York, Harper & Row, 1971), p. 333.

7. U.S. Dept. of Health, Education and Welfare, *Welfare Myths versus Facts,* Social and Rehabilitation Service (Washington: SRS 72–02009, 1971), p. 5.

8. Lewis A. Coser, "The Sociology of Poverty," *Social Problems* 13 (Fall 1965): 144.

9. Lorin A. Baumhover and Joan D. Jones, *Handbook of American Aging Programs* (Westport, Conn.: Greenwood Press, 1977), pp. 5–12.

10. Andrew Achenbaum, *Shades of Gray,* pp. 7–20.

11. P. N. Stearns, "Modernization and Social History," *Journal of Social History* 14 (1980): 189–249.

12. R. Wiebe, "Modernizing the Republic," in Bailyn et al, eds., *The Great Republic,* 2d edition (Boston: D. C. Heath, 1981), pp. 215–30.

13. Martha Baum and Rainer C. Baum, *Growing Old: A Societal Perspective* (New York: Prentice-Hall, 1980), pp. 93–95.

14. See, for example, Robert H. Binstock, "Interest Group Politics and the Field of Aging," *The Gerontologist,* 12 (1972): 265–70; Henry J. Pratt, *The Politics of Old Age* (Chicago: University of Chicago Press, 1976), pp. 15–30.

15. For the titles of the reports, see *Congressional Record,* January 13, 1961, p. 692.

16. Senate Resolution 33, ibid., p. 691.

17. Ibid.

18. Ibid.

19. Dale Vinyard, "The Senate Special Committee on Aging," *The Gerontologist* 12 (1972): 299.

20. The campaign for the retention was organized by William C. Oriol, then staff director of

the committee. *The New York Times* reported that the vote "was considered recognition that the nation's 23 million senior citizens vote a much higher percentage of the time than does the average voter." *New York Times,* February 2, 1977, p. B4.

21. For a list of committee hearings and reports, see *Developments in Aging: 1981,* a report of the Special Committee on Aging, U.S. Senate, 97th Congress, 2d Session, Report No. 97–314, pp. 507–24.

22. See, for example, Bennett M. Rich, "Developments in Aging: 1978," *The Gerontologist,* (February 1980): 7–9.

23. *Toward a National Policy on Aging,* 1971 White House Conference on Aging, Final Report, vol. 2, p. 83.

24. *Congressional Record,* October 2, 1974, H9809–9813. The excerpt from the Congressional Record is contained in the House of Representatives Select Committee on Aging, *Annual Report for the year 1975,* (1976), pp. 61–65.

25. Select Committee on Aging, *Annual Report for the year 1975,* p. 8.

26. The tables are based on *Federal Responsibility to the Elderly,* Select Committee on Aging, U.S. House of Representatives, January 2, 1979 (Washington: U.S. Government Printing Office), pp. 15–16 (with modifications).

27. *Federal Responsibility to the Elderly,* Select Committee on Aging, U.S. House of Representatives, January 2, 1979 (1979), p. 1.

28. *NRTA News Bulletin,* 19, no. 3, (March 1978): 1.

29. *NRTA Journal,* May–June 1979, p. 24. See also *NRTA News Bulletin* 19, no. 3 (March 1978): 1, 4–5.

30. *NRTA News Bulletin* 22, no. 6 (June 1981): 8.

31. Henry J. Pratt, "Old Age Associations in National Politics," *The Annals,* 415 (September 1974): 112. For the types of linkages with Congress, see Pratt's *The Gray Lobby* (Chicago: The University of Chicago Press, 1976), pp. 145–51.

32. *NRTA News Bulletin,* 19, no. 3, (March 1978): 4.

33. Richard Harris, "Annals of Legislation," *The New Yorker,* July 16, 1966, pp. 50–51.

34. Ibid., p. 51.

35. Pratt, *The Gray Lobby,* p. 89.

36. William R. Hutton, *Senior Citizen News,* September 1979, p. 1.

37. *Senior Citizen News,* November 1982, p. 3.

38. Constitution, article XI, section 1. See *Senior Citizen News,* September 1979, p. 10.

39. *Senior Citizen News,* December 1979, p. 7.

40. *Senior Citizen News,* November 1982, p. 6.

41. Pratt, *The Gray Lobby,* p. 93.

42. *The National Council on Aging,* Spring 1978, pp. 20–22.

43. Ibid., p. 11.

44. Quoted in Pratt, *The Gray Lobby,* p. 99.

45. Ibid.

46. Ibid.

47. Stanley Earley and Maggie Kuhn, *Gray Panthers History* (mimeographed, n.d.), p. 4.

48. *The Gray Panther Movement* (The Gray Panthers, 3700 Chestnut Street, Philadelphia, 1974), p. 1.

49. Ibid., pp. 10–11.

50. *Gray Panther Network,* January/February 1982, pp. 20–22.

51. Ibid., May/June 1979, p. 9.

52. Robert H. Binstock, "Aging and the Future of American Politics," *Annals of the American Academy of Political and Social Sciences* 415 (1974): 201–12.

53. NARFE, *The Retirement Organization of the Federal Civilian Service* (Washington, n.d.), p. 2.

54. Ibid.

55. Pratt, *The Gray Lobby*, p. 103.

56. *Shaping America's Aging Agenda for the 80's,* a report by the Leadership Council of Aging Organizations on the 1981 White House Conference on Aging, (Washington National Council on the Aging, Inc., 1982), pp. vii–viii.

57. Ibid., p. ii. For a statement of the purpose, background, and issues of special interest to thirty national groups, see National Association of State Units on Aging, *An Orientation to the Older Americans Act* (Washington: 1982), pp. 63–76.

Chapter II. The Aging Network

1. The "Aging network," defined narrowly, consists of those public and semi public agencies responsible for implementing the requirements of the Older Americans Act. Included are the Administration on Aging, the regional offices of the Department of Health and Human Services, state offices on aging, area agencies on aging, and the groups with which the area agencies have contracted for the provision of services.

2. Herman B. Brotman, in *Funding of Federal Programs Benefiting Older Persons (Employment),* hearings before the Select Committee on Aging, House of Representatives, 94th Congress, 2d session, June 1976, p. 7.

3. Henry J. Pratt, "Symbolic Politics and White House Conferences on Aging," *Society* 15, no. 5 (July–August 1978): 67–72. See also Dale Vinyard, "White House Conferences and the Aged," *Social Service Review,* (December 1979): 655–71.

4. For the executive order see *Public Papers of the Presidents,* March 21, 1956.

5. The Council of State Governments, *The States and Their Older Citizens* (Chicago, 1955), pp. 161–64.

6. *The 1961 White House Conference on Aging: Basic Policy Statements and Recommendations,* prepared for the Special Committee on Aging, U.S. Senate, 87th Congress, 1st session, Committee Print, May 15, 1961.

7. *Congressional Record,* February 21, 1963, p. 2693.

8. Henry J. Pratt, *The Gray Lobby* (Chicago: University of Chicago Press, 1976), pp. 113–16.

9. Public Law 89–73, July 14, 1965.

10. For a fascinating account of the early years, see Pratt, *The Gray Lobby,* pp. 117–28.

11. Public Law 90–526, September 28, 1968.

12. *Developments in Aging: 1969,* a report of the Special Committee on Aging, U.S. Senate, 91st Congress, 2d session, Report No. 91–875, p. 145.

13. *Developments in Aging: 1972 and January–March 1973,* a report of the Special Committee on Aging, U.S. Senate, 93d Congress, 1st session, Report No. 93–147, p. 3.

14. Pratt, *The Gray Lobby,* pp. 130–36.

15. 1971 White House Conference on Aging, *Toward a National Policy on Aging,* Final Report, vol. 1, pp. 9–10.

16. Ibid., pp. 11–13.

17. *Developments in Aging: 1971 and January–March 1972,* a report of the Special Committee on Aging, U.S. Senate, 92d Congress, 2d session, Report No. 92–784, p. ix.

18. *Developments in Aging: 1972,* p. 3.

19. Public Law 93–29, May 3, 1973.

20. *Developments in Aging: 1977,* a report of the Special Committee on Aging, U.S. Senate, 95th Congress, 2d session, Report No. 95–771, part 1, p. 113.

21. *Older Americans Act: A Summary,* Staff Study, Select Committee on Aging, U.S. House of Representatives, 94th Congress, 2d session, August 1976, p. 1.

22. Public Law 95–478, October 18, 1978. For a summary of the several amendments over the years, see J. William Norman, "The Older American Act: Meeting the Needs of the Elderly," *Aging,* January–February 1982, pp. 2–10. See also Susan R. Coombs, *An Orientation to the Older Americans Act* (Washington: National Associaton of State Units on Aging, 1982), pp. 3–7.

23. *Developments in Aging: 1977,* part 1, pp. 247–49.

24. Title II, Section 202 of Public Law 95–478, October 18, 1978.

25. *The White House Conference on Aging Community Forums Handbook,* (Washington: U.S. Government Printing Office, 1980), 0–316–734/60988, p. 1.

26. *Developments in Aging: 1980,* a report of the Special Committee on Aging, U.S. Senate, 97th Congress, 1st session, Report No. 97–62, part 1, pp. 175–76.

27. *Congressional Quarterly,* November 28, 1981, p. 2332.

28. Ibid.

29. *Older American Reports* (Washington: Capitol Publications, Inc.), December 9, 1981, p. 2. See also *Senior Citizens News* (Washington, National Council of Senior Citizens), January 1982, pp. 1–2.

30. For the full resolution see *Committees' Recommendations from the White House Conference on Aging,* November 30–December 3, 1981, no. 53, p. 6.

31. *Older American Reports,* p. 3.

32. *New York Times,* January 13, p. A13.

33. Janice Caldwell, director of the Gerontology Society of America, in *Gerontology News,* December–January 1981, p. 1, and Jacob Clayman, president, National Council of Senior Citizens, in *Senior Citizens News,* January 1982, p. 2.

34. Caldwell, *Gerontology News,* December–January 1981, p. 1.

35. Edward F. Howard, "WHCOA and LCOA Reports 'Strikingly Different'," *Perspective on Aging* 11, no. 3 (May–June 1982): 6.

36. Paul Kerschner, quoted in ibid.

37. Public Law 97–115, December 29, 1981. For a summary of the 1981 amendments and of the Older Americans Act as amended, see Coombs, *An Orientation to the Older Americans Act,* pp. 77–82.

38. *Comprehensive Older Americans Act Amendments of 1978,* Conference Report, House of Representatives, 95th Congress, 2d session, Report No. 95–1618, p. 54.

39. *Developments in Aging: 1981,* a report of the Special Committee on Aging, U.S. Senate, 97th Congress, 2d session, Report No. 97–314, vol. 1, pp. 394–98.

40. The role of the Administration on Aging has been described as "one of oversight, monitoring, assessing, approving State program plans, authorizing Federal funding, and providing technical assistance." *Annual Report for the Year 1976 of the Select Committee on Aging, U.S. House of Representatives,* 94th Congress, 2d session (Washington: U.S. Government Printing Office, 1977), p. 17.

41. Title I, Section 102.

42. In 1976, the AoA expanded its research support in order to promote the establishment of multidisciplinary centers for gerontology. The purpose of multidisciplinary centers, located principally at universities, is to coordinate the various teaching and research units concerned with programs for the aging. A multidisciplinary center may receive grants to start up or operate programs to train professional personnel, conduct basic and applied research, and develop informational repositories for the use of universities and communities.

43. *Developments in Aging: 1974 and January–March 1975,* a report of the Special Committee on Aging, U.S. Senate, 94th Congress, 1st session, Report No. 94–250, p. 284.

44. *Developments in Aging: 1978,* a report of the Special Committee on Aging, U.S. Senate, 96th Congress, 1st session, Report No. 96–55, part 2, p. 18.

45. For illustrations of the activities of state agencies, see *Developments in Aging: 1981,* vol. 2, pp. 36–42.

46. Public Law, Section 304c, May 3, 1973.

47. *Developments in Aging: 1973 and January–March 1974,* a report of the Special Committee on Aging, U.S. Senate, 93d Congress, 2d session, Report No. 93–846, p. 107.

48. Code of Federal Regulations, 45–903.66 (6), (ii), (1976, p. 153).

49. For comments on the growing pains of the Area Agency on Aging, see the annual reports of the Senate Special Committee on Aging. Amendments in 1975 extended the Older Americans Act through 1978. Public Law 94–135, November 28, 1975.

50. The planning and service areas include the fifty states, the District of Columbia, American Samoa, Guam, Puerto Rico, the Trust Territory of the Pacific Islands, and the Virgin Islands.

51. *Developments in Aging: 1978,* part 1, p. 174.

52. *Developments in Aging: 1981,* vol. 2, pp. 94–95, vol. 1, pp. 414–18.

53. Carroll L. Estes, *The Aging Enterprise* (San Francisco: Jossey-Bass, 1979), p. 182.

54. Conference Report, *Comprehensive Older Americans Act Amendments of 1978,* 95th Congress, 2d session, House of Representatives, Report No. 95–1618, p. 62.

55. *Major Themes and Additional Budget Details, Fiscal Year 1984,* Executive Office of the President, Office of Management and Budget, p. 132.

56. *Appendix, Budget of the United States Government, Fiscal Year 1984,* Executive Office of the President, Office of Management and Budget, p. I-K 45.

57. James Tobin, "Reaganomics and Economics," *New York Review* 28 (December 3, 1981): 11–14.

58. CBS Newscast, Friday, April 8, 1983.

59. Public Law 95–478, October 18, 1978. See also *Comprehensive Older Americans Act Amendments of 1978,* p. 12.

60. *Amendments of 1978,* p. 64.

61. For a brief review of the literature and an examination of nutritional deficiencies as evidenced by a survey of one Area Agency on Aging, see Ian G. Rawson, Edward I. Weinberg, Jo Ann Herold, and Judy Holtz, "Nutrition of Rural Elderly in Southwestern Pennsylvania," *The Gerontologist* 18, no. 1 (February 1978): 24–29. See also Robert L. Schneider, "Barriers to Effective Outreach in Title VII Nutrition Programs," Ibid. 19, no. 2 (April 1979): 163–68.

62. Jeanette Peclovits, "Nutrition for Older Americans," quoted in *Developments in Aging: 1970,* a report of the Special Committee on Aging, U.S. Senate, 92d Congress, 1st session, Report No. 92–46, p. 67.

63. Public Law 92–258, March 22, 1972.

64. Public Law, 94–135, November 26, 1975.

65. *Developments in Aging: 1981,* vol. 1, pp. 398–99.

66. Ibid., pp. 400–01.

67. *Minority Elderly Services, New Programs, Old Problems, Part II,* a report of the U.S. Commission on Civil Rights, November 1982, p. 4.

68. Ibid., p. 50.

69. Ibid., p. 63.

70. Ibid., pp. 47–55.

71. Older Americans Programs, Hearings before the Select Committee on Aging, U.S. Senate, (Washington: U.S. Printing Office, 1981).

72. Martha Baum has worked with the Allegheny County Area Agency on Aging in developing plans for the Commonwealth of Pennsylvania and in trying to solve problems having to do

with compliance with regulations. She can personally attest to the burdensomeness of the data-gathering process and the complexity of the regulatory maze.

73. Carroll L. Estes, *The Aging Enterprise,* p. 182.

74. Phillip L. Nathanson, "Planning in State Agencies on Aging," in Baumhover and Jones, *Handbook of American Aging Programs* (Westport, Conn: Greenwood Press, 1977), pp. 23–30.

75. James R. Jones, "Title III Programs: The Area Agency Concept," in ibid., pp. 31–46.

Chapter III. General Financial and Retirement Programs

1. Frances Perkins, *The Roosevelt I Knew* (New York: Viking Press, 1946), p. 278.

2. "Social Security Forty Years Later," *Social Security Bulletin,* August 1975.

3. Robert Bremner, *From the Depths: The Discovery of Poverty in the United States* (New York: New York University Press, 1956), pp. 1–18.

4. Arthur Schlesinger, *The New Deal in Action* (Folcroft, Pa: Folcroft Library Editions, 1977), p. 43.

5. Paul H. Douglas, *Social Security in the United States* (New York: McGraw-Hill, 1939), pp. 110–17.

6. Daniel Nelson, *Unemployment Insurance* (Madison: University of Wisconsin Press, 1969), pp. 26–27.

7. W. Andrew Achenbaum, *Old Age in a New Land* (Baltimore: The Johns Hopkins University Press, 1978), pp. 110–17.

8. See, for example, Ernest W. Burgess, *Aging in Western Societies* (Chicago: University of Chicago Press, 1960); Donald O. Cowgill and Lowell D. Holmes, eds., *Aging and Modernization* (New York: Appleton-Century-Crofts, 1972), Irving Rosow, *Socialization to Old Age* (Berkeley and Los Angeles: University of California Press, 1974).

9. Achenbaum, Old Age, pp. 121–23.

10. See, for example, Arthur Altmeyer, *The Formative Years of Social Security* (Madison: University of Wisconsin Press, 1968); William Leuchentenberg, *Franklin Roosevelt and the New Deal* (New York: Harper & Row, 1963).

11. Edwin Witte, *The Development of the Social Security Act* (Madison: University of Wisconsin Press, 1962).

12. Ibid., pp. 144–45.

13. Perkins, *Roosevelt,* pp. 297–98.

14. Paul H. Douglas, *Social Security in the United States: An Analysis* (New York: Da Capo Press, 1971).

15. J. Douglas Brown, *An American Philosophy of Social Security* (Princeton: Princeton University Press, 1972), p. 3. For a comprehensive account and analysis of early issues, see Martha Derthick, *Policy Making for Social Security* (Washington: The Brookings Institution, 1979).

16. *U.S. News and World Report,* April 30, 1979, p. 24.

17. *New York Times,* March 26, 1983, p. 4.

18. *Survey Graphic,* September 1945, quoted in William Haber and Wilbur J. Cohen, *Social Security: Programs, Problems and Policies* (Homewood, Ill: Richard D. Irwin, Inc., 1960), p. 5. See also Altmeyer, *The Formative Years.*

19. Alicia H. Munnell, *The Future of Social Security* (Washington: The Brookings Institution, 1977), p. 6.

20. Ibid., pp. 18–24.

21. *Social Security Financing and Benefits,* reports of the 1979 Advisory Council on Social Security, Department of HEW, 1979, p. 35.

22. Ibid., p. 41.

23. *Social Security Bulletin* 6, no. 1 (January 1983): 46.

24. *Impact of Administration's Social Security Proposals on the Elderly,* Hearing before the Select Committee on Aging, House of Representatives, 97th Congress, 1st session, May 22, 1981, pp. 143–144. See also: Congressional Budget Office, *Reducing the Federal Deficit: Strategies and Options,* report to the Senate and House Committees on the Budget, part III, February 1982, p. A89.

25. Munnell, *Future of Social Security,* pp. 38–39.

26. 1979 Advisory Council Report, p. 66.

27. Ibid., p. 71.

28. Robert M. Ball, *Social Security Today and Tomorrow* (New York: Columbia University Press, 1978), p. 290.

29. Ibid., p. 44.

30. *Reducing the Federal Deficit,* p. 157.

31. For an explanation of the theory, see Brown, *An American Philosophy,* pp. 125–29.

32. *Reducing the Federal Deficit,* p. A91.

33. 1979 Advisory Council Report, p. 356. For a recent discussion and series of papers, see *Social Security Earnings Test,* Hearing before the Subcommittee on Retirement Income and Employment of the Select Committee on Aging, House of Representatives, 96th Congress, 2d session, June 26, 1980.

34. "Social Security and the Changing Roles of Men and Women," Department of Health, Education, and Welfare, 1979, in: *Treatment of Women under Social Security,* Hearings before the Task Force on Social Security and Women of the Subcommittee on Retirement Income and Employment and the Select Committee on Aging, U.S. House of Representatives, 96th Congress, 1st session, vol. II, 1980, p. 40.

35. 1979 Advisory Council Report, p. 89.

36. Ibid., p. 94.

37. Ibid., p.104.

38. Ibid., pp. 80, 82.

39. *Treatment of Women under Social Security* vol. I, 245.

40. *Social Security Financing: Issues and Options,* Senate Special Committee on Aging, July 1981 (mimeographed), p. 2.

41. Harris poll reported in *Aging Info.,* Select Committee on Aging, House of Representatives, December 1981, p. 2.

42. *Developments in Aging: 1981,* A Report of the Special Committee on Aging, U.S. Senate, 97th Congress, 2d session, Report No. 97–314, vol. 1, pp. 69–82; and *Social Security Oversight: Short-Term Financing Issues,* Hearing before the Special Committee on Aging, U.S. Senate, 97th Congress, 1st session, part 1, Washington, June 16, 1981, pp. 54–55, 83–95.

43. 1979 Advisory Council Report, pp. 178–79, 295–303.

44. *Impact of Administration's Social Security Proposals on the Elderly,* pp. 148–50; and *Reducing the Federal Deficit,* pp. A89–90.

45. 1979 Advisory Council Report, p. 74.

46. Ibid., p.75.

47. *Reducing the Federal Deficit,* p. B49. See also *Developments in Aging: 1981,* pp. 83–84.

48. Executive Order 12335, December 16, 1981.

49. Public Law 92–603, October 30, 1972.

50. Public Law 92–603, October 30, 1972.

51. Lenna D. Kennedy, "SSI: Trends and Changes, 1974–80," *Social Security Bulletin* 45, no. 7 (July 1982); table 3, pp. 5, 9. Recipients over sixty-five are not classified as aged recipients if they qualified initially for reasons of blindness or disability. In 1982, 34 percent of blind recipients and 20 percent of disabled recipients were thus not classified as aged. *Congressional*

Action on the Fiscal Year 1983 Budget: What It Means for Older Americans, an information paper prepared by the staff of the Special Committee on Aging, U.S. Senate, 97th Congress, 2d session, November 1982, p. 3.

52. Charles I. Schottland, *The Social Security Program in the United States* (New York: Appleton-Century-Crofts, 1968), pp. 96–109.

53. Lenna D. Kennedy, Dorothea Thomas, and Jack Schmulowitz, "Conversions to Supplemental Security Income from Assistance: A Program Records Study," *Social Security Bulletin* 38, no. 6 (June 1975): table A, p. 30.

54. Statement of James B. Cardwell, in *Future Directions in Social Security*, Hearings before the Special Committee on Aging, Senate, 93d Congress, 2d session, part 7, 1974, p. 566.

55. *Report to the Commissioner of Social Security and the Secretary of Health, Education, and Welfare on the Supplemental Security Program*, SSI Study Group, January 1976, p. 34.

56. *Social Security in America's Future*, final report of the National Commission on Social Security, March 1981, p. 248.

57. *The Supplemental Security Income Program for the Aged, Blind and Disabled: Selected Characteristics of State Supplementation Programs as of October 1979* (Washington: Social Security Administration, April 1980), p. 5. For details relating to each state, see pp. 11-98.

58. For a chart listing optional state supplements for special needs, see Donald E. Rigby and Elsa Orley Ponce, "Supplemental Security Income: Optional State Supplementation, October 1979," *Social Security Bulletin* 42, no. 10 (October 1979): 12–13.

59. Statement of Chauncey A. Alexander, executive director, National Association of Social Workers, in *Future Directions*, part 7, p. 639.kk.

60. Statement of Jack Ossofsy, executive director of the National Council on Aging, ibid., part 8, p. 748.

61. Statement of Attorney Robert N. Brown, ibid., part 7, pp. 607–612.

62. Testimony of Attorney Patricia Butler, ibid., p. 622.

63. John A. Menafee, Bea Edwards, and Sylvester J. Schieber, "Analysis of Nonparticipation in the SSI Program," *Social Security Bulletin* 44 (June 1981): 3–21.

64. *Social Security Financing and Benefits*, report of the 1979 Advisory Council on Social Security, pp. 201–05.

65. *Social Security in America's Future*, p. 250.

66. *Congressional Quarterly*, August 21, 1982, p. 2046.

67. Richard P. Nathan, senior fellow, The Brookings Institution, *Food Stamp Reform*, Hearings before the Subcommittee on Agricultural Research and General Legislation of the Committee on Agriculture and Forestry, U.S. Senate, 94th Congress, 1st session, part I (Washington, 1975), p. 213.

68. William E. Simon, *The Food Stamp Controversy of 1975: Background Materials*, prepared by the staff of the Select Committee on Nutrition and Human Needs, U.S. Senate, Washington, 1975, p. 36.

69. *Congressional Action on the Fiscal Year 1983 Budget: What It Means for Older Americans*, an information paper prepared by the staff of the Special Committee on Aging, U.S. Senate, 97th Congress, 2d session, November 1982, p. 13.

70. *Impact of the Federal Budget on the Future of Services for Older Americans*, Joint Hearing before the Select Committees on Aging, House of Representatives and the Special Committee on Aging, U.S. Senate, 97th Congress, 2d session, April 1, 1982, Comm. Pub. No. 97-339, p. 95.

71. "Surplus Food Donation Programs: 1932–1964," *Congressional Digest* 43, no. 5 (June–July 1964): p. 165.

72. Public Law 88–525, August 31, 1964.

73. Quoted in *Congressional Digest* 43, no. 5 (June–July 1964): 176.

74. Public Law 93–86, August 10, 1973.

75. *Food Stamp Program: A Report in Accordance with Senate Resolution 58,* prepared by Food and Nutrition Service, U.S. Department of Agriculture, for the Committee on Agriculture and Forestry, U.S. Senate, Washington, 1975, pp. 35–38.

76. *Food Stamp Reform,* p. 390.

77. The text of the report of the comptroller is given in ibid., pp. 704–21.

78. Carol Tucker Foreman, as quoted in *Developments in Aging: 1977,* a report of the Special Committee on Aging, Senate, 95th Congress, 2d session, Report No. 95–771, part 2, p. 208.

79. Kathryn Waters Gest, "Food Stamp Program Overhauled by Congress," *Congressional Quarterly,* September 24, 1977, p. 2017.

80. 7 Code of Federal Regulations 273.8 (h) (6) 1982.

81. *Developments in Aging: 1981,* a report of the Special Committee on Aging, U.S. Senate, 97th Congress, 2d session, Report No. 97–314, vol. 2, pp. 43–45.

82. 7 Code of Federal Regulations, 274.2 (a), 1982.

83. *Food Stamp Program,* p. 67.

84. Ibid., p. 71.

85. *Food and Nutrition,* 10, no. 1 (February 1980): 2.

86. Ibid., p. 4.

87. Ibid., 9, no. 5 (October 1979): 14.

88. *Food Stamp Reform,* p. 638.

89. Richard P. Nathan, the *New York Times,* February 23, 1983, p. D21.

90. *Major Themes and Additional Budget Details, Fiscal Year 1983,* Office of the President, Office of Management and Budget, pp. 44–45.

91. Ibid.

92. Martha Baum and Rainer C. Baum, *Growing Old: A Societal Perspective* (New York, Prentice-Hall, 1980), p. 44.

93. See, for example, James Schultz, "Income Distribution and Aging," in Robert H. Binstock and Ethel Shanas, eds., *Handbook of Aging and the Social Sciences* (New York: Van Nostrand Reinhold, 1976), pp. 561–91; U.S. Bureau of the Census, Series P-60, No. 106. (Washington: U.S. Government Printing Office, 1977), table 15; U.S. Bureau of the Census, *Statistical Abstracts of the United States,* 99th Edtion (Washington: U.S. Government Printing Office, 1978).

Chapter IV. Other Selected Financial and Retirement Programs

1. Edward Berkowitz and Kim McQuaid, *Creating the Welfare State: The Political Economy of Welfare Reform* (New York: Praeger, 1980), pp. 2–3.

2. U.S. Bureau of the Census, *Statistical Abstracts of the United States, 97th Edition* (Washington: U.S. Government Printing Office, 1976).

3. Charles S. Harris, *Fact Book on Aging: A Profile of America's Older Population* (Washington: National Council on Aging, 1978).

4. Stephen Crystal, *America's Old Age Crisis: Public Policy and the Two Worlds of Aging* (New York: Basic Books, 1982).

5. Richard C. Crandall, *Gerontology: A Behavioral Science Approach* (Reading, Mass.: Addison-Wesley, 1980), p. 518.

6. Ralph Dolgoff and Donald Feldstein, *Understanding Social Welfare* (New York: Harper & Row, 1980), p. 189.

7. "A pension plan is any plan, fund, or program which provides retirement income to

employees or results in a deferral of income by employees until the termination of employment or beyond." U.S. Department of Labor, Labor Management Services Division, *Employee Retirement Income Security Act,* 1975 report to Congress, p. 3.

8. Ibid., p. 1.

9. Public Law 93–406, September 2, 1974. For an account of pre-ERISA problems, see Frank Cummings, "Reforming Private Pensions," *The Annals* 415 (September 1974): 80–94.

10. For a more detailed explanation, see *What You Should Know about the Pension and Welfare Law,* a guide to the Employee Retirement Security Act of 1974, U.S. Department of Labor, Labor Management Services Administration, Pension and Welfare Benefit Programs, January 1978, and *Often Asked Questions about the Employee Retirement Security Act of 1974.* U.S. Department of Labor, Labor Management Services Division (1976).

11. A defined benefit plan specifies the benefit, or the method of determining the benefit, such as $10 monthly for each year of service. The employer's contribution is based on an actuarial estimate of the benefits to be paid. A defined contribution plan is one in which the employer's (or in some plans the employer's and the employee's) contribution is specified, such as 6 percent of monthly compensation. The benefit then becomes whatever the total amount accumulated in the individual's account will earn.

12. An explanation for employees is contained in *What You Should Know about the Pension and Welfare Law,* pp. 27–29.

13. Ibid., p. 35.

14. Statement of Robert Tilove, "Private Pensions and Public Policies," *Employee Benefits Journal* 2, no. 4 (Summer 1977): 3.

15. Approximately 8 million workers are participants in the nation's 2,000 multiemployer plans, that is plans whose participants work for unrelated companies. Half of these are in plans developed through collective bargaining, such as coal mining, construction, trucking, and others characterized by irregular employment. Employees contribute to a central pension fund.

16. For details, see the Pension Benefit Guaranty Corporation's *Annual Report to the President and Congress.*

17. Tilove in "Private Pensions and Public Policies," pp. 3, 7.

18. *Congressional Quarterly,* October 11, 1980, pp. 3117–18.

19. Robert Frumkin and Donald Schmitt, "Pension Improvements Since 1974 Reflect Inflation, New U.S. Law," *Monthly Labor Review* 102, no. 4 (April 1979): 32–37. For the characteristics of earlier plans, see Alfred M. Skolnik, "Private Pension Plans, 1950–74," *Social Security Bulletin* 39, no. 6 (June 1976): 3–17.

20. "Congress Opens New Debate on Private Pension System," *Congressional Quarterly,* March 17, 1979, p. 450. See also James F. A. Biggs, "Living with ERISA," *Management Controls,* December 1976, pp. 186–91.

21. Gayle B. Thompson, "Impact of Inflation on Private Pensions of Retirees, 1970–74: Findings from the Retirement History Study," *Social Security Bulletin* 41, no. 11 (November 1978: 16–26.

22. *Coming of Age: Toward a National Retirement Income Policy,* President's Commission on Pension Policy, February 26, 1981, pp. 43–45.

23. *U.S. News and World Report,* March 9, 1981, p. 77.

24. Alicia H. Munnell, *The Economics of Private Pensions* (Washington: The Brookings Institution, 1982), p. 169. See also James H. Schulz, "The Other Face of Income Maintenance Policies: Private and Public Employee Pensions," in *Proceedings of a Symposium on Income Maintenance,* May 17, 1982, The Florence Heller Graduate School, Brandeis University, Waltham, Mass. pp. 20–35.

25. For a discussion of various facets of the government's role in the regulation of private

pensions, see *Developments in Aging: 1981*, a report of the Special Committee on Aging, U.S. Senate, 97th Congress, 2d session, Report No. 97-314, pp. 123–53.

26. *Overview of U.S. Retirement System, Background Papers*, President's Commission on Pension Policy, February 1979, p. 79.

27. *Restructuring the Civil Service Retirement System: Analysis of Options to Control Costs and Maintain Retirement Income Security*, prepared for the Subcommittee on Civil Service, Post Office, and General Services of the Committee on Governmental Affairs, U.S. Senate, by the Congressional Research Service, Library of Congress, January 1982, pp. 7, 12.

28. *Civil Service Retirement: Financing and Costs*, Congressional Budget Office, May 1981, p. 1. See also *Options for Federal Civil Service Retirement: An Analysis of Costs and Benefit Programs*, Congressional Budget Office, December 1978.

29. Maurice C. Hart, "Civil Service Program, October 20, 1969," *Social Security Bulletin* 33, no. 2 (February 1970): 33.

30. Public Law 91–93, October 20, 1969.

31. *Developments in Aging: 1981*, vol. 1, p. 154.

32. Public Law 97–35, August 13, 1981.

33. Public Law 95–256, April 6, 1978.

34. Public Law 83–598, August 17, 1954.

35. *Federal Personnel Manual, Supplement 870–1, Life Insurance*, pp. 9, 11, 19–22.

36. Public Law 86–382, 1959.

37. *Federal Personnel Manual, Supplement 890–1, Federal Employees Health Benefits*, pp. 5, 47.

38. *Developments on Aging: 1981*, pp. 157–159. See also *Restructuring the Civil Service Retirement System*, pp. 29–54.

39. "Civil Service Retirement System Annuitants and Social Security," *Social Security Bulletin* 46, no. 2 (February 1983): 40.

40. The three-tiered plan is discussed in "Federal Pension Plans Lure Budget-Cutters," *Congressional Quarterly*, June 26, 1982, pp. 1529–32.

41. *State and Local Pension Systems, Federal Regulatory Issues* (Washington: Advisory Commission on Intergovernmental Relations, December 1980), pp. 20–21.

42. Robert Tilove, *Public Employee Pension Funds* (New York: Columbia University Press, A Twentieth Century Fund Report, 1976), pp. 261–62.

43. Ibid., p. 319.

44. "Public Retirement Systems in Wisconsin," *The Wisconsin Taxpayer* 47, no. 6 (June 1978): 1–8.

45. Speech of Representative Dan Angel, quoted in *Overview of U.S. Retirement Systems, Background Papers*, President's Commission on Pension Policy, February 21, 1979, p. 57.

46. *The Book of the States, 1982–83* (Lexington, Ky.: The Council of State Governments, 1982), p. 324.

47. Tilove, *Public Employee Pension Funds*, p. 193.

48. Alicia H. Munnell and Ann M. Connolly, *Pensions for Public Employees* (Washington: National Planning Association, 1979), p. 62.

49. Ibid., p. 63.

50. Ibid., p. 64.

51. *State and Local Government Terminations of Social Security Coverage*, Senate Special Committee on Aging, 96th Congress, 2d session, Committee Print, December 1980, p. 6.

52. Munnell and Connolly, *Pensions*, p. 79.

53. *State and Local Government Terminations*, pp. 13–14.

54. Ibid., p. 11.

55. Ibid., p. 7.

56. *State and Local Pension Systems,* p. 55. See also *Public Employee Retirement Income Security Act of 1978,* Hearing before the Subcommittee on Education and Labor, House of Representatives, 95th Congress, 2d session (1979).

57. *Coming of Age: Toward a National Retirement Income Policy,* President's Commission on Pension Policy, February 26, 1981, p. 46.

58. *Developments in Aging: 1982,* A report of the Special Committee on Aging, U.S. Senate, 98th Congress, 1st session, Report No. 98–13, part 2, p. 265.

59. *The Railroad Retirement System: Analysis of Its Historical Development, Statistical Trends, Structure, and Adequacy,* vol. 2 of staff papers supporting the report to the President and the Congress by the Commission on Railroad Retirement, August 1972, House Document 92–350, p. 71.

60. Ibid., p. 68.

61. *The RRB Quarterly Review,* U.S. Railroad Retirement Board, March 1981, p. 34.

62. *The Railroad Retirement System,* p. 55.

63. *Restructuring of the Railroad Retirement System, 1974,* Hearings before the Subcommittee on Railroad Retirement of the Committee on Labor and Public Welfare, U.S. Senate, 93d Congress, 2d session, part I (Washington: 1974), table I, p. 247.

64. Public Law 93–445, October 16, 1974. For the veto message of President Ford, see *Restructuring,* part II, pp. 1213–14.

65. For details of the act, see Alfred M. Skolnik, "Restructuring the Railroad Retirement System," *Social Security Bulletin* 38, no. 4 (April 1975): 23–29.

66. *Railroad Retirement and Survivor Benefits for Railroad Workers and Their Families,* U.S. Railroad Retirement Board, July 1978, pp. 6–11. See also *January 1981 Supplement.*

67. *Social Security Bulletin* (December 1981): 20–22.

68. Ibid., p. 11.

69. *Congressional Quarterly,* April 16, 1983, p. 741.

70. *The Railroad Retirement System: Benefits and Financing,* Congressional Budget Office, December 1981, pp. 27–33.

71. *New York Times,* August 13, 1983, p. 8.

72. *Congressional Quarterly,* August 6, 1983, pp. 1621–22.

73. "Windfall Payments," *The RRB Quarterly Review,* March 1983, p. 25.

74. Data supplied by Col. Leon S. Hirsh, Jr., Director of Compensation, Department of Defense, December 3, 1979.

75. *Report of the President's Commission on Military Compensation,* April 1978, pp. 43–46.

76. *Major Themes and Additional Budget Details,* Fiscal Year 1984, Executive Office of Management and Budget, p. 213.

77. Stanford G. Ross, *Income Security Programs: Past, Present and Future,* working paper for the President's Commission on Pension Policy, October 1980, pp. 24–25.

78. *The Military Retirement System: Options for Change,* Congressional Budget Office, January, 1978, p. 6.

79. *President's Commission on Military Compensation,* p. 35.

80. *The Military Retirement System,* p. 7.

81. Ibid., p. 12.

82. Ibid., p. 13.

83. "DOD's new Proposed Military Retirement Plan," *Command Policy* 2, no. 7 (July 1979): 25–26.

84. Ibid., p. 12.

85. "Historical Summary of the Survivor Benefit Plan for Members of the Uniformed Services," in *Study of the Survivor Benefit Plan for Members of the Uniformed Services,* February 1,

1979, rev. ed. Office of the Assistant Secretary of Defense Manpower, Reserve Affairs and Logistics, pp. 1–2.

86. Public Law 87–381, October 4, 1961.

87. Public Law 92–425, September 21, 1972.

88. *Study of the Survivor Benefit Plan,* pp. 1–19.

89. Ibid., pp. 3–4.

90. Analysis of the Military Survivor Benefit Plan, Congressional Budget Office, March 1981, pp. 1–15.

91. President's Commission on Pension Policy, *Coming of Age: Toward a National Retirement Income Policy, February 26, 1981, p. 46; see also Accrual Accounting for Military Retirement: Alternative Approaches,* July 1983.

92. "Black Lung Benefits: An Administrative Review," *Social Security Bulletin* 34, no. 10 (October 1971): 18.

93. Public Law 91–173.

94. See statement of Congressman Phillip Burton in *Black Lung Benefits,* Hearing before the General Subcommittee on Labor of the Committee on Education and Labor, House of Representatives, 92d Congress, 1st session (1971), p. 149.

95. Statement of Congressman Ken Hechler, ibid., p. 29.

96. See statement of Arnold Miller, president of the Black Lung Association, ibid., p. 92.

97. Statement of Congressman Ken Hechler, ibid., p. 29.

98. Statement of Congressman John P. Saylor, ibid., p. 36. The word *pneumoconiosis* is used in connection with other "dusty trades." The largest industries, aside from coal mining, in which diseases of the lung are said to be work related are (1) paper and pulp mills, (2) sawmills and planing mills, (3) masonry, stonework and plastering, and (4) glass or glassware. *Black Lung Legislation, 1971–72,* Hearings before the Subcommittee on Labor of the Committee on Labor and Public Welfare, U.S. Senate, 92d Congress, 1st and 2d sessions (1972), pp. 388–89.

99. "Black Lung Benefits: An Administrative Review," p. 17.

100. Public Law 92–303.

101. Ibid., Section 411, c4.

102. *Black Lung Benefits Reform Act of 1975,* Report No. 94–770, U.S. House of Representatives, 94th Congress, 1st session, December 31, 1975, p. 84.

103. Ibid., p. 19.

104. Ibid., p. 73.

105. Testimony of Gail Falk, staff attorney, in *Black Lung Benefits Reform Act of 1975,* p. 58.

106. Ibid., p. 61.

107. Ibid., p. 73.

108. Ibid., p. 11. The review and appeals procedures are spelled out in Code 20 of Federal Regulations 410.601–707 (1980).

109. Public Law 95–239, March 1, 1978, and Public Law 95–227, February 10, 1978.

110. Code 20 of Federal Regulations 410.702 (h), 1980.

111. Ibid., 410.702 (g).

112. Calvin Cook, "The 1977 Amendments to the Black Lung Benefits Law," *Monthly Labor Review,* May 1978, pp. 25–29. For an account of the administration of the act, see *Black Lung Benefits Act: Annual Report on Administration of the Act during Calendar Year 1978 and January 1, 1979–June 30, 1979,* U.S. Department of Labor, Employment Standards Administration (1979).

113. *Congressional Quarterly,* December 26, 1981, p. 2569.

114. *Social Security Bulletin,* 46, no. 1 (January 1983): 64.

115. *New York Times,* October 19, 1979.

116. Ibid., December 3, 1979, pp. B1, 9.

117. Ibid., May 27, 1980, p. C1.

118. *Congressional Quarterly*, February 23, 1980, p. 550.

119. *Pittsburgh Post Gazette*, August 15, 1979, p. 7.

120. See *Tax Benefits for Older Americans*, Publication 554, Department of the Treasury, Internal Revenue Service, 1982.

121. Congressional Budget Office, *The Tax Treatment of Homeownership: Issues and Options*, September 1981, p. 15.

122. Congressional Budget Office, *Tax Expenditures: Current Issues and Five-Year Budget Projections for Fiscal Years 1981–1985*, a report to the Senate and House Committees on the Budget, April, 1980, p. 1.

123. Ibid., pp. 28–34.

124. *Developments in Aging: 1979*, a report of the Special Committee on Aging, U.S. Senate, 95th Congress, 2d session, Report No. 95–613, part 1, pp. 100–04.

125. *Developments in Aging: 1977*, a report of the Special Committee on Aging, U.S. Senate, 95th Congress, 2d session, Report No. 95–613, pp. 100–04.

126. Public Law 96–223.

127. *Developments in Aging: 1980*, a report of the Special Committee on Aging, U.S. Senate, 97th Congress, 1st session, Report No. 97–62, part 1, p. 99.

128. *Energy and the Aged*, Hearing before the Special Committee on Aging, U.S. Senate, 97th Congress, 1st session, Washington, April 9, 1981, p. 130.

129. *Developments in Aging: 1981*, a report of the Special Committee on Aging, U.S. Senate, 97th Congress, 2d session, Report No. 97–314, vol. 1, p. 239.

130. Leadership Council of Aging Organizations, *The Administration's 1984 Budget: A Critical View from an Aging Perspective*, March 15, 1983, p. 17.

131. *Developments in Aging: 1980*, p. 103.

132. *Developments in Aging: 1979*, p. 110. during 1976–1977, no fewer than four federal agencies were conducting weatherization activities: Community Services Administration, Federal Energy Administration, Department of Housing and Urban Development, and Farmer's Home Administration. Manpower was supplied by the Labor Department under the Comprehensive Employment and Training Act (CETA) and by community service employment programs under the Older Americans Act. *Developments in Aging: 1977*, a report of the Special Committee on Aging, U.S. Senate, 95th Congress, 2d session, Report No. 95–771, part 1, p. 43.

133. *Developments in Aging: 1982*, a report of the Special Committee on Aging, U.S. Senate, 98th Congress, 1st session, Report No. 98–13, vol. 2, p. 26.

134. Public Law 95–617–21, November 9, 1978.

135. *Development in Aging: 1978*, a report of the Special Committee on Aging, U.S. Senate, 96th Congress, 1st session, Report No. 96–55, part 1, p. 166.

136. Projection of David Marlin, Director of Legal Research and Services for the Elderly in *Developments in Aging: 1976*, a report of the Special Committee on Aging, U.S. Senate, 95th Congress, 1st session, Report No. 95–88, part 1, p. 195.

137. *Developments in Aging: 1972 and January–March, 1973*, a report of the Special Committee on Aging, U.S. Senate, 93rd Congress, 1st session, Report No. 93–147, pp. 90–91.

138. Public Law 93–355, July 25, 1974.

139. *Congressional Digest*, May 1981, p 133.

140. *Developments in Aging: 1982*, a report of the Special Committee on Aging, U.S. Senate, 98th Congress, 1st session, Report No. 98–13, vol 2, pp. 244–45.

141. For the operations in one state, see William M. Stephens, "Legal Aid Programs in Tennessee," *Aging*, November–December 1977, pp. 16–17.

142. *New York Times*, December 14, 1981, p. A22.

143. *Developments in Aging: 1980,* a report of the Special Committee on Aging, U.S. Senate, 97th Congress, 1st session, Report No. 97–62, part 2, p. 373.

144. *Developments in Aging: 1976,* part 1, pp. 192–98.

145. *Developments in Aging: 1982,* vol. 2, p. 245.

146. National Council of Senior Citizens, Inc., *Senior Citizens News,* February 1983, p. 5.

147. *The Administration's 1984 Budget,* p. 36.

148. Ibid., pp. 37–38.

Chapter V. Major Medical Programs

1. Mathilda W. Riley and Anne Foner, *Aging and Society,* vol. 1 (New York: Russell Sage Foundation, 1968), pp. 473–75.

2. P. R. Kaim-Caudle, *Comparative Social Policy and Social Security: A Ten-Country Study,* (New York: Dunnellen, 1973).

3. U.S. Department of Health, Education, and Welfare, *Facts about Older Americans* (Washington: U.S. Government Printing Office, 1977).

4. Robert M. Gibson, "Age Differences in Health Care Expenditures," *Social Security Bulletin* 40: 3–14.

5. Ibid., p. 10.

6. James J. Callahan, Jr., et al., "Responsibility of Families for Their Severely Disabled Elders," *Health Care Financing Review,* Winter 1980, p. 43.

7. J. Douglas Brown, *An American Philosophy of Social Security: Evolution and Issues* (Princeton: Princeton University Press, 1972), p. 195.

8. Theodore R. Marmor, *The Politics of Medicare* (Chicago: Aldine, 1973), p. 8.

9. Martha Derthick, *Policymaking for Social Security,* (Washington: The Brookings Institution, 1979), p. 318.

10. Public Law 89–97. For a most interesting account of the struggle, see Marmor, *Politics,* pp. 35–74.

11. Rosemary Stevens, *American Medicine and the Public Interest* (New Haven: Yale University Press, 1971), p. 440.

12. Arthur E. Hess, "Medicare's Early Months: A Program Round-Up," *Social Security Bulletin* 30, no. 7 (July 1967): 408.

13. Marian Gornick, "Ten Years of Medicare: Impact on the Covered Population," *Social Security Bulletin* 39, no. 7 (July 1976): 4.

14. *Medicare and Medicaid Problems, Issues, and Alternatives,* report of the staff to the committee on Finance, U.S. Senate, 91st Congress, 1st session, Committee Print (1970), pp. 113–116.

15. National Commission on Social Security, *Materials Prepared for Working Group on Health Care,* 1980, p. T-2.

16. *Health Care Financing Review* 4, no. 4 (Summer 1983): 115.

17. For example, assume that the patient has already paid the deductible. Assume also that the physician charges $50 for a particular service. Medicare, however, declares that a reasonable charge for that service is $30. Medicare then pays 80 percent of the reasonable charge, or $24. The patient co-insurance payment of 20 percent is $6. In addition, the patient pays the difference between the physicians's charge of $50 and the reasonable charge of $30 for a total of $26. Had the physician accepted assignment, the patient's bill would have been $6.

18. Thomas P. Ferry, et al., "Physicians'-Charges Under Medicare: Assignment Rates and Beneficiary Liability," *Health Care Financing Review,* Winter, 1980, pp. 49–73. See also Lynn Paringer, "Medicare Assignment Rates of Physicians: Their Responses to Changes in Reimburse-

ment Policy," ibid., pp. 75–89. The expression "reasonable charge" is in itself quite complex. For an extended explanation, see Health Care Financing Administration, *Determination of Reasonable Charges Under Part B of Medicare: A Basic Text* (Washington: U.S. Government Printing Office: 1980), 620-233/4315.

19. *Health Care Financing Review,* Winter 1980, p. 50. The data included Medicare beneficiaries who were also enrolled in Medicaid. The rate would have been still lower had it covered voluntary assignments only.

20. Ira L. Burney et al., "Medicare and Medicaid Physician Payment Incentives," *Health Care Financing Review,* Summer 1979, p. 66.

21. *Health Care Financing Review* 4, no. 4 (Summer 1983): 117.

22. Karen Davis, "Hospital Costs and the Medicare Program," *Social Security Bulletin,* Vol. 36, No. 8, pp. 18–36.

23. *Medicare and Medicaid Problems,* p. 5.

24. *Developments in Aging: 1982,* a report of the Special Committee on Aging, U.S. Senate, 98th Congress, 1st session, report no. 98-13, vol. 1, pp. 394–97. See also *Congressional Quarterly,* March 26, 1983, pp. 599–600.

25. *Major Themes and Additional Budget Details, Fiscal Year 1984,* Executive Office of the President, Office of Management and Budget, p. 62.

26. *Containing Medical Care Costs Through Market Forces,* Congressional Budget Office, May 1982, p. 52.

27. Public Law 92–603.

28. Ruth M. Covell, "The Impact of Regulation on Health Care Quality," in Arthur Levin, ed., *Regulating Health Care; The Struggle for Control* (New York: The Academy of Political Science, 1980), p. 120.

29. *The Effect of PSRO's on Health Care Costs: Current Findings and Future Evaluations,* Congressional Budget Office, June 1979, pp. 3–10.

30. Ibid., pp. 42–57. See also "Doctors' Panels under Scrutiny on Cost Benefit," *New York Times,* August 5, 1980, pp. C1, C4.

31. *Major Themes and Additional Budget Details,* p. 64.

32. Public Law 97–248. See also *The Hospice Alternative,* Hearing before the Special Committee on Aging, U.S. Senate, 97th Congress, 2d session, Pittsburgh, May 24, 1982.

33. Karen Davis, *National Health Insurance: Benefits, Costs, and Consequences,* (Washington: The Brookings Institution, 1975), p. 51.

34. National Commission on Social Security, *Materials,* p. T-6.

35. Jay A. Winsten, Harvard School of Public Health, *New York Times,* May 5, 1983, p. A31.

36. Ibid.

37. Data from *Health Care Financing Review* 4, no. 4 (Summer 1983): 120–21.

38. Advisory Commission of Intergovernmental Relations, *Intergovernmental Problems in Medicaid* (Washington: 1968), p. 1. For an account of early developments, see pp. 3–9.

39. Ibid., p. 6.

40. Ibid., pp. 19–40 for an extensive review. See also *Medicare and Medicaid Problems,* pp. 41–44; Rosemary Stevens, *American Medicine and the Public Interest* (New Haven: Yale University Press, 1971), pp. 473–91; John Holahan, *Financing Health Care for the Poor: The Medicaid Experience* (Lexington, Mass.: Lexington Books, D. C. Heath, 1975), pp. 9–32.

41. Connecticut, Hawaii, Illinois, Indiana, Minnesota, Mississippi, Missouri, Nebraska, New Hampshire, North Carolina, North Dakota, Ohio, Oklahoma, Utah, and Virginia.

42. See Marilyn Rymer et al., "Evaluation of Medicaid Spend-Down," in Allen D. Spiegel, ed., *The Medicaid Experience* (Germantown, Md.: Aspen Systems Corporation, 1979), pp. 211–24.

43. Burney, "Medicare and Medicaid Physician Payment Incentives," p. 63. See also Stephen F. Loebs, "Medicaid—A Survey of Indicators and Issues," in Spiegel, *Medicaid Experience*, p. 13.

44. *Developments in Aging: 1982*, a report of the Special Committee on Aging, U.S. Senate, 98th Congress, 1st session, Report No. 98–13, vol. 1, p. 400.

45. National Commission on Social Security, *Materials*, 1980, pp. T10–15. See also *Minutes of the National Commission on Social Security*, July 11 and 12, 1980, p. 26.

46. Alma McMillan, et al., "A Study of the 'Crossover Population': Aged Persons Entitled to Both Medicare and Medicaid," *Health Care Financing Review* 4, no. 4 (Summer 1983): 19–46.

47. For an extended discussion of cost-reduction possibilities, see *Medicaid: Choices for 1982 and Beyond*, Congressional Budget Office, June 1981.

48. Peter D. Fox and Steven B. Clauser, "Trends in Nursing Home Expenditures: Implications for Aging Policy," *Health Care Financing Review* 2, no. 2 (Fall 1980): 65–67.

49. Bruce C. Vladeck, *Unloving Care: The Nursing Home Tragedy*, A Twentieth Century Fund Study (New York: Basic Books, 1980), p. 43.

50. Ibid., p. 42.

51. Ibid., pp. 107–33.

52. *Standard and Poor's Industry Surveys*, July 1982, p. H23.

53. Christine E. Bishop, "Nursing Home Studies and Reimbursement Issues," *Health Care Financing Review* 1, no. 4 (Spring 1980): 47.

54. Vladeck, *Unloving Care*, pp. 147–53.

55. *Developments in Aging: 1979*, a report of the Special Committee on Aging, U.S. Senate, 96th Congress, 2d session, Report No. 96-613, part 1, p. 90. In the mid seventies, the Special Committee was responsible for the extensive study entitled *Nursing Home Care in the United States: Failure in Public Policy*.

56. Callahan, "Responsibility of Families," pp. 35–40.

57. Fox and Clauser, "Trends," p. 69.

58. *Public Policy and the Frail Elderly*, U.S. Department of Health, Education, and Welfare, Office of Human Development Services, Federal Council on Aging, December 1978, p. 4.

59. *Developments in Aging: 1979*, op. cit., p. 88. See also *Developments in Aging: 1982*, vol. 1, p. 430.

60. Ibid., (1979), pp. 83–84.

61. *To Understand the Aging Process: The Baltimore Longitudinal Study of the National Institute on Aging*, U.S. Department of Health, Education, and Welfare, Public Health Service, National Institutes of Health, DHEW Publication No. (NIH) 78-134, pp. 407.

62. *The Budget of the United States Government, Fiscal Year 1981*, Executive Office of The President, Office of Management and Budget, Appendix (1980), p. 446.

63. Public Law 93–296, May 31, 1974.

64. *National Institute on Aging*, U.S. Department of Health, Education, and Welfare, Public Health Service, National Institutes of Health, DHEW Publication No. 78–1129, n.d., unpaged.

65. *Special Report on Aging 1980*, U.S. Department of Health and Human Services, Public Health Service, National Institutes of Health (1980), pp. 3–6. See also National Institute on Aging, *Annual Report*, 1980.

66. *The Budget, Fiscal Year 1981*, p. 447.

67. *Developments in Aging: 1982*, vol. 2, pp. 28–29.

68. Ibid., pp. 270, 275–79.

69. *The Budget of the United States Government, Fiscal Year 1984*, Executive Office of the President, Office of Management and Budget, pp. 8–89.

70. Ibid., p. 5–109.

71. Statement of Dr. Robert Butler, director, National Institute on Aging, *Future of Health*

Care and the Elderly (Geriatric Medicine), Joint Hearing before the Subcommittee on Health and Long Term Care and the Subcommittee on Human Services of the Select Committee on Aging, U.S. House of Representatives, 95th Congress, 2d session, May 17, 1978, p. 80.

72. *Developments in Aging: 1982,* vol. 2, pp. 106–08.

73. *Health Care Financing Review* 1, no. 4 (Spring 1980): 95.

74. Ibid., p. 97.

Chapter VI. Two Auxiliary Programs

1. See statement of Frances M. Carp in *Transportation and the Elderly: Problems and Progress,* Hearings before the Special Committee on Aging, U.S. Senate, 93d Congress, 2d session, February 25, 1974, part 1, p. 67.

2. *Senior Transportation—Ticket to Dignity,* Report by the Subcommittee on Federal, State, and Community Services of the Select Committee on Aging, U.S. House of Representatives, 94th Congress, 2d session, May 20, 1976, p. 19.

3. For a more extensive list of travel barriers, see *Transportation for the Elderly: The State of the Art,* U.S. Department of Health, Education, and Welfare, Office of Human Development, Administration on Aging (January 1975), p. 111.

4. *Summary Report of Data from National Survey of Transportation Handicapped People,* U.S. Department of Transportation, Urban Mass Transportation Administration (1978), p. 7.

5. Public Law, 83–364, July 7, 1964. The amendment is Public Law 91–453, October 15, 1970.

6. Public Law 93–113, September 26, 1973.

7. *Congressional Quarterly,* May 31, 1980, p. 1506.

8. 49 CFR 609.3 (1982).

9. 49 CFR 609.15 g (3) (1982).

10. *New York Times,* September 20, 1980, p. 1.

11. *Congressional Quarterly,* December 6, 1980, p. 3521.

12. Ibid., March 14, 1981, p. 484.

13. *Developments in Aging: 1978,* a report of the Special Committee on Aging, U.S. Senate, 96th Congress, 1st session, Report No. 96–55, part 2, pp. 177–82; *Developments in Aging: 1979,* a report of the Special Committee on Aging, U.S. Senate, 96th Congress, 2d session, Report No. 96–613, part 2, pp. 241–45.

14. Public Law 95–478, October 18, 1978, Section 321.

15. 45 CFR 1321.171 (1982).

16. *Senior Transportation—Ticket to Dignity,* p. 31.

17. Ibid., p. 32.

18. From a statement of New Jersey Assemblyman David Schwarts, *The Impact of Federal Transportation Policies on the Elderly,* Hearing before the Subcommittee on Human Services of the Select Committee on Aging, U.S. House of Representatives, 96th Congress, 1st session, October 13, 1979, (1980), p. 9.

19. *Senior Transportation—Ticket to Dignity,* p. 34.

20. *Elderly and Handicapped Transportation: Local Government Approaches,* Public Technology, Inc., for the Urban Consortium for Technology Initiatives, Washington, 1979, p. 32.

21. *Senior Transportation—Ticket to Dignity,* p. 4.

22. Statement of Representative James J. Florio, *The Impact of Federal Transportation Policies on the Elderly,* p. 5.

23. Report of the President's Committee on Urban Housing, *A Decent Home* (Washington, 1968), pp. 54–55.

24. Irving Welfeld and Raymond J. Struyk, "Housing Options for the Elderly," in *Occasional*

Papers in Housing and Community Affairs, Department of Housing and Urban Development, 1978, vol. 3, pp. 18–21.

25. James Follein, Jane Kats, and Raymond J. Struyk, "Programmatic Options to Encourage Home Ownership," ibid., vol. 2. p. 53.

26. Joseph P. Fried, *Housing Crisis U.S.A.* (New York: Praeger, 1971), p. 63.

27. Public Law 412, September 1937.

28. Public Law 171, July 15, 1949.

29. The National Commission on Urban Problems, *More Than Shelter,* Research Report No. 8, (Washington: 1968), p. 11.

30. *Statement of Policies for Housing Authority of the County of Greene* (Waynesburg, Pennsylvania, 1966).

31. Public Law 1020, August 7, 1956. See Marie McGuire Thompson, "The Elderly in Our Environment: Yesterday and Today," HUD, *Challenge* (HUD) 10, no. 8 (August 1979): 4–6.

32. *1979 Statistical Yearbook* (Washington: U.S. Department of Housing and Urban Development), table 65, p. 207.

33. Ibid., table 64, p. 206.

34. *Developments in Aging: 1971 and January–March 1972,* a report of the Special Committee on Aging, U.S. Senate, 92d Congress, 2d session, Report No. 92–784, p. 178.

35. Morton Leeds, "Housing: Serving the Aged," *Challenge* (HUD) 10, no. 8 (August 1979): 7.

36. Public Law 95–557, October 31, 1978.

37. *Developments in Aging: 1978,* part 1, p. 131.

38. *Developments in Aging: 1979,* part 2, p. 216.

39. Public Law 93–383, August 22, 1974.

40. Report of the Department of Housing and Urban Development, in *Developments in Aging: 1974 and January–March 1975,* a report of the Special Committee on Aging, U.S. Senate, 94th Congress, 1st session, Report No. 94–250, pp. 246–47.

41. *Challenge* (HUD) 6, no. 7 (July 1975): 28.

42. Public Law 96–153, December 21, 1979; Public Law 97–35, August 13, 1981.

43. *Developments in Aging: 1981,* a report of the Special Committee on Aging, U.S. Senate, 97th Congress, 2d session, Report No. 97–314, vol. 1, pp. 214–16. See also *Developments in Aging: 1982,* a report of the Special Committee on Aging, U.S. Senate, 98th Congress, 1st session, Report No. 98–13, vol. 1, pp. 301–06.

44. Public Law 86–372, September 23, 1959.

45. Public Law 93–383, August 22, 1974.

46. *Developments in Aging: 1981,* part 2, p. 220.

47. Ibid.

48. Report of the Department of Housing and Urban Development in *Developments in Aging: 1970,* a report of the Special Committee on Aging, U.S. Senate, 92d Congress, 1st session, Report No. 92–46, p. 214.

49. Report of the Department of Housing and Urban Development in *Developments in Aging: 1974 and January–April 1975,* a report of the Special Committee on Aging, U.S. Senate, 94th Congress, 1st session, Report No. 94–250, p. 248.

50. Housing and Urban Development Act of 1968, Public Law 90–448, August 1, 1968.

51. National Association of Housing and Development Officials, *The NAHRO Letter* 9, no. 43 (October 27, 1975): 2.

52. *Developments in Aging, 1981,* vol. 2, pp. 223–24. See also *Federal Housing Assistance: Alternative Approaches,* Congressional Budget Office, May 1982, pp. 23–24.

53. Morton J. Schussheim, Joshua M. Kay, and Richard L. Wellons, *Rural Housing: Needs, Credit Availability, and Federal Programs,* Committee on Agriculture and Forestry, U.S. Sen-

ate, 94th Congress, 1st session, Committee Print (1975), p. 1. For a recent study, see *Rural Housing Programs: Long Term Costs and Their Treatment in the Federal Budget*, Congressional Budget Office, June 1982.

54. *Developments in Aging: 1981*, vol. 2, p. 9.

55. Ibid., pp. 9–10.

56. L. D. Elwell, "FMHA Means Housing in Rural Areas," *Challenge* (HUD) 6, no. 7 (July 1975): 20–21.

57. "Commissioner Flemming Stresses Support for Winterization Programs," *Aging*, nos. 256–57 (February–March 1976): 4.

58. *Developments in Aging: 1981*, vol. 2, p. 9.

59. "Federal, State, and Local Programs Help Elderly Reduce Heating Costs," *Aging*, nos. 256–57 (February–March 1976): 16–19.

60. For a discussion of some of the problems in the operation of the weatherization programs, see *Developments in Aging: 1979*, part 1, pp. 109–12.

61. Welfeld and Struyk, *Housing Options*, pp. 47–52.

62. Ibid., p. 63.

63. Ibid., pp. 68–69.

64. *Developments in Aging: 1978*, part 1, pp. 136–39. See also "Condos: High Rises All Around" in *Gray Panther Network*, March–April 1980, pp. 1–4.

65. Welfeld and Struyk, *Housing Options*, pp. 74–75.

66. *Developments in Aging: 1978*, part 1, p. 141.

67. Welfeld and Struyk, *Housing Options*, pp. 76–80. For an evaluation of the options for elderly homeowners, see Follein, "Programmatic Options," pp. 109–23.

68. For an extended discussion of the voucher system and the housing assistance block grant, see *Federal Housing Assistance: Alternative Approaches*, pp. 29–64. See also *Developments in Aging: 1981*, vol. 1, pp. 221–23.

69. Report of the President's Commission on Housing, April 1982, pp. 49–56. See also *Turning Home Equity into Income for Older Homeowners*, an information paper prepared by the staff of the Special Committee on Aging, July 1982; and *Opportunities in Home Equity Conversion for the Elderly*, Hearing before the Special Committee on Aging, U.S. Senate, 97th Congress, 2d session, Washington, July 20, 1982 (1983).

Chapter VII. Government and the Older Worker

1. *Developments in Aging: 1981*, a report of the Special Committee on Aging, U.S. Senate, 97th Congress, 2d Session, Report No. 97–314, pp. 260–64.

2. Ibid., p. 270.

3. Ibid., p. 271.

4. Public Law 90–202, December 15, 1967. The Age Discrimination in Employment Act of 1967 is to be distinguished from the Age Discrimination Act of 1975 (Public Law 94–135, November 28, 1975). The goal of the latter is to eliminate discrimination in programs receiving federal financial assistance.

5. *Developments in Aging: 1981*, p. 272.

6. Public Law 95–256. Enforcement responsibility under ADEA was initially placed in the Department of Labor. However, in 1979 the authority for enforcement was transferred by executive order to the Equal Employment Opportunity Commission. The reason advanced for the change was "to consolidate all Federal enforcement of job related civil rights in one agency." *Developments in Aging: 1981*, p. 273.

7. *Toward a National Older Worker Policy*, an information paper for use by the Special

Committee on Aging, U.S. Senate, 97th Congress, 1st session, (September 1981) Committee print, p. 19.

8. *Developments in Aging: 1981,* p. 275.

9. Ibid., p. 278.

10. For example, see the report prepared by the National Council on the Aging, Inc., *The Senior Community Service Project: Activities and Accomplishments, The 1973–1977 SCSP Report* (1978), p. 58.

11. "The Federal Older Worker Program: Its History, Funding, Administration, and Operations," in *Funding of Federal Programs Benefiting Older Persons (Employment),* Hearings before the Select Committee on Aging, U.S. House of Representatives, 94th Congress, 2d session (1976), pp. 140–55.

12. Statement of Leon Henderson, *Oversight Hearings, Older Americans act, Title IX Hearings before the Subcommittee on Retirement Income and Employment of the Select Committee on Aging,* U.S. House of Representatives, 95th Congress, 1st session, October 5, 1977 (1978), p. 39.

13. *The Federal Older Worker Program,* pp. 184–85.

14. 29 Code of Federal Regulations 89.15 (b) (1) (ii) (1982).

15. *Developments in Aging: 1979,* a report of the Special Committee on Aging, U.S. Senate, 96th Congress, 2d session, Report No. 96–613, part 2, pp. 228–29.

16. *Developments in Aging: 1982,* a report of the Special Committee on Aging: U.S. Senate, 98th Congress, 1st session, Report No. 98–13, pp. 154–55.

17. See statement of Thomas Bradley, associate director, National Council on the Aging, in *Funding of Federal Programs,* p. 43.

18. *The Administration's 1984 Budget: A Critical View from an Aging Perspective,* Leadership Council of Aging Organizations, March 15, 1983, p. 20.

19. *Developments in Aging: 1981,* a report of the Special Committee on Aging, U.S. Senate, 97th Congress, 2d Session, Report No. 97–314, vol. 1, p. 226.

20. Public Law 93–203, December 28, 1973.

21. *Developments in Aging: 1978,* a report of the Special Committee on Aging, U.S. Senate, 96th Congress, 1st session, Report No. 96–55, part 1, pp. 182–83.

22. Ibid., part 2, p. 173.

23. *Developments in Aging: 1982,* a report of the Special Committee on Aging, U.S. Senate, 98th Congress, 1st session, Report No. 98–13, vol. 1, pp. 109–12.

24. *Funding of Federal Programs,* p. 43.

25. Various possibilities for increasing elderly employment are examined: *Work and Retirement: Options for Continual Employment of Older Workers,* Congressional Budget Office, July 1982, pp. 35–50.

26. *Developments in Aging: 1979,* a report of the Special Committee on Aging, U.S. Senate, 96th Congress, 2d session, Report No. 96–613, part 2, pp. 250–51.

27. 45 Code of Federal Regulations 1209. 1–1 (1979).

28. *Program Information Statement RSVP,* ACTION, January 1972, p. 1.

29. *Developments in Aging: 1971* and *January–March 1972,* a report of the Special Committee on Aging, U.S. Senate, 92d Congress, 2d session, Report No. 92–784, p. 152.

30. ACTION, *Annual Report,* 1979, p. 9.

31. Ibid., p. 11.

32. Statement of Mary E. King, deputy director of ACTION, in *Impact on the Elderly of the Fiscal Year 1979 Budget,* Hearing before the Select Committee on Aging, U.S. House of Representatives, 95th Congress, 2d session, March 2, 1978, p. 39.

33. *Annual Report,* pp. 7–8.

34. Public Law 93–113, Oct. 1, 1973.

35. *Cost Benefit Profile of the Foster Grandparents Program* (ACTION, 1972), p. 10.
36. Ibid., p. 11.
37. *Developments in Aging: 1969*, a report of the Special Committee on Aging, U.S. Senate, 91st Congress, 2d session, Report No. 91–875, p. 177.
38. *Developments in Aging: 1982*, a report of the Special Committee on Aging, U.S. Senate, 98th Congress, 1st session, Report No. 98–13, vol. 2, part 2, p. 230.
39. ACTION, *Annual Report*, 1979, pp. 7–8.
40. 45 Code of Federal Regulations 1207. 1–1 (1979).
41. Ibid., 1207. 2–1 (c).
42. Ibid., 1207. 3–2.
43. Ibid., 1207. 4–3.
44. *Developments in Aging: 1982*, vol. 2, part 2, p. 267.
45. ACTION, *Annual Report*, 1979, p. 18.
46. Ibid., p. 18.
47. "Funding of Older American Volunteer Programs," in *Funding of Federal Programs Benefiting Older Persons (Volunteer Opportunities)*, Hearings before the Select Committee on Aging, U.S. House of Representatives, 94th Congress, 2d session (1976), pp. 127–88.

Chapter VIII. The Aging Veteran

1. *Annual Report, 1982*, Administrator of Veterans Affairs, table 3, p. 147.
2. Quoted from Robinson E. Adkins, *Medical Care of Veterans* (Washington: U.S. Government Printing Office, 1967), p. 21, in Sar A. Levitan and Karen Cleary, *Old Wars Remain Unfinished: The Veterans Benefits System* (Baltimore: The Johns Hopkins Press, 1973), p. 7.
3. Ibid., p. 9. The survivors of Confederate veterans were made eligible for pensions in 1958.
4. *Annual Report, 1982, Administrators of Veterans Affairs*, p. 5.
5. Bennett M. Rich, *The Presidents and Civil Disorder* (Washington: The Brookings Institution, 1941), pp. 167–76.
6. Bill Keller, "How a Unique Lobby Force Protects over $21 Billion in Past Veterans' Programs," *Congressional Quarterly*, June 14, 1980, p. 1628.
7. Ibid., p. 1627. See also Levitan and Cleary, *Old Wars*, pp. 15–27; and Phil Keisling, "Old Soldiers Never Die," *The Washington Monthly*, March 1982, pp. 23–26.
8. Keller, "Unique Lobby," p. 1628.
9. Ibid., p. 1627.
10. Ibid., p. 1629.
11. *Developments in Aging: 1982*, a report of the Special Committee on Aging, U.S. Senate, 98th Congress, 1st session, Report No. 98–13, vol. 2, p. 281.
12. Veterans Administration, *Federal Benefits for Veterans and Dependents*, January 1, 1982, p. 2.
13. Veterans Administration, *Federal Benefits for Veterans and Dependents*, January 1, 1980, p. 1.
14. *Analysis and Evaluation of the Non Service-Connected Pension Program*, a study submitted by the Veterans Administration to the Committee on Veterans' Affairs, U.S. Senate, 95th Congress, 2d session, January 30, 1978, Senate Committee Print No. 13, p. 2.
15. Public Law 95–599, November 4, 1978.
16. Veterans Administration, *Federal Benefits for Veterans and Dependents*, January 1983, pp. 3–4.
17. *Annual Report, 1981, Administrator of Veterans Affairs*, table 67, p. 207.
18. *Analysis and Evaluation*, p. 7.
19. *Study of Health Care for American Veterans*, a report prepared by the National Academy

of Sciences' National Research Council, submitted to the Committee on Veterans' Affairs, U.S. Senate, 95th Congress, 1st session, June 7, 1977, Committee Print No. 4, p. 17.

20. Ibid., p. 16.

21. Ibid., p. 32.

22. Ibid., p. 24.

23. *The Aging Veterans' Present and Future Medical Needs,* Veterans Administration, October 1977, pp. 11–12.

24. *Study of Health Care for American Veterans,* p. 24.

25. *Developments in Aging: 1982,* vol. 2, p. 268.

26. *Annual Report, 1982,* Administrator of Veterans Affairs, p. 14.

27. *The Aging Veteran's Medical Needs,* p. 29.

28. Ibid., p. 30.

29. *Study of Health Care for American Veterans,* p. 212.

30. *Developments in Aging: 1982,* vol. 2, p. 268.

31. *Study of Health Care for American Veterans,* p. 214.

32. Ibid., p. 216.

33. Ibid., p. 225.

34. *Developments in Aging, 1982,* vol. 2, p. 269.

35. Ibid., p. 269.

36. *Developments in Aging: 1979,* a report of the Special Committee on Aging, U.S. Senate, 96th Congress, 2d session, Report No. 96–613, part 2, p. 328.

37. *Study of Health Care for American Veterans,* p. 279.

38. Ibid., p. 280.

39. *Congressional Quarterly,* June 14, 1980, p. 1632.

40. *Developments in Aging: 1979,* pp. 333–34.

41. *Congressional Quarterly,* October 28, 1978, p. 3165.

42. Keisling, *Old Soldiers,* pp. 26–29.

Chapter IX. Public Policy and the Aging Summarized

1. *Developments in Aging: 1982,* a report of the Special Committee on Aging, U.S. Senate, 98th Congress, 1st session, Report No. 98–13, vol. 1, p. 3.

2. *Future Directions for Aging Policy: A Human Service Model,* a report by the Subcommittee on Human Services of the Select Committee on Aging, U.S. House of Representatives, 96th Congress, May 1980, p. 16.

3. Robert H. Binstock, "Federal Policy toward the Aging," *National Journal,* November 1978, p. 1845.

4. *Future Directions,* p. 24.

5. Ibid., p. 89.

6. Ibid., p. 89–90.

7. *Federal Responsibility to the Elderly (Executive Programs and Legislative Jurisdiction),* Select Committee on Aging, U.S. House of Representatives, 96th Congress, 1st session, Comm. Pub. No. 95–167, January 2, 1979, p. 1.

8. *Future Directions,* p. 54.

9. Editorial, "For Their Own Good," *New York Times,* February 5, 1984, p. 18E.

10. Robert Peal, "Making Some Entitled to Less," *New York Times,* February 5, 1984, p. 4E.

11. Ibid.

Index

Contemporary Community Health Series

The Psychiatric Halfway House: A Handbook of Theory and Practice
Richard D. Budson

Racism and Mental Health: Essays
Charles V. Willie, Bernard M. Kramer, and Bertram S. Brown, Editors

The Sociology of Physical Disability and Rehabilitation
Gary L. Albrecht, Editor

In cooperation with the Institute on Human Values in Medicine:

Medicine and Religion: Strategies of Care
Donald W. Shriver, Editor

Nourishing the Humanistic in Medicine: Interactions with the Social Sciences
William R. Rogers and David Barnard, Editors

Pitt Series in Policy and Institutional Studies

Bert A. Rockman, Editor